A TEXT BOOK OF

WATER RESOURCES ENGINEERING - I

FOR
SEMESTER – V
THIRD YEAR DEGREE COURSE IN
CIVIL ENGINEERING

As Per the New Revised Syllabus of
Shivaji University, Kolhapur.

H.K. GITE
Assistant Engineer Grade-1
Water Resource Department, Govt. of Maharashtra
Formerly Assistant Professor, Civil Engg. Department
JSPM's Rajarshi Shahu College of Enginering,
Tathwade, Pune.

A.B. LANDAGE
M. Tech. (WRE)
Assistant Professor, Civil Engg. Department
Govt. College of Engineering
Karad, (Dist. Satara)

N3401

WATER RESOURCES ENGINEERING - I (SU) ISBN : 978-93-5164-773-7

First Edition : August 2015
© : Authors

The text of this publication, or any part thereof, should not be reproduced or transmitted in any form or stored in any computer storage system or device for distribution including photocopy, recording, taping or information retrieval system or reproduced on any disc, tape, perforated media or other information storage device etc., without the written permission of Authors with whom the rights are reserved. Breach of this condition is liable for legal action.

Every effort has been made to avoid errors or omissions in this publication. In spite of this, errors may have crept in. Any mistake, error or discrepancy so noted and shall be brought to our notice shall be taken care of in the next edition. It is notified that neither the publisher nor the authors or seller shall be responsible for any damage or loss of action to any one, of any kind, in any manner, therefrom.

Published By :	POLYPLATE	Printed By :
NIRALI PRAKASHAN Abhyudaya Pragati, 1312, Shivaji Nagar, Off J.M. Road, PUNE – 411005 Tel - (020) 25512336/37/39, Fax - (020) 25511379 Email : niralipune@pragationline.com		**REPRO INDIA LTD.** 50/2 T.T.C. MIDC, Industrial Area, Mahape, Navi Mumbai Tel - (022) 2778 2011

☞ DISTRIBUTION CENTRES

PUNE
Nirali Prakashan : 119, Budhwar Peth, Jogeshwari Mandir Lane, Pune 411002, Maharashtra
Tel : (020) 2445 2044, 66022708, Fax : (020) 2445 1538
Email : bookorder@pragationline.com, niralilocal@pragationline.com

Nirali Prakashan : S. No. 28/27, Dhyari, Near Pari Company, Pune 411041
Tel : (020) 24690204 Fax : (020) 24690316
Email : dhyari@pragationline.com, bookorder@pragationline.com

MUMBAI
Nirali Prakashan : 385, S.V.P. Road, Rasdhara Co-op. Hsg. Society Ltd.,
Girgaum, Mumbai 400004, Maharashtra
Tel : (022) 2385 6339 / 2386 9976, Fax : (022) 2386 9976
Email : niralimumbai@pragationline.com

☞ DISTRIBUTION BRANCHES

JALGAON
Nirali Prakashan : 34, V. V. Golani Market, Navi Peth, Jalgaon 425001,
Maharashtra, Tel : (0257) 222 0395, Mob : 94234 91860

KOLHAPUR
Nirali Prakashan : New Mahadvar Road, Kedar Plaza, 1st Floor Opp. IDBI Bank
Kolhapur 416 012, Maharashtra. Mob : 9850046155

NAGPUR
Pratibha Book Distributors : Above Maratha Mandir, Shop No. 3, First Floor,
Rani Jhanshi Square, Sitabuldi, Nagpur 440012, Maharashtra
Tel : (0712) 254 7129

DELHI
Nirali Prakashan : 4593/21, Basement, Aggarwal Lane 15, Ansari Road, Daryaganj
Near Times of India Building, New Delhi 110002
Mob : 08505972553

BENGALURU
Pragati Book House : House No. 1, Sanjeevappa Lane, Avenue Road Cross,
Opp. Rice Church, Bengaluru – 560002.
Tel : (080) 64513344, 64513355,Mob : 9880582331, 9845021552
Email:bharatsavla@yahoo.com

CHENNAI
Pragati Books : 9/1, Montieth Road, Behind Taas Mahal, Egmore,
Chennai 600008 Tamil Nadu, Tel : (044) 6518 3535,
Mob : 94440 01782 / 98450 21552 / 98805 82331,
Email : bharatsavla@yahoo.com

niralipune@pragationline.com | www.pragationline.com
Also find us on www.facebook.com/niralibooks

PREFACE

It gives us immense pleasure to present this book on **Water Resources Engineering – I** for the Students of Third Year Degree Course in Civil Engineering of Shivaji University, Kolhapur. It is strictly written as per the New Revised Syllabus with effective from 2015.

The basic objective of this book is to bridge the gap between the reference books written by the renowned International Authors and the requirements of undergraduate students. This book has been written in a simple language, keeping in mind student's requirements. The main emphasis has been given on exploring the basic concepts rather than merely the information. Solved Examples have been provided throughout the text at the end of the topics.

We are sure the book will also be useful to the teaching faculties while teaching this subject and also student communities.

We gratefully acknowledge this co-operation from **Shri. Dineshbhai Furia, Shri. Jignesh Furia Mrs. Nirali Verma**, **Shri. M.P. Munde** and Mrs. Deepali Lachake (Co-ordinator) of **Nirali Prakashan**.

Our special thanks to our family members, students, and all those who directly or indirectly supported us in this project.

We are also thankful to **Mr. Virdhaval Shinde**, Branch Manager, Kolhapur Office and **Mr. Ashok Nanaware**, Branch Manager, Sangli District for their valuable help and efforts for promotion of the book.

Any suggestions and feedback shall be appreciated and acknowledged.

Pune   **Authors**

SYLLABUS

SECTION – I

Unit – I (8 Hrs)

Introduction of Hydrology : Definition, Importance and scope of hydrology, the hydrologic cycle.

Precipitation : Forms and types of precipitation, Methods of measurement, Graphical representation of rainfall, Mass rainfall curves, Hyetograph, Determination of average precipitation over the catchment.

Evaporation : Process, factors affecting, measurement, and control of evaporation.

Infiltration : Process, Factors affecting and measurement of Infiltration.

Unit – II (6 Hrs)

Runoff : Factors affecting runoff, Determination of annual runoff, Rainfall runoff relationship

Hydrograph : Storm hydrograph, Base flow and Separation of base flow, direct runoff hydrograph, Unit hydrograph, theory, assumptions and limitations, Derivation and use of unit hydrograph, S-curve hydrograph.

Unit – III (6 Hrs)

Stream Gauging : Selection of site, discharge measurement by Area velocity method, slope Area method.

Floods : Estimation of peak flow, empirical equations, rational method, Importance of Design flood, standard project flood, maximum probable flood, Introduction to flood frequency analysis.

SECTION – II

Unit – IV (6 Hrs)

Ground Water Hydrology : Occurrence, distribution and classification of ground water, Darcy's law, Acquifer parameters, permeability, specific yield, specific retention, porosity, storage coefficient, Transmissibility, Hydraulics of well under steady flow conditions in confined and unconfined aquifers, Specific capacity of well, Recuperation Test, constructional features of Tube wells and Open wells.

Unit – V (8 Hrs)

Introduction to Irrigation : Definition and necessity of irrigation, ill-effects of irrigation, surface, sub-surface, sprinkler irrigation, Water logging and land drainage,

Water Requirement of Crops : Principal crops and crop seasons, cropping pattern and crop rotation, Classes and availability of soil water, depth and frequency of irrigation, Duty, delta, base period and their relationship, factors affecting duty, methods of improving duty, Assessment and efficiency of irrigation water. Gross command area, culturable command area and command area calculations based on crop water requirement.

Estimation of evapo-transpiration by blaney-criddle method and penman method.

Unit – VI (6 Hrs)

Minor Irrigation Works : General layout, main components and functioning of : 1. Percolation tanks, 2. K. T. Weir, 3. Bandhara irrigation, 4. Lift irrigation.

Watershed Management : Need and importance of watershed management, Soil conservation measures, Techniques of Rainwater and groundwater harvesting.

CONTENTS

SECTION – I

Unit I : Hydrology, Precipitation, Evaporation and Infiltration   1.1 – 1.48

Unit II : Run-Off and Hydrograph   2.1 – 2.48

Unit III : Stream Gauging and Floods   3.1 – 3.42

SECTION – II

Unit IV : Ground Water Hydrology   4.1 – 4.48

Unit V : Irrigation and Crop Water Requirement   5.1 – 5.50

Unit VI : Minor Irrigation Works and Watershed Management   6.1 – 6.38

✠ ✠ ✠

UNIT – I

HYDROLOGY, PRECIPITATION, EVAPORATION AND INFILTRATION

1.1 INTRODUCTION

'**Hydrology**' is defined as the science of the waters of the earth, that deals with its properties, origin, circulation and distribution. The study of hydrology includes the assessment, proper utilization and efficient management of the available water for the overall development of the region. It includes the surface waters of the lakes, streams, rivers etc. and also ground water occurring below the earth's surface. Thus, hydrology is mainly concerned with the occurrence and subsequent transportation through the atmosphere as vapour, over the earth's surface as water and underground as ground water. The other allied branches such as meteorology, hydraulics, physics and chemistry of water and geology also play an important role in hydrology. The development of hydrology on scientific basis has started from 1930 onwards. The basic knowledge of hydrology is essential for any civil engineer dealing with the planning, designing and execution of structures such as dams, bridges, flood control works etc. Even though considerable progress has been made since 1930 in the branch of hydrology, there are certain factors which are still indeterminate and as such it is not accepted as perfect science as even today empirical formulae are still to be utilized for evaluation of certain quantities (related to hydrology).

1.2 WATER RESOURCES

The total water resources of the world is approximately estimated as 1.358×10^2 million cubic metres. Out of this, about 97.1% is available in the form of salty sea water and the remaining 2.9% is made up of fresh surface water (about 2.25%) and ground water (about 0.65%). The entire world has two-thirds of water and only one-third of land surface.

As regards our country (India), the total geographical area is 3.15 million km^2 and the average annual rainfall is approximately 1150 mm, the run-off and evaporation expressed as percentage of annual rain fall being 46% and 54% respectively. The approximate annual surface run off is 167.2 million cubic metre, out of which only 40% can be utilized, due to limitations of topography of our country. India being an agricultural country, more stress must be laid on the proper utilization of the available water resources for the development of our country.

1.3 HYDROLOGIC CYCLE

The **'hydrologic cycle'** is a term applied to the general circulation of water from the oceans to the atmosphere, to the ground surface and back to the oceans again.

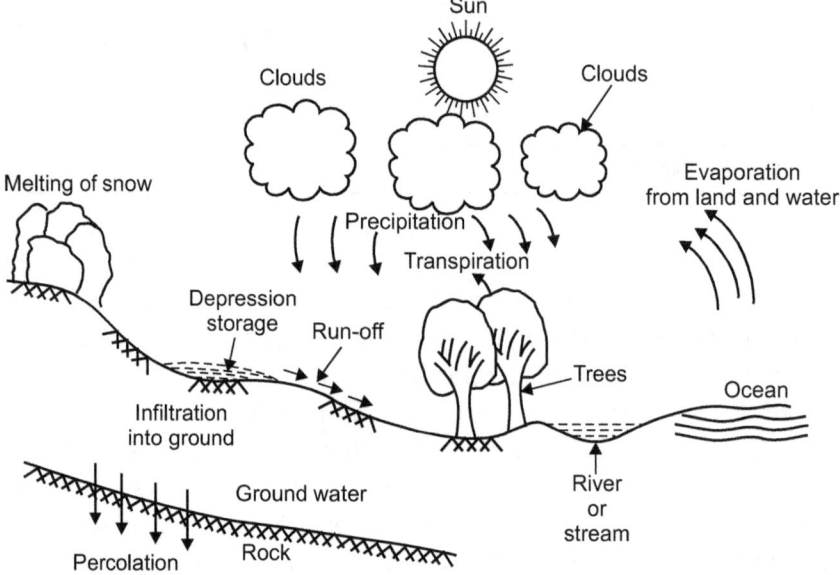

Fig. 1.1 : Hydrologic cycle

The *'hydrologic cycle'* (Fig. 1.1) begins with the waters of the oceans. Due to solar radiation, the water from the oceans gets evaporated into the atmosphere and the water vapours are formed resulting in cloud formation that condenses by the various processes which results in precipitation. Some of the precipitation occurs on the ocean surface itself whereas some falls on the land surface. The part of the precipitation on the land surface is retained in the soil, the surface depressions and on vegetation, which is again released to the atmosphere by the process of evaporation (from land surface) and transpiration (from vegetation) and the remaining flows back into the oceans by moving through devious surfaces and underground channels. All phases of the hydrologic cycle take place simultaneously and is a never ending continuous process which maintains balance between the waters of the earth and the moisture in the atmosphere.

Thus, the important phases of the hydrologic cycle can be expressed as :

- Evaporation from land and water surfaces i.e. lakes, oceans etc. and transpiration from the vegetation.
- Precipitation i.e. moisture falling on the surface of the earth in the form of drizzle, rain, glaze, sleet, snow, hail, dew, frost etc.
- Run-off i.e. portion of the precipitation that ultimately reaches the stream channel over the land surface and beneath the surface of the earth. The part of the run-off is stored in

the reservoirs, and rest flows back to the ocean. Again due to solar radiation, (which provides required energy for hydrologic cycle), evaporation of water surfaces take place and the hydrologic cycle is repeated.

1.4 SCOPE AND APPLICATIONS OF HYDROLOGY

1.4.1 Scope of Hydrology

The scope of hydrology, in terms of hydrologic cycle is that part of the cycle from precipitation to the water in the form of run-off joining the oceans. The remaining part of the hydrologic cycle is related to the oceanography and meteorology. The main aspects of hydrology involves :

- Measurement of different phases of hydrologic cycle (related to civil engineering) and recording of up-to-date data.
- Analysis of the above data to develop new concepts (or theories).
- The application of the above data and concepts (or theories) for the solution of practical civil engineering problems especially related to water resources projects. e.g. Irrigation, hydro-power, flood control, drinking water supply, navigation etc.

1.4.2 Applications of Hydrology

Hydrology finds its greatest application in the design and operation of water resources engineering projects, such as those for irrigation, water supply, flood control, water power, and navigation. In all these projects hydrological investigations for the proper assessment of the following factors are necessary. The various applications of hydrology to engineering are :

- Hydrology is used to find out maximum probable flood at proposed sites e.g. Dams.
- The variation of water production from catchments can be calculated and described by hydrology.
- Engineering hydrology enables us to find out the relationship between a catchments' surface water and groundwater resources
- The expected flood flows over a spillway, at a highway Culvert, or in an urban storm drainage system can be known by this very subject.
- It helps us to know the required reservoir capacity to assure adequate water for irrigation or municipal water supply in droughts condition.
- It tells us what hydrologic hardware (e.g. rain gauges, stream gauges etc.) and software (computer models) are needed for real-time flood forecasting
- Used in connection with design and operations of hydraulic structure
- Used in prediction of flood over a spillway, at highway culvert or in urban storm drainage

- Used to assess the reservoir capacity required to assure adequate water for irrigation or municipal water supply during drought
- Hydrology is an indispensable tool in planning and building hydraulic structures.
- Hydrology is used for city water supply design which is based on catchments area, amount of rainfall, dry period, storage capacity, runoff evaporation and transpiration.
- Dam construction, reservoir capacity, spillway capacity, sizes of water supply pipelines and affect of afforest on water supply schemes, all are designed on basis of hydrological equations.
- Determining the water balance of a region. Determining the agricultural water balance.
- Designing riparian restoration projects. Mitigating and predicting flood, landslide and drought risk.
- Real-time flood forecasting and flood warning. Designing irrigation schemes and managing agricultural productivity.
- Part of the hazard module in catastrophe modeling.
- Providing drinking water. Designing dams for water supply or hydroelectric power generation.
- Designing bridges, Designing sewers and urban drainage system.
- Analyzing the impacts of antecedent moisture on sanitary sewer systems.
- Predicting geomorphologic changes, such as erosion or sedimentation.
- Assessing the impacts of natural and anthropogenic environmental change on water resources.
- Assessing contaminant transport risk and establishing environmental policy guidelines.

1.5 HYDROLOGY IN RELATION TO WATER RESOURCES DEVELOPMENT

The most importance use of hydrology in water resources engineering is in the structural and hydraulic design of water control structures, municipal and industrial water supply, irrigation, power, flood control, navigation, erosion control and pollution abatement.

(1) Structural and Hydraulic Design : In any type of reservoir, provision must be made for passing flood flows over or around the dam. The spillway section capacity, the height of dam. Downstream protection works etc. depends on the correct assessment of flood flow and routing. An under estimate may result an unsafe design and an over estimate may lead to un-necessary expenditure.

(2) Irrigation : The hydrologic problems in irrigation are similar to those in water supply but on a larger scale. Today we increasingly find ourselves confronted with limiting conditions because of more ambitious program of irrigation and complexities of the problem correspondingly increase. On some rivers requirements of water to irrigate the available cultivable land far exceed the total flow and downstream projects have to depend on "return flow" from upstream projects. More and more, the hydrologist is called upon to evaluate new projects in area where the margin of safety is already low or to discover new sources of water for projects in difficulty or to develop more economical methods of water use.

(3) **Municipal and Industrial Water Supply :** The location and development of sources adequate to the needs of urban area and industries is a matter of increasing concern. This concern is being felt even in India in most of the cities and great efforts are made to obtain water supply even from great distances.

(4) **Power :** Hydrologic studies are essential to the planning of any water power development and for many existing plants the operating schedule is depends upon a perpetual hydrologic inventory and prediction system. To determine the feasibility of a "run-of-river" plant, operating with poundage, just sufficient to tide over the peak demand hours of each day, a reliable prediction is needed of the absolute minimum daily flow that may be expected of the stream and of the percentage of time that various other low rates of flow may be expected to exist. For the storage plant low seasonal flow rather than low daily flows are the important items and reservoir draw down studies must be made to determine the prime power possibilities of the site and relative economic of various heights of dams and capacities of turbine generator units.

(5) **Flood Control :** Flood control projects range from small improvements such as localized dredging or channel straightening to gigantic, basin wide development involving outlays of crores of rupees. For such projects, it is necessary first to analysis statistically the probable future flood of various magnitudes so that potential future flood losses may be predicted. Next a design flood must be synthesized and a variety of preliminary plans prepared for works that might protect against it. After this a number of the more promising alternatives must be studied in detail, either analytically or by means of hydraulic method.

(6) **Navigation :** If the stream is non-alluvial, the hydrologic studies are relatively simple and consist mainly of hydraulic computations to determine the effect of the proposed improvements or water surface for various rates of flow. Streams carrying sediment pose much more complex problems.

(7) **Erosion Control :** Erosion control is basically allied to the sedimentation of reservoirs, the problem which affects reservoir operation and its life.

(8) **Environmental Aspects :** The enormous growth of population and large scale industrialization in many countries of the world have brought about many public health problems, not be the least important of which is that of the pollution of streams. Many rivers downstream from cities have become open sewer dangerous To public health and destructive of fish and other wild life and natural beauty. Complete prevention of stream

pollution, although possible on some streams, is not economically feasible. it is here that the hydrologist comes to the assistance of the sanitary engineer. A complete stream pollution control study must include an investigation of stream flow, particularly the magnitude and duration of low flows. in some instances, the augmentations of low flow by means of reservoirs, has proved to be at least as important to the control of stream pollution as have investments in additional sewage treatment plants.

1.6 PRECIPITATION

The term *'Precipitation'* includes all forms of water from the atmosphere that ultimately reaches the earth surface. In our country, most of the precipitation is the form of rainfall, the other forms being snowfall, hail, dew, frost etc. In addition to the rainfall, snowfall in the Himalayan ranges after it melts contributes appreciable amount of water. However, the term *'Precipitation'* usually refers to the 'rainfall' from the atmosphere. It has been found that about one-fourth of the total amount of precipitation that falls on the continental areas flows back to the oceans by surface and sub-surface flow. Thus, the evaporation from the continental areas form the main source of moisture for the precipitation that occurs on the continent.

The study of 'precipitation' deals with its occurrence, measurement and analysis of the rainfall data over the area. It also enables to determine the run-off that will be available from such rainfalls. For land surfaces the relation between rainfall run-off and evaporation may be expressed as :

$$\text{Precipitation} = \text{Evaporation} + \text{Run-off}$$

Thus knowing the 'precipitation' and any one of the remaining two, the third variable can be determined.

1.7 TYPES OF PRECIPITATION

For the formation of clouds and subsequent precipitation, it is necessary for moist, air masses to cool below the saturation point. Usually adiabatic cooling of moist air takes place by reduction of pressure through lifting it to higher elevation.

Thus, for the precipitation to occur, the moist air masses should ascend and according to the causes of upward motion of moist air masses, the various types of precipitation are classified as follows :

1.7.1 Convectional Precipitation

In this type of precipitation, the air masses close to the warm earth get heated and ascend because of its low density. This upward movement of the air which is warmer than its surrounding cools adiabatically to form clouds that ultimately results in precipitation, the intensity of which varies from light showers to thunder storm. When such a precipitation is accompanied by devastating winds, it results into *'tornadoes'*.

1.7.2 Cyclonic Precipitation

A large low pressure zone with a circulating wind is known as a cyclone. Cyclonic precipitation occurs when the lifting of moist air masses results in the formation of low pressure belt. Such a low pressure belt is formed due to the unequal heating of the earth's mass that result in the difference of pressure head in the air masses.

The two main types of cyclones are known as 'tropical cyclones' and 'extra-tropical cyclones'. The 'tropical cyclone' also known as 'hurricane' or 'typhoon' which has diameter varying from 200 to 1600 km is accompanied by very high wind velocity that results in heavy precipitation. The 'extra-tropical cyclone' on the other hand has much larger diameter (even upto 3000 km) that results in precipitation over a very wide area.

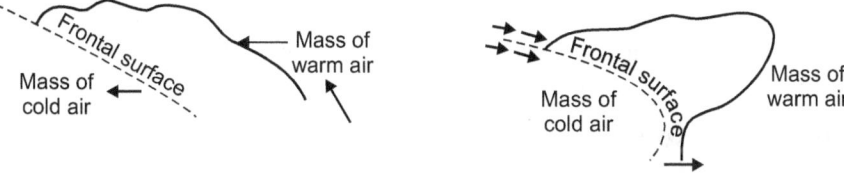

Fig. 1.2 : Warm front precipitation   Fig. 1.3 : Cold front precipitation

'Cyclonic precipitation' is also classified as 'frontal' and 'non-frontal' type. When warm air is lifted over cold, it results in frontal precipitation. The 'frontal precipitation' may be either *warm-front precipitation* (Fig. 1.2) or *cold-front precipitation* (Fig. 1.3).

In the former, the warm air mass moves upward over a cold air mass which results in the precipitation of light to moderate intensity whereas in the latter the advancing mass of cold air forces the warm air upwards resulting in the precipitation of the showery nature.

1.7.3 Orographic Precipitation

Orographic precipitation occurs when an air mass is forced by topographic barriers to higher altitude where the temperature is cooler. This type of precipitation is common in mountainous regions where air currents are forced up over the tops of the mountains by wind movement. When the air rises to a cooler altitude, condensation occurs. Orographic precipitation can be quite pronounced on the windward side of a mountain range while there is often a relatively little precipitation on the leeward side. (Fig. 1.4). e.g. Cherapunjee in the Himalaya Ranges receives highest rainfall in our country of the order of 1200 cm because of Orographic precipitation.

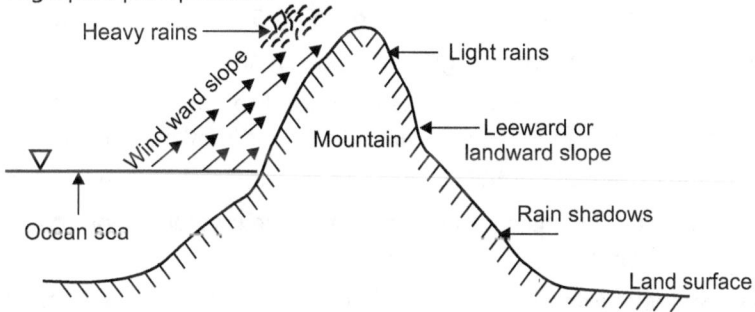

Fig. 1.4 : Orographic precipitation

1.8 PRECIPITATION IN INDIA

Precipitation in India is mainly due to –

- South-West monsoon and
- Winter monsoon.

1.8.1 South-West Monsoon

The major portion of India receives rainfall during South-West monsoon (June to September) every year which amounts to more than 75% of annual rainfall in our country. The South-West monsoon popularly known as Kerala monsoon becomes active by the end of May every year and advances in two branches known as the Arabian Sea branch (Kerala) and the Bay of Bengal branch (Assam). Our Capital city Delhi receives rainfall from both the branches in the last week of June or first week of July.

1.8.2 Winter Monsoon

During the months of December to February, due to western disturbances, the northern part of our country i.e. Jammu and Kashmir and Himalayan region receives rainfall and snowfall. Creation of low pressure in the Bay of Bengal during this period causes rainfall in the south India.

1.8.3 Forms of Precipitation

The forms of precipitation that are commonly seen are as follows :

Drizzle : It is a uniform precipitation of water droplets of size less than 0.5 mm and of intensity less than 1 mm/hour.

Rain : Rain forms the main form of precipitation in our country. Water vapours in the atmosphere gets condensed and fall from the cloud in the form of water drops of size larger than 0.5 mm, with a maximum size of 6 mm.

The intensity of rain fall is divided into the following three categories :

    (1) **'Light Rain'** for the intensity varying from trace to 2.5 mm/hour.

    (2) **'Moderate Rain'** for the intensity varying from 2.5 mm to 7.5 mm/hour and

    (3) **'Heavy Rain'** whose intensity is greater than 7.5 mm/hour.

Glaze : It is the freezing of rain or drizzle as if comes into contact with the cold objects or ground (at about 0°C). Such an ice coated rain or drizzle is known as 'glaze'.

Sleet : These are the frozen rain drops while falling through air below freezing temperature.

Snow : It is the precipitation which falls in the form of **ice crystals.** In our country, snow falls in the northern Himalayan ranges.

Snow Flakes or Snow Pellets : The ice crystals combine together to form snow flakes or snow pellets.

Hail : These are lumps of ice of size more than 6 to 8 mm diameter. They occur during violent thunder storms. The above forms of precipitation refer to *'falling moisture'*. The other forms not included above are haze, dew, frost etc.

1.9 MEASUREMENT OF PRECIPITATION

1.9.1 Introduction

As most of the **'precipitation'** that occurs in our country is through **'rainfall'**, these two terms will be treated as synonymous. The first meteorological element measured by man was probably the rainfall (i.e. precipitation). It has been found that rainfall records were maintained in our country in the fourth century B.C. In order to estimate total run-off that may be available it is necessary to measure the 'precipitation'. Precipitation is measured in terms of vertical depth to which the water from the rainfall would stand on a level surface if all the rain water were collected on it, assuming no losses by evaporation or run-off.

1.9.2 Raingauge

As the amount of precipitation is not same throughout the country, but varies from place to place, certain precipitation measuring devices called as *'raingauges'* are to be installed at selected key points. A raingauge is a device that collects and measures the precipitation in mm occurring over that area.

1.9.3 Selection of Site for Raingauge Station

In order that the raingauge installed at a particular place should collect and measure the rainfall accurately, the following points need consideration during its installation.

- The installation of the raingauge should be on a level ground and open to the sky.
- The raingauge should have a true horizontal surface which can easily *catch* the rain drops falling over it.
- In order that the wind effects should not disturb the *'catch'* the gauge should as far as possible be installed at the ground level. Proper care should also be taken to see that there is no splashing or flooding of raingauge from the adjoining area.
- An open fence of the size about six meter square should surround the raingauge station to protect it from cattles. The minimum distance of any obstruction from the raingauge station should not be less than two times the height of obstruction.
- As measurement of precipitation by raingauge at a particular place is never subject to check by repetition, utmost precautions should be taken to collect the rainfall in the raingauge and to measure it accurately.

1.9.4 Installation of Non-Recording Raingauge

The raingauge is fixed on a masonry or concrete foundation 600 x 600 mm sunk into the ground. Into this foundation, the base of the gauge is cemented so that the rim of the gauges is exactly 300 mm above ground level.

1.9.5 Protection of Raingauge

The raingauge is protected from being damaged particularly by stray cattle by erecting a fence around it as shown in Fig. 1.5.

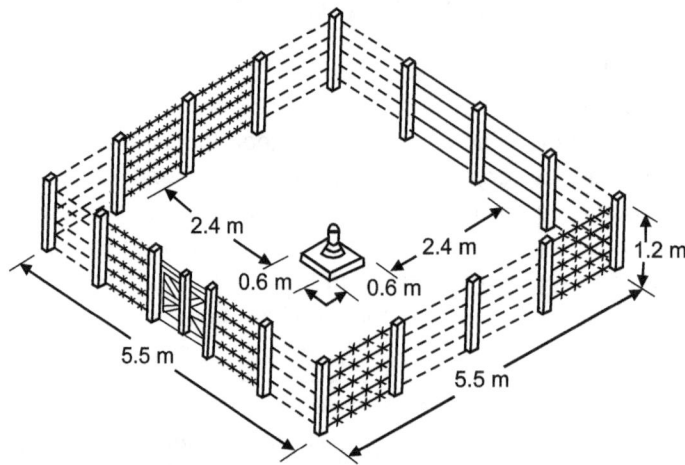

Fig. 1.5 : Raingauge installed within a barbed wire fence

The raingauge should be kept locked and periodically got painted to prevent its surface from corroding. The rain water in the gauge is measured every day at 0.8.30 am Indian Standard time each day. If it is raining at the time of observation, all operations should be completed as quickly as possible to avoid errors. If rainfall is heavy at the time of observation, a spare bottle should be used.

1.10 TYPES OF RAINGAUGES

The two types of *'raingauges'* commonly used for measurement of rainfall are classified as *'non-recording'* and *'recording or automatic raingauges'*.

1.10.1 Non-Recording Raingauges

Any open receptacle having vertical sides may be used for measurement of rainfall. To permit more accurate measurements certain refinements are made in receptacles and are knows as raingauges. The most common type of non-recording raingauges used in our country is the *'Symons raingauge'*. It consists of a circular rim of 127 mm diameter placed over a funnel as shown in Fig. 1.6.

The glass bottle below the funnel collects the rain falling over the rim. The funnel and the receiving glass bottle are placed in a metal casing. The rim which is in horizontal position is placed 305 mm above the ground level. The rainfall collected in the glass bottle is then measured by a glass tube graduated in mm and tenth of mm.

It is usual practice to measure the rainfall everyday morning at 8.30 hours (I.S.T) and is said to be the rainfall of that day. However, if the rainfall in a day exceeds 100 mm which is the maximum capacity of the glass bottle, it should be measured frequently before the bottle overflows.

Thus, it can be seen that the Symon's raingauges measures only the total (depth of) rainfall for the past 24 hours but does not furnish any information about the intensity and duration of rainfall that has occurred at different times of the day.

In places where snowfall is expected, the outer funnel and the receiving bottle of the raingauge are removed and the snow is collected in the outer metal casing. After melting of the snow the resulting depth of water is measured by a graduated measuring glass tube. These gauges are called as non-recording as they do not record the rainfall directly, but simply collect it.

The modified form of Symon's raingauge as recommended by Indian Meteorological Department in 1969 known as *'Standard raingauge'* is being used now-a-days in our country. The *'Standard raingauge'* is available in two different sizes of 100 and 200 sq. cm. aperture size, having 112.9 and 159.6 mm diameters respectively.

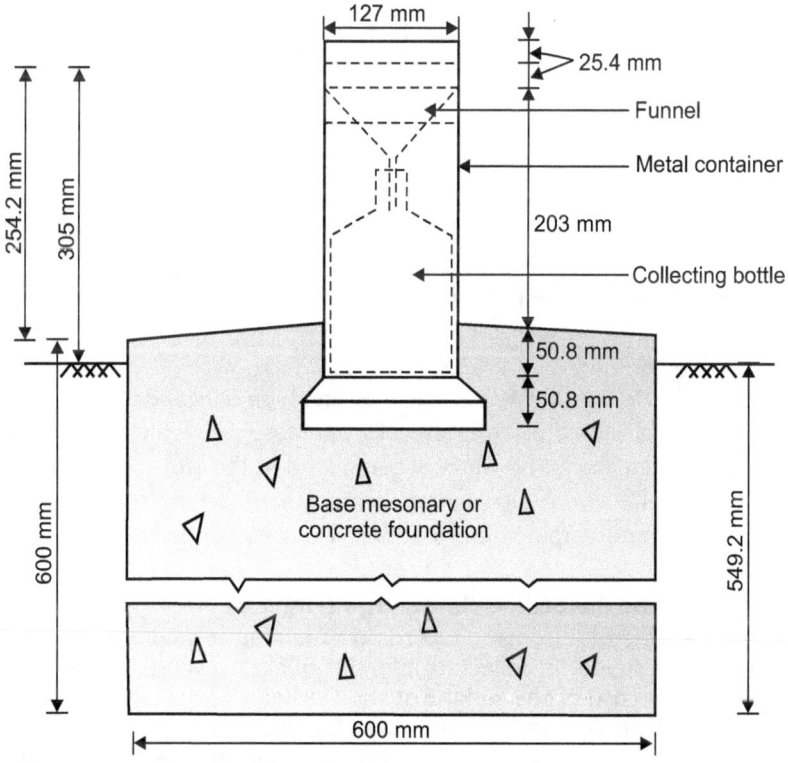

Fig. 1.6 : Symon's type non-recording raingauge

1.10.2 Recording or Automatic Raingauges

The difficulty of recording the intensity and duration of rainfall experienced in *'non-recording'* is overcome by installation of *'recording type raingauges'*. Recording raingauges furnish a continuous plot of precipitation against time in the form of pencil point trace on a clock driven chart.

1.10.2.1 U.S.W.B. Tipping Bucket Type Gauge (Fig. 1.7)

The tipping bucket type recording gauge as suggested by United State Weather Bureau, for first order rain gauge stations consists of 300 mm size funnel that collects the precipitation (i.e. rainfall) and transfers it to a pair of small buckets.

These buckets are so arranged that when 0.25 mm of rainfall is collected in one bucket it tips and spills water into a storage can and automatically brings the other bucket in position.

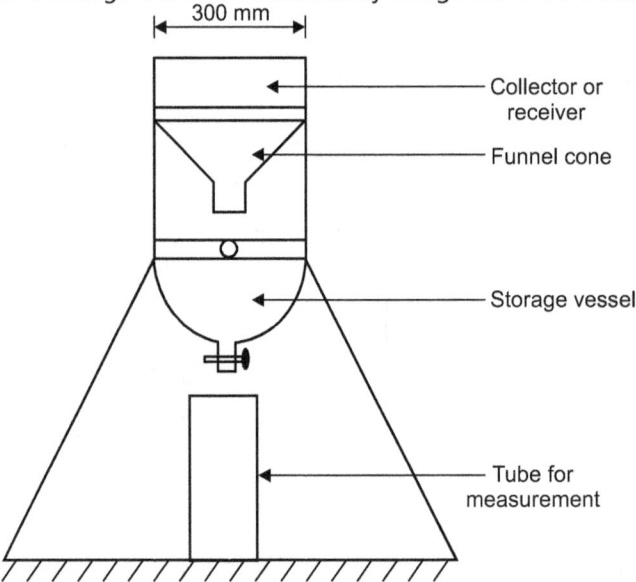

Fig. 1.7 : U.S.W.B. tipping bucket type raingauge

The tipping of the bucket actuates an electrically operated pen which goes on continuously plotting on a clock driven chart. The water accumulated in the storage can is then measured to obtain the total rainfall which also serves as a check. This type of gauge is adopted for recording rainfall of remote raingauge stations. However, it is unsuitable for recording snowfalls.

1.10.2.2 Weighing Type Recording Raingauge (Fig. 1.8)

These gauges are capable of automatic recording of rainfall as well as snowfall. The amount of rainfall through the funnel is collected into the bucket resting on a spring balance or weighing scale. The increase in the weight of the bucket and its contents are continuously recorded on a chart wrapped round a drum driven by clock mechanism.

The movement of the pen in vertical plane on the chart records the cumulative rainfall against the time scale obtained by the regular rotation of the drum.

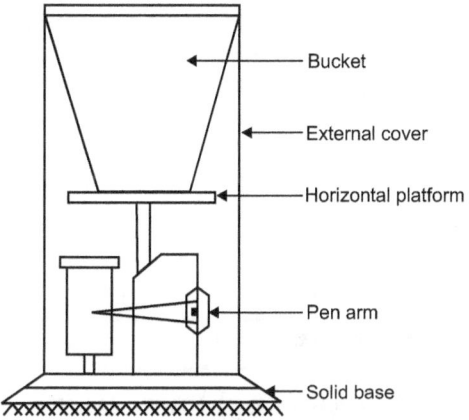

Fig. 1.8 : Weighing type raingauge

1.10.2.3 Float Type Recording Raingauge (Fig. 1.9)

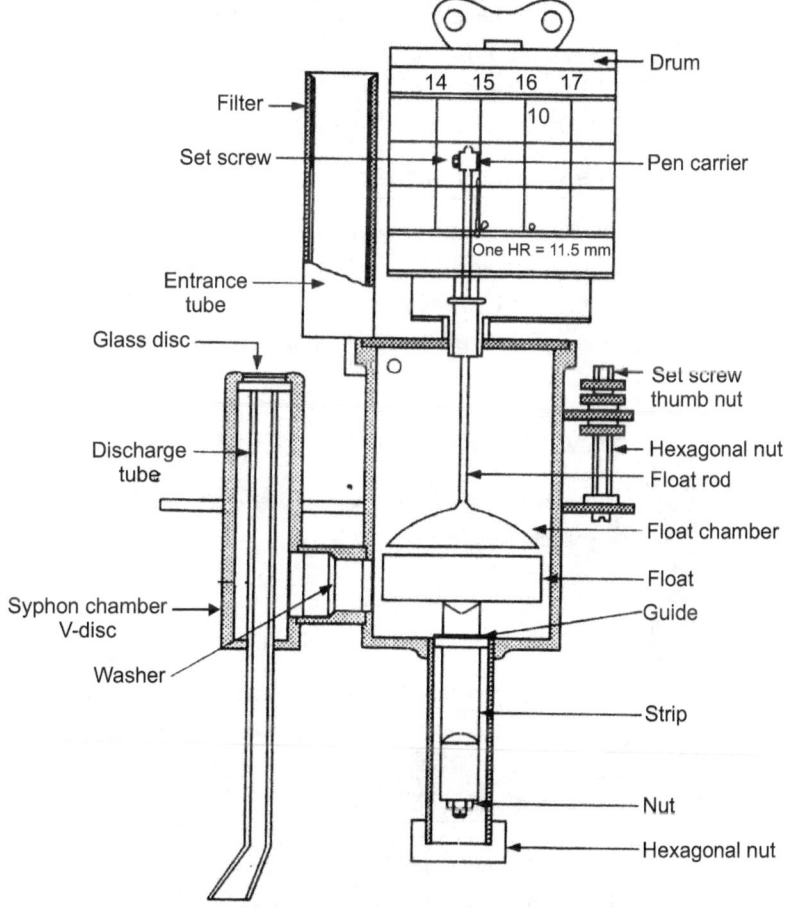

Fig. 1.9 : Float type (Automatic) gauge

In this type of raingauge, the rainfall is collected, through the funnel into the float chamber, which causes the float to rise. The movement of the float is transferred to the pen attached to it which goes on continuously moving on a chart wound round a drum, driven by clock mechanism. The moment the float chamber is filled up with water, a siphon arrangement empties the float chamber automatically. The whole mechanism works continuously for one week after which the chart surrounding the drum is also to be replaced. The Indian Meteorological Department has recommended this type as a standard type of recording raingauge for our country.

The above gauge can also be used for recording the moderate snowfall.

1.11 MODERN METHODS OF MEASUREMENT OF PRECIPITATION

1.11.1 Telemetering (Self Reporting) Raingauge

If a raingauge is installed in an inaccessible mountainous region, it will not be possible to collect the daily rainfall data. In such cases, telemetering (or self reporting) raingauge can be used conveniently. As already explained in the tipping bucket type of raingauge, the moment the buckets fill and tips, an electronic unit installed at the raingauge station sends the message regarding the millimeters of rainfall collected to the base station.

1.11.2 Rainfall Measurement by Radar

Radar transmits a pulse of electromagnetic energy as a beam in a direction determined by a movable antenna. The beam width and shape are determined by the antenna size, and configuration. The radiated wave which travels at the speed of light, is partially reflected by could or precipitation particles and returns to the radar, where it is received by the same antenna.

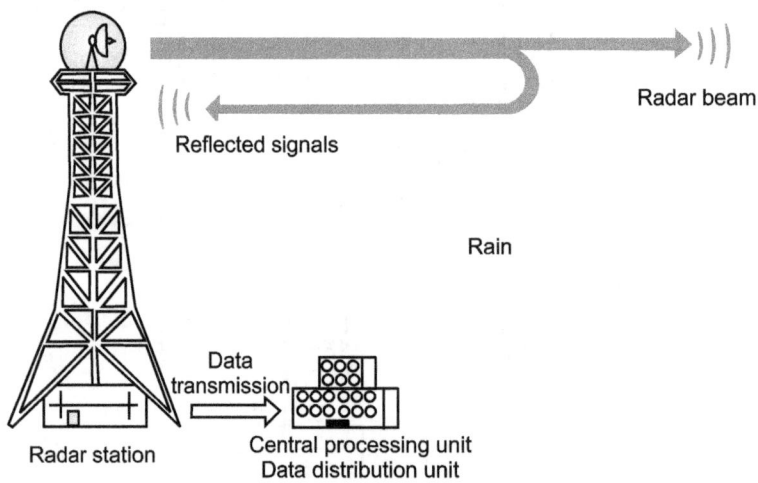

Fig. 1.10 : Rainfall measurement by radar

Energy returned to the radar and displayed on the radarscope, is called echo. The brightness of an indication of the magnitude of returned power, which in turn is a measure of the radar reflectively of the hydrometeors. The reflectivity of a group of hydrometers depends on such factors as

- Drop size distribution
- Number of particles per unit volume
- Physical state a solid or liquid
- Shape of individual elements
- If a symmetrical, their aspects with respect to the radar.

Generally speaking the more intense the precipitation, the greater the reflectivity. the areal extent of rainfall may be depicted reliably by radar for ranges up to 230 km. Beyond this range the beam is at such a high altitude and is so broad that results become distorted in azimuth. Intense rainfall centers, however, can be detected beyond this range. Photographic procedures for integrating radar echoes and correlating them with precipitation consist of exposures at 5 minutes intervals over a period of from 1 to 3 hrs. An experienced radar operator can them make a fairly good quantitative analysis of the rainfall distribution.

However recently at some places, special equipment automatically measures electronically the returned power for incremental area within the beam and converts it into equivalent rainfall rates, which are then integrated with respect to time. The totals for any duration are equal precipitation, can be drawn. Indian Meteorological Department has a net work of ten 3 cm radar at various airports in the country and net work of eight 10 cm 8 band Radars along the coast. The Indian Meteorological Department has already installed such remote sensing radar gauges for the early detection of thunder storms in coastal regions of Tamil Nadu, West Bengal and Andhra Pradesh.

Such a radar raingauge should be installed in a plane ground free from solid obstructions etc.

1.12 OPTIMUM NUMBER OF RAINGAUGE STATIONS

As the raingauge station represents a very small area of the entire extent of the storm, it is necessary to have sufficient number of raingauges installed in the area so as to get the real information of the storm over the entire catchment. It has been found that smaller the catchment area covered by the each raingauge, better will be the accuracy of the measurement of precipitation. However, installation of large number of raingauge stations may not be economical. Thus, it is necessary to ascertain the optimum number of raingauge stations to be installed consistent with their true representation and fairly accurate measurement of the precipitation of the area. The guide lines recommended by the Indian Standard (4987 of 1968) for the 'raingauge density' (i.e. optimum number of raingauges to be installed in a given area) are as follows.

The Indian Standard for the installation of Raingauge stations in our country are :

Serial No.	Topography	Criteria for Installation of Raingauge Station
1.	Flat, plains.	1 raingauge station for 520 km².
2.	Undulating or elevated or somewhat mountainous region.	1 raingauge station for 260 to 390 km².
3.	Highly hilly (or mountainous area having heavy rainfall).	1 raingauge station for 130 km² (with 10% of automatic recording types).

WMO Suggestion for Density of Raingauge Network :

World Meteorological Organization has given a minimum density for precipitation gauge network: (at least 10% are automatic recording gauges)

Region Type	Range of Norms for Minimum Network (km²/gauge)	Range of Provisional Norms in Difficult Conditions (km²/gauge)
I	600-900	900-3000
II-A	100-250	250-1000
II-B	25	
III	1500-1000	

I : Flat region of temperature, Mediterranean and tropical zones;

II-A : Mountain region of temperate, Mediterranean and tropical zones

II-B : Small Mountains island with very irregular precipitation requiring very dense hydrographic network

III : Arid and polar zones

1.13 STATISTICAL METHOD FOR DETERMINATION OF OPTIMUM NUMBER OF RAINGAUGES

As per statistical analysis, it is possible to determine the optimum number of raingauge stations required in an area to give an average or mean rainfall with a certain allowable percentage error. Smaller the permissible percentage error, larger will be the number of raingauge stations and vice a versa.

The statistical equation used for optimum number of raingauge stations is as follows :

$$N = \left(\frac{C_V}{e}\right)^2$$

where, N = Optimum number of raingauge stations

C_V = Coefficient of variation of rainfall of already existing n_e stations expressed in per cent.

e = Allowable error (in percentage) in estimation of mean rainfall.

where $\quad C_V = \left(\dfrac{\sigma}{P_{mean}}\right)$

in which $\quad \sigma^2 = (\text{Standard deviation})^2 = \dfrac{\Sigma P^2 - (P_{total})^2 / n}{n - 1}$

where, $\quad \Sigma P^2 = P_1^2 + P_2^2 + P_3^2 + P_N^2 \ldots$

$P_{total} = P_1 + P_2 + \ldots + P_N$

n = Number of raingauge stations

N = Optimum number of raingauges required

1.14 ESTIMATION OF MISSING RAINFALL DATA

If the annual rainfall data of a particular station is found to be missing due to non-functioning of the instrument etc. it can be determined from the values of the annual rainfall data of the neighbouring raingauge stations, as explained below.

- When *normal* (average) annual precipitation is at nearby raingauge stations are within 10% of the normal annual precipitation at a missing station say x, then annual precipitation at the station x, will be $P_x = \dfrac{(P_1 + P_2 + P_3 + \ldots + P_n)}{n}$, where $P_1, P_2, P_3, \ldots, P_n$ are the annual rainfall of the neighbouring n stations.

- When the normal (average) annual rainfall of the neighbouring stations vary by more than 10% of the normal (average) annual run-off of the missing station x, then the *"normal rational method"* is to be used. In this method, the precipitations (i.e. rainfall) at the neighbouring stations are weighted by the ratios of their normal (average) annual precipitation.

Thus, $\quad P_N = \dfrac{1}{n}\left\{\dfrac{N_x}{N_1} \cdot P_1 + \dfrac{N_x}{N_2} \cdot P_2 + \ldots \dfrac{N_x}{N_n} \cdot P_n\right\}$

where $N_1, N_2, N_3, \ldots, N_n$ are the normal average annual precipitation of the 'n' neighbouring stations and N_x refers to the normal average annual precipitation of the missing raingauge station x.

1.15 DOUBLE MASS CURVE ANALYSIS (FIG. 1.11)

Sometimes the existing external conditions at a particular raingauge station may significantly change due to changes in the environment such as afforestation, deforestation, construction of multi-storeyed buildings near the site of raingauge station. This may result in the inconsistency of the rainfall data at such affected stations. The technique called as *'Double mass curve'* is adopted to check such inconsistencies. A double mass curve consists of a systematic plot of cumulative annual rainfall at such a station against the cumulative values of annual rainfall for the surrounding raingauge stations. The rainfall data of the affected as well as the surrounding raingauge stations is then entered in chronological order arranged in reverse direction. From such a plot, the year in which inconsistency has taken place is indicated by the abrupt change in the slope of the plotted graph (Fig. 1.11).

Procedure :

- Select group of convenient number of base stations lying in the vicinity of selected problem station Q.
- Arrange in the reverse chronological order the annual rainfall of selected station Q and the mean rainfall of group of stations and calculate the accumulated rainfall of station Q and also the accumulated values of mean of the group stations.
- Plot a graph of accumulated mean annual rainfall (of group of station) versus the accumulated annual rainfall of station Q for corresponding time period as shown in the Fig. 1.11.
- A change in the consistency is indicated from the graph at the point where the slope of the line changes i.e. break point in the year 1984.
- Correct the rainfall values at station Q beyond this break point (i.e. inconsistency point) by the equation,

$$C_p = O_p \times \text{Correction factor}$$

$$= O_p \times \frac{M}{N}$$

$$= O_p \cdot \frac{S_C}{S_O}$$

where, C_P = Correction for rainfall of precipitation at Q

O_P = Original rainfall or precipitation

S_C = Corrected slope

S_O = Original slope

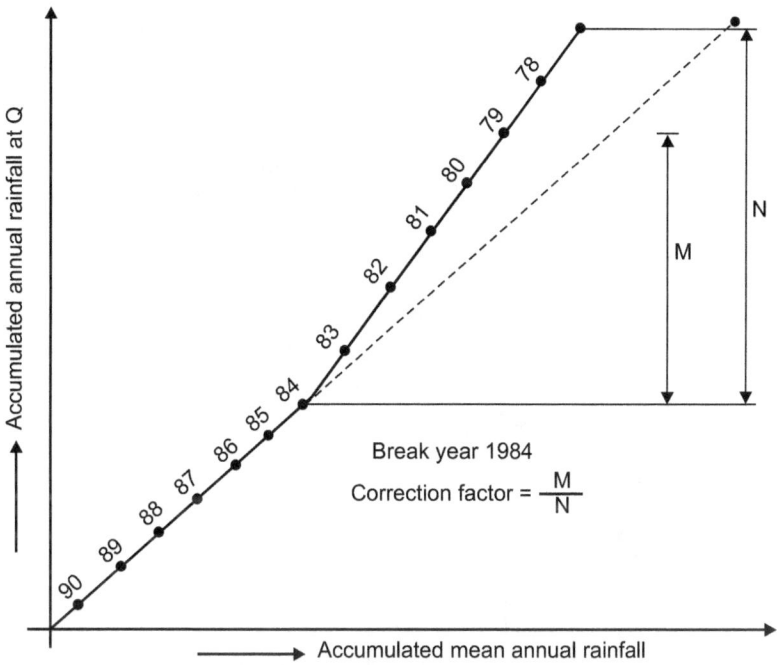

Fig. 1.11 : Double mass curve analysis

1.16 REPRESENTATION OF RAINFALL DATA

The rainfall data is generally represented either in the form of *'mass rainfall curve'* or *'hyetograph'*.

1.16.1 Mass Rainfall Curve

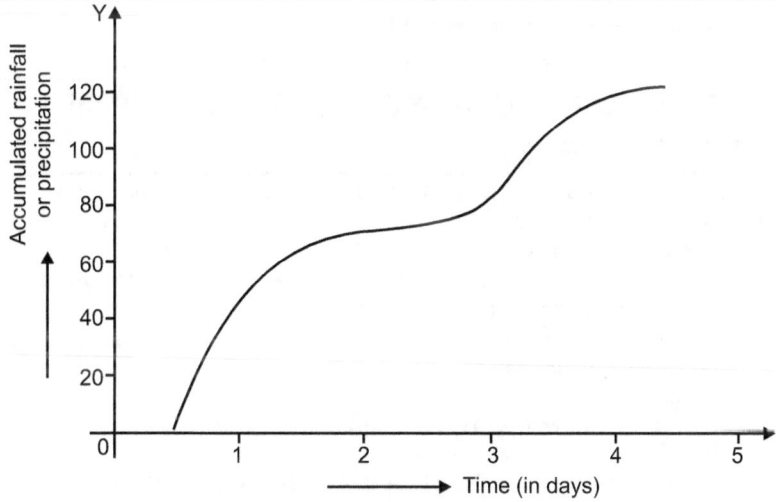

Fig. 1.12 : Mass rainfall curve

Mass rainfall curve is a systematic plot of cumulative precipitation (or rainfall) against time arranged in the order of their occurrence. Such mass rainfall curves enable to determine the duration and total amount of precipitation or (rainfall) and also the intensity of precipitation (or rainfall) at any particular time of the day.

The precipitation recorded by the recording type of raingauges are the typical cases of mass rainfall curves. Fig. 1.12 indicates a plot of accumulated rainfall or precipitation in mm versus the time in days i.e. mass rainfall curve.

1.16.2 Hyetograph (Fig. 1.13)

If the intensity of rainfall in mm/hour is plotted against the time in hours, a typical bar chart is obtained and is called as hyetograph. It is derived from the mass rainfall curve as explained earlier. Obviously the area covered by the hyetograph indicates the total rainfall (or precipitation) recorded during that period (Fig. 1.13).

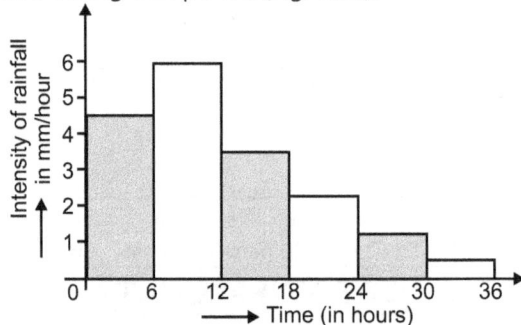

Fig. 1.13 : Hyetograph

1.16.3 Point Rainfall or Station Rainfall

Point or station rainfall is defined as 'the data of rainfall of a particular station' and may be designated as hourly, daily, weekly, monthly and yearly etc. This can be represented graphically in the form of bar chart (i.e. magnitude of rainfall versus time).

1.17 INTENSITY-DURATION AND DEPTH-DURATION FREQUENCY CURVES

It is a common knowledge that intensity of the storm (i.e. precipitation) is seen to decrease with the increase in the storm duration. Moreover, for a storm of given duration, its intensity will be more if its return period is very large. Often, the knowledge of rainfall intensities of different durations having different return periods is essential in the design of quick disposal of run-off, soil conservation, sediment transport etc.

The three factors the intensity of rainfall (i), its duration in hours (D) and the return period in years (T) are related to each other as follows :

$$i = \frac{C(T)^a}{(D+b)^n}$$ where C, a, b and n are constants of the catchment or watershed.

Intensity-duration frequency curve in Fig. 1.14 indicates the plot of variation of intensity (i) on Y-axis with duration (D) on X-axis for return period T of 25, 50, 75 and 100 years.

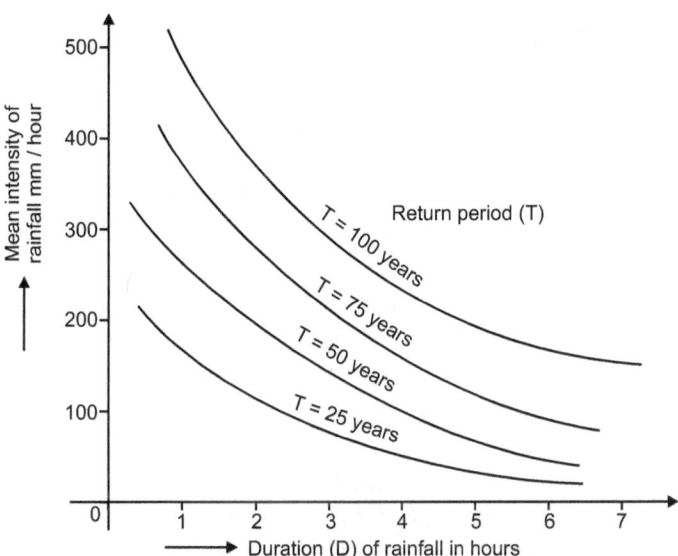

Fig. 1.14 : Intensity-Duration frequency curves

Depth-duration frequency curve in Fig. 1.15 shows the plot of depth of rainfall (in mm) along Y-axis versus the duration (D) in hours along X-axis for the various return periods.

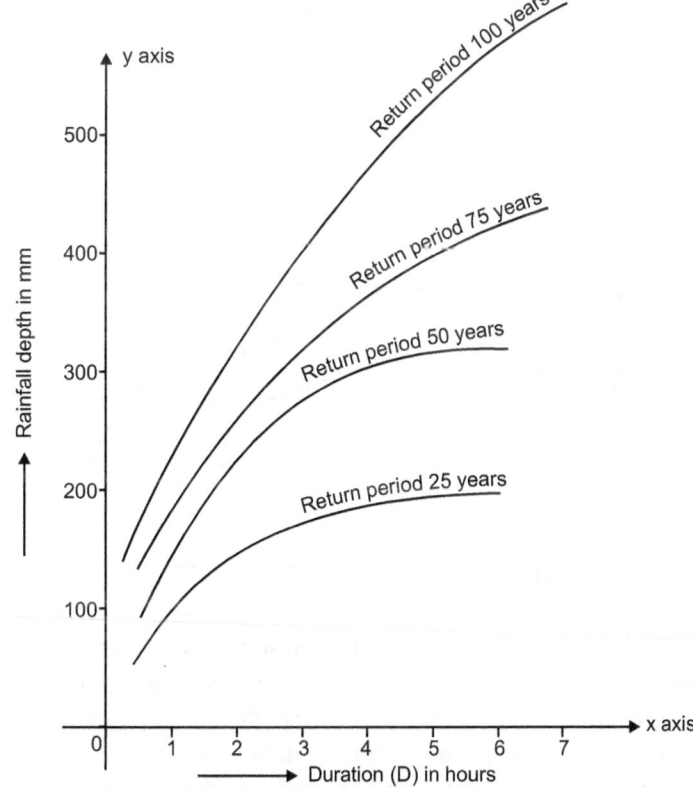

Fig. 1.15 : Depth-Duration (frequency) curves

1.18 DEPTH-AREA-DURATION (D.A.D.) ANALYSIS

The characteristics of areal distribution of a given storm of specified duration are indicated in its depth-area relationship. It has been observed that for a storm of specified duration, the mean or average depth decreases with the increase in the area of catchment in an exponential form. Such depth area duration curves are useful in determining the size of design rainfall and design floods. Moreover, it can be seen that higher intensities of storm usually occurs in the earlier part of the storm.

The object of D.A.D. analysis is to ascertain the largest average depth of rainfall that has occurred over catchment of various sizes during specified time which may be in hours or days. e.g. maximum depth that has occurred during 12 hours over 1000 sq. km. catchment area. The establishment of relationship between maximum depth-area-duration for an area is called as D.A.D. analysis.

To start with, select a storm of severe intensity that has occurred over the given area and prepare mass curve and isohyetal maps for this area. Now, plot depth-area curve of specified duration of the storm. Now from the mass curve of rainfall for various durations, find out the maximum depth of rainfall during this duration, and a curve of maximum depth - area for the specified duration D hours is prepared.

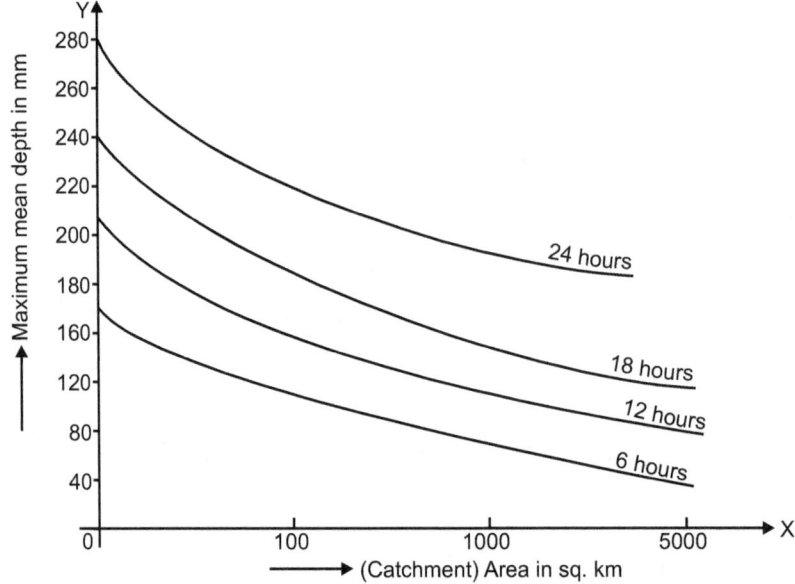

Fig. 1.16 : Depth-Area-Duration curve

Further by repeating the same procedure for different storms, maximum depth-area curves are prepared for D-duration. By following the same procedure for different values of D, a series of envelope curves for maximum depth versus area for different duration is prepared and is known as Depth-area-duration curves as shown in Fig. 1.16.

From the D.A.D. curves, the following conclusion can be drawn.
- The maximum depth for a specified storm is found to decrease with the increase in area of catchment.
- Maximum depth is found to increase with the duration for a specified area of catchment.

1.19 DETERMINATION OF AVERAGE (OR MEAN) PRECIPITATION OVER AREA

A raingauge at a particular station indicates a *'point rainfall'* which may be considered as mean precipitation over small areas less than about 50 sq. km. However, in case of hydrological problems, a knowledge of the mean depth of precipitation over large areas such as catchment basins is required to be ascertained as the rainfall over such a large areas will not be uniform i.e. same at all the raingauge stations installed in the area. The methods commonly adopted to determine the average or mean precipitation over the given area are as follows :

1.19.1 Arithmetic Average or Mean Method

The simplest method of determining the mean precipitation (or rainfall) over a given catchment area is to take a simple arithmetic mean of all the rainfall recorded at the various raingauges in the area i.e. if $P_1, P_2, P_3, ..., P_n$ are the amount of rainfall recorded at the n raingauge stations installed in the catchment basin, then mean or average precipitation is

$$= \frac{P_1 + P_2 + P_3 + ... + P_n}{n} = \frac{\Sigma P}{n}$$

The method is very simple and is usually adopted in a flat area where the raingauges are uniformly distributed and where the variation in the rainfall recorded at various stations installed in the area is very small.

1.19.2 Thiessen (Polygon) Method (Fig. 1.17)

The method described above gives unsatisfactory results when there is non-uniform distribution of raingauges that are installed in the catchment area. In such cases, *'Thiessen polygon method'* is adopted. The method consists in assigning certain weightage to each raingauge station depending upon its areal distribution i.e. area of influence.

The procedure of determining the area of influence by Theissen polygon consists in first locating the position of the raingauge station on a map and then drawing perpendicular bisectors of the lines connecting the raingauge stations. Thus, the polygon formed by such lines around each ringuage station represents the area of influence controlled by that station.

The areas of such polygons are computed by a planimeter and are expressed in terms of percentage of the entire area of the catchment. This assigned percentage area is then multiplied by the precipitation (i.e. rainfall) at that station and the summation of all such results will be the weighted mean or average precipitation for the catchment.

Thus, if $A_1, A_2, A_3, ..., A_n$ are the areas of influence (i.e. polygons) of raingauge stations 1, 2, 3, ..., n and $P_1, P_2, P_3, ..., P_n$ are the magnitudes of precipitation recorded by the raingauge stations respectively, then (the mean or average precipitation)

$$P_{mean} = \frac{P_1 A_1 + P_2 A_2 + P_3 A_3 + ... + P_n A_n}{(A_1 + A_2 + A_3, ..., A_n)}$$

or

$$P_{mean} = \frac{\Sigma P_1 A_1}{\Sigma A_1}$$

and

$$\begin{bmatrix} \text{Weightage factor for} \\ \text{each raingauge station} \end{bmatrix} = \frac{\begin{bmatrix} \text{Area of influence for the raingauge station} \\ \text{(as determined by Thiessen polygon method)} \end{bmatrix}}{\text{Total area of the catchment basin}}$$

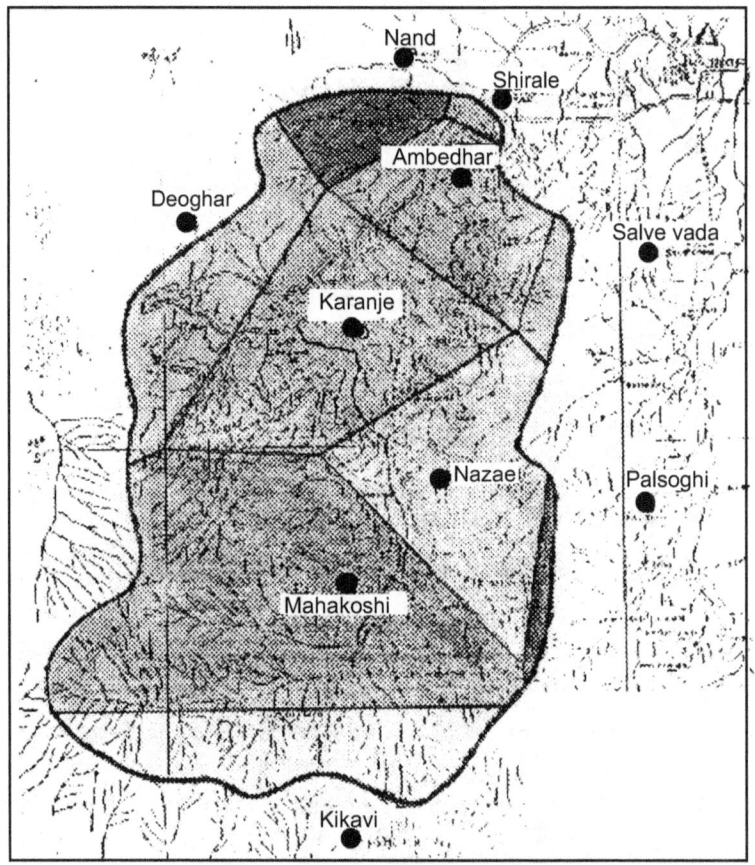

Fig. 1.17 : Thiessen polygon method

The Thiessen method is superior to the arithmetic mean or average method. Moreover, the raingauge stations installed outside the catchment area are also incorporated. However, its serious limitation is that every time a new raingauge station is added to or deleted from the network, a new Thiessen polygon diagram will have to be constructed.

1.19.3 The Isohyetal Method (Fig. 1.18)

It is the most accurate method of determining the mean or average precipitation over a given catchment area. An *'isohyet'* is defined as the line joining all points having same or equal rainfall. The method consists in marking the positions of raingauge stations with their recorded rainfall on a catchment area drawn to suitable scale on the drawing paper. The lines of equal rainfall are then drawn by using the interpolation technique. The respective areas between the adjacent isohyets are then determined either graphically or by a planimeter, say $A_1, A_2, A_3, ..., A_n$. The mean value of the rainfall indicated by the two consecutive isohyets is then supposed to be representing the inter-isohyetal area. Then mean or average rainfall

$$\frac{\left\{\frac{(P_1 + P_2)}{2} A_1 + \frac{(P_2 + P_3)}{2} A_2 + ... + \frac{(P_{n-1} + P_n)}{2} A_{n-1}\right\}}{\text{Total area of catchment (A)}}$$

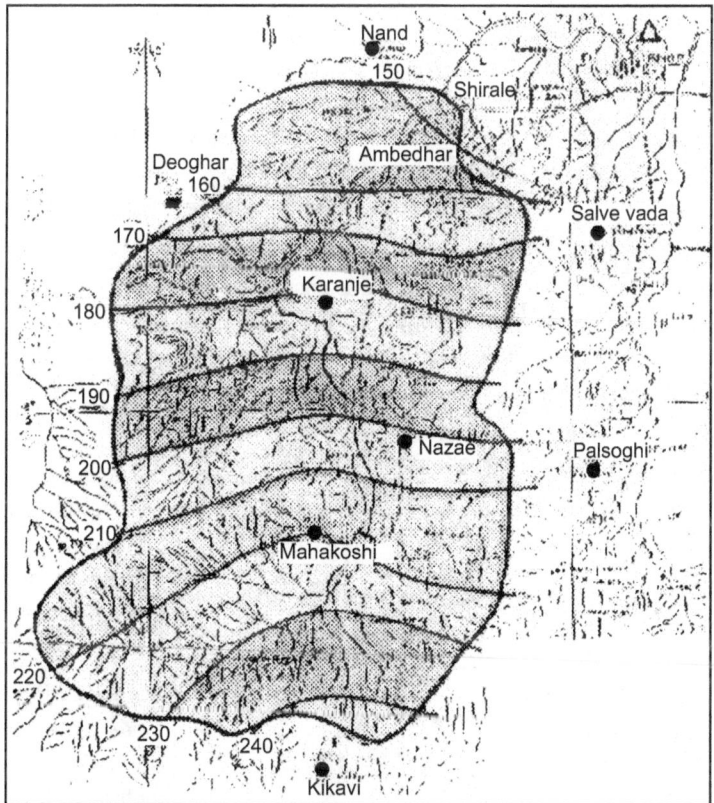

Fig. 1.18 : Isohyetal method

1.19.4 Merits and Demerits of above Three Methods

Arithmetic mean method (I)	Thiessen polygon method (II)	Isohyetal method (III)
(1) It is a simple method and requires no skill.	It is to be preferred to the arithmetic mean method as due weightages are assigned to all raingauge stations on sound rational basis.	The method is superior to the first two methods.
(2) If the raingauge stations are distributed uniformly over the entire catchment area, and when there is no appreciable variation in the rainfall, the method gives satisfactory results.	The method also accounts for the raingauges just lying outside the catchment area that influence the rainfall.	At the time of plotting for isohyets due consideration is given to rainfall at each raingauge station.
(3) Raingauge station lying just outside of the boundary of the catchment area is not considered even though it has influence over the area within the boundary.	The method is inferior to isohyetal method as regards the accuracy of the results. The method does not account for rainfall when different polygons are plotted around raingauge station.	The method also considers raingauge stations lying just beyond the boundary of the catchment to calculate mean rainfall but their influence goes on reducing with the increase in the distance from the boundary.
(4) If there is appreciable difference in the topography and rainfall varies consider-ably then the method is not suitable.	If there is abrupt change in the topography of the catchment the rainfall as recorded by raingauge station may not be truly repre-sentative for that polygon under consideration.	The method also accounts for the changes in the topography of catchment.
(5)		The accuracy of the isohyetal plotting depends upon the skill, judgement and experience of the person sketching the isohyets.
(6)		However, the method requires more care and time as compared to the other two methods.

1.20 EVAPORATION

Of the precipitation (i.e. rainfall) that occurs on the surface of the earth, part of it is lost as :

(i) *'Interception'* loss due to vegetation, plant leaves etc.

(ii) *'Evaporation'* from water bodies and soil surfaces.

(iii) *'Transpiration'* from vegetation, plant leaves.

A term evapo-transpiration is usually used for (ii) and (iii) combined.

(iv) *'Infiltration'* into the soil at ground surface level.

(v) *'Depression storage'* that accumulates in the low-lying area, and after all the above requirements are met with, the remaining portion that flows on the surface as 'runoff'.

Thus, as per the equation of continuity called as water budget equation,

Precipitation (i.e. rainfall) = Run-off + Total loss of water

'Evaporation' that forms a part of the hydrologic curve is the process by which the precipitation that falls on the earth's surface is returned to the atmosphere as vapour. In addition to the evaporation losses from water bodies, soil and vegetation, *'transpiration'* from the vegetation and plant leaves, is also considered. The total loss due to both is called as *'evapo-transpiration'* or total evaporation, or total loss.

1.21 EVAPORATION AND FACTORS AFFECTING EVAPORATION

As already stated, evaporation is the process by which the precipitation (i.e. rainfall) is returned to the atmosphere as *'vapour'* i.e. the liquid stage is transferred to the gaseous stage at the free surface. The study of *'evaporation'* and *'transpiration'* is very important to the hydrologist as it enables in determining the *'run-off'* of the area.

The factors affecting evaporation or rate of evaporation are as follows :

- Difference in vapour pressure at the water surface and air above.
- Temperatures of air and water.
- Wind velocity.
- Atmospheric pressure.
- Quality of water,
- Surface area of the water body exposed.

Above factors are explained below :

- **Difference in Vapour Pressure :** It has been observed that the evaporation rate depends on the difference between the vapour pressure of the water (e_w) and actual vapour in the air (e_a). Mathematically, by Dalton's law,

$$\text{Evaporation} \propto (e_w - e_a)$$

or   Evaporation in mm/day = $K (e_w - e_a)$

where, K = Constant and e_w and e_a are recorded in mm of mercury. The process of evaporation is continued until $e_a = e_w$.

- **Temperatures of Air and Water :** The rate at which molecules are released from water body depends upon its temperature. Higher the temperature, greater will be the evaporation rate. However, there is no fixed relation between temperature of air and its evaporation, eventhough the rate of evaporation increases with the rise in temperature.

- **Wind Velocity :** The wind velocity is related to the turbulence in the water. Higher the wind velocity and temperature, greater will be the rate of evaporation. However, the rate of evaporation is not affected when the wind velocity increases beyond certain limit. This critical velocity of the wind depends upon the size and surface area of the water body exposed.

- **Atmospheric Pressure :** It has been found that decrease in the pressure with increase in elevation i.e. altitude, increases the evaporation rate.

- **Quality of Water :** As compared to fresh water, the rate of evaporation is less for water containing salt. For each one per cent increase in the specific gravity of water, there is decrease of about one per cent in the rate of evaporation. Thus, the rate of evaporation from sea water (which has higher specific gravity as compared to fresh water) is found to be 2 to 3% less than from the fresh water, when there is no change in other conditions. There appears to be no appreciable effect on the evaporation rate of water due to its turbidity.

- **Surface Area of the Water Body :** The depth and the surface area of the water body affects the rate of evaporation to certain extent. More heat will be stored in large and deep water bodies as compared to small and shallow one. However, this factor affects the seasonal evaporation rates, the mean or average annual evaporation rate remaining practically unaffected.

1.22 MEASUREMENT OF EVAPORATION

As the *'evaporation'* has an important role in the hydrologic cycle, it is necessary to estimate its rate by some methods, even though such as estimation may not be cent per cent accurate.

The most direct method of ascertaining the evaporation from water bodies such lakes, reservoirs etc. would be from the computed values of *'precipitation'*, *'inflow into the water body'* and *'outflow'* from it and the seepage that has taken place. However, as the *'seepage'* cannot be measured directly and the computations of other factors cannot be carried out precisely, the results obtained by direct measurement are far from satisfactory. It has been found to be more convenient to measure the evaporative power of the air by using certain equipment rather than to measure the actual evaporation that takes place.

The methods commonly adopted for measurement of evaporation from water bodies are :

- Data collected from evaporimeters,
- By empirical formulae and
- By analytical methods.

1.22.1 Data Collected from Evaporimeters

Evaporimeters or *Evaporometers* are water circular pans containing water, made of galvanized iron, zinc or copper, which may be painted or unpainted with their tips either screened or unscreened that are exposed to the atmosphere. The loss of water that takes place due to evaporation from such pans is recorded at specified intervals. As evaporation depends upon atmospheric changes, the meteorological data related to water and air temperatures, wind movement, humidity and the precipitation (i.e. rainfall) are also be to recorded. The evaporation pans may be installed in the or above the ground or may even float on the surface of water. It has been observed that evaporation from pan surfaces is more than that from the adjacent water bodies, the difference being inversely proportional to the area of the water pan.

'Pan coefficient' is defined as 'the ratio of evaporation that takes place from the surface of the water body to that from the evaporimeter (i.e. pan)'. The value of pan coefficient changes with the season, being greater in winter than in the summer. The actual evaporation from the water body is determined from the inflow to the water body and outflow from it. Some of the evaporation pans in common use are as described below.

(1) **U.S. Weather Services Class A Land Pan (Fig. 1.19 (a) and (b)) :** This standard pan commonly used for measurement of evaporation from water bodies is made of unpainted galvanized iron 1220 mm in diameter and 255 mm deep installed on a 150 mm high wooden grillage to permit circulation of air below the pan. The depth of water in the pan is maintained at 180 mm to 200 mm. The stilling well and hook gauge provided with the pan enables to measure the amount of water lost by evaporation. The measurements are recorded twice daily at 8.30 a.m. and 5.30 p.m.

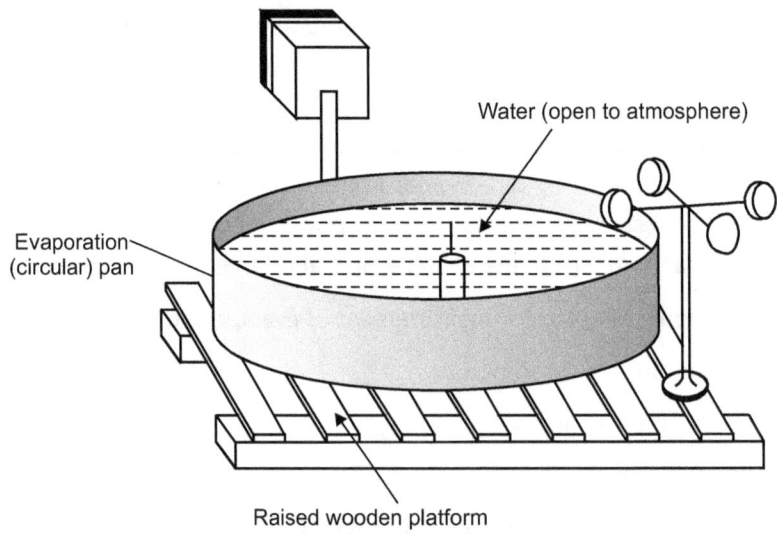

Fig. 1.19 (a) : U.S. Weather service class A land pan

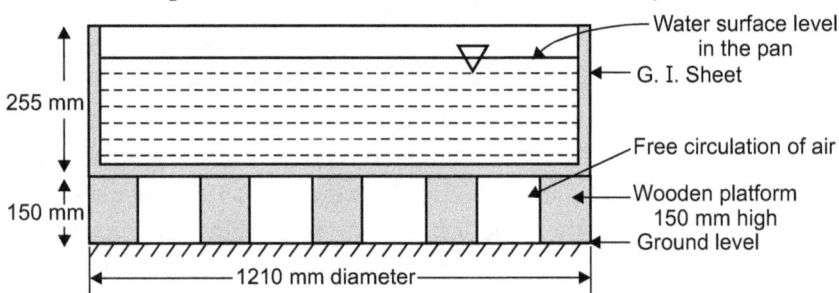

Fig. 1.19 (b) : U.S. Weather service class A land pan

The water is added into the pan from a graduated cylinder so as to bring the level of water to the original mark (which is 50 to 75 mm below the rim of the pan). Due to the protection offered by the rim of the pan and the objects surrounding it, the pan is not subject to the wind effect. The day time temperature of the water in the pan is higher than that of the nearby water body, whereas during night time it will be reversed. As the evaporation from such land pan is higher than that from nearby bodies, the measurements recorded by the pan are to be multiplied by the *'pan coefficient'*, whose value varies from 0.60 during summer to 0.80 in winter, the average value being 0.70.

(2) **Standard I. S. Land Pan (Fig. 1.20) :** The I. S. 5973-1970 standard pan (called as modified class A pan) has a diameter of 1220 mm and depth of 255 mm. It is made of 0.9 mm thick copper sheet, tinned inside and painted white from outside.

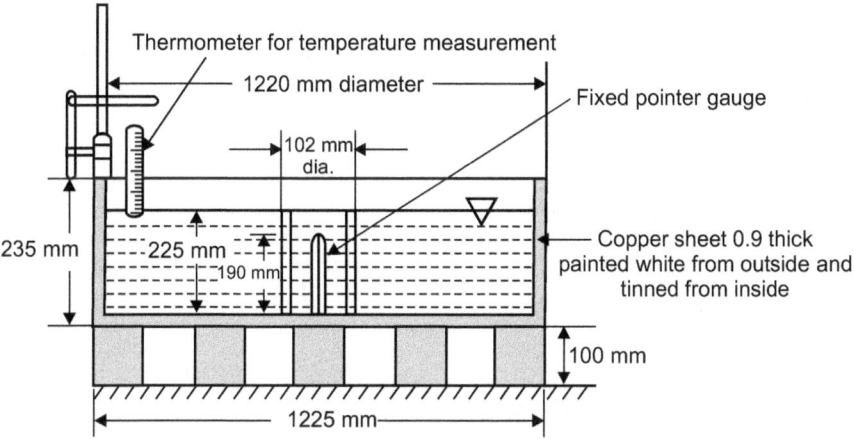

Fig. 1.20 : (Bureaus of Indian) Standard I.S. evaporation (land) pan on raised wooden platform

The fixed point gauge provided with the pan is used to record the level of water. The pan is covered from the top, with a galvanized iron wire mesh to protect the water in the pan from birds etc. The wire mesh covering the pan helps in maintaining the temperature of the water in the pan more uniform both during day and night. The pan rests on a wooden platform 1225 mm square in size and 100 mm high to permit free circulation of air below the pan.

(3) **Colorado Sunken Pan (Fig. 1.21) :** It is a 920 mm square sized pan, 460 to 920 mm deep, prepared from galvanized unpainted iron sheet, sunk into the ground in such a way that about 100 mm of the top projects above the ground surface.

The idea in sinking the pan underground is to create conditions similar to those of a water body. However, installation of such pans becomes costly and it is very difficult to detect any leakage that may take place from these pans.

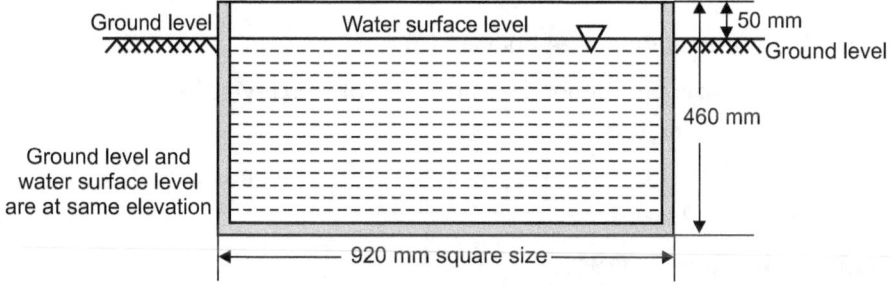

Fig. 1.21 : Colorado sunken pan

(4) Floating Evaporation Pan : The floating pan, (called as U.S. Geological Survey Floating Pan) is 900 mm square size and 450 mm deep and is supported on the raft floating in water, with a view to obtain evaporation results under the conditions which are identical with the actual water bodies. The level of the water in the pan is maintained at the same level of water body on which it floats. Baffles provided in the pan prevents it from surging due to wave action. The demerits of the pan are its high cost of installation and its proper maintenance and difficulty in recording the measurement. The value of pan coefficient is 0.80.

1.22.2 By Empirical Formulae

The various empirical formulae used for the determination of evaporation which expresses it as a function of atmospheric elements and adopt the mass transfer approach are as follows :

(1) Meyer's Formula (1915) :

$$E_l = C(e_s - e_a)\left(1 + \frac{u}{16}\right)$$

where, E_l = Evaporation from water body in mm/day.

e_s = Vapour pressure of water surface in mm of mercury.

e_a = Actual vapour pressure of overlying air in mm of mercury.

u = Mean monthly velocity of wind in km/hour measured at 9 m above the ground level.

C = Coefficient varying from 0.36 to 0.50.

(2) U.S.B.R. Formula : The United States Bureau of Reclamation's formula for evaporation is

$$E_l = 4.57\,T + 43.3$$

where, E_l = Annual evaporation of the water body in cm.

T = Annual mean temperature in °C.

(3) Horton's Formula (1917) :

$$E_l = 0.635\,(\theta v_w - v)$$

where, E_l = Evaporation in 24 hours in cm.

v_w = Maximum vapour pressure in cm of mercury at water surface temperature.

v = Vapour pressure (actual) in the air in cm of mercury.

θ = Wind factor.

(4) Thornthwaite Formula (1948) :

$$\text{Evaporation expressed in mm/month} = 16\left[\frac{10\,T}{I}\right]^a$$

where, T = Monthly mean temperature

a = Function of I

$$I = \sum_{1}^{12} \left(\frac{T}{S}\right)^{1.51}$$

where, S = Total solar radiation for clear skies for given month and latitude

1.22.3 By Analytical Method

The two commonly adopted analytical methods for determination of evaporation are :

(1) Water budget equation (i.e. conservation of mass)

(2) Energy budget equation (i.e. conservation of energy)

(1) Water Budget Equation :

$$P + Q_I \pm Q_S = O + E \pm S_C$$

where, P = Precipitation i.e. rainfall.

Q_I = Surface inflow.

Q_S = Inflow or outflow from the subsurface.

O = Outflow from the surface.

E = Evaporation loss.

S_C = Change in the storage of surface water.

(2) Energy Budget Equation :

$$H_N = H_S + H_E + H_F + H_s + H_O$$

where, H_N = Net heat energy received in the water body.

H_S = Sensible heat transfer from water body to air.

H_E = Heat energy consumed in evaporation process.

H_F = Heat flux to the ground.

H_s = Heat stored in the water surface.

H_O = Heat going out of system by flow of water.

At the end, it can be summed up that though analytical methods yield better results, it is somewhat difficult to obtain the various parameters involved in the equation. The empirical formulae are approximate one and may be applicable under particular conditions for certain places. Hence, the measurement of evaporation by pans will be the most practical methods that can be applied.

1.23 METHODS OF REDUCING EVAPORATION FROM LAKES OR RESERVOIRS

In India, the yearly evaporation losses from lakes or reservoirs is found to be about 1.5 to 1.6 m. Efforts are being made by scientists to reduce the evaporation losses. The various methods that are adopted for reducing evaporation losses from water bodies are as follows :

(1) **Minimizing the Surface Area of Water Bodies :** As the evaporation varies directly with the surface area of the water body exposed, attempts should be made to reduce the surface area by selecting suitable sites of reservoirs that give more depth and less surface area exposed to atmosphere.

(2) **By Covering the Water Spread by Certain Chemical Films :** In this method a thin film of chemical such as acetyl alcohol (hexadeconol) or certain oil is spread over the surface of water body that reduces the evaporation rate. Such a thin film of about 0.015 µm thickness will allow rainfall that will be falling over it, but will not permit any molecule of water to escape from the water body. However, this method will not be practicable if strong wind is blowing over the surface. Such a wind will sweep the thin film to one side of the bank and the water will be exposed to solar radiation.

(3) **By Suitable Wind Breakers :** Tall trees are generally grown on the windward side of the reservoir or lake which act as wind breakers and thus reduce the rate of evaporation.

(4) **By Artificial Covers :** The entire water surface can be covered by temporary roofs etc. if the water body is small.

(5) **Other Methods :** Other methods like releasing warmer water from the water body by suitable arrangement, clearing the weeds and water loving plants etc. surrounding the water body, and adoption of certain measures that will cool down the water body, can also be adopted to reduce the rate of evaporation.

1.24 EVAPORATION FROM LAND SURFACES

When precipitation falls on the land surface, the soil becomes wet. Evaporation that takes place from such surfaces is known as 'evaporation from land surface, the evaporation rate from land surface depends upon the type of soil and depth of the water table. This evaporation is expressed as percentage of evaporation that takes place from free water surface and is known as *'evaporation opportunity'* (E.O.).

$$\text{i.e. E.O.} = \left[\frac{\text{Evaporation from the land surface}}{\text{Evaporation from an equal water surface}}\right] \times 100$$

For measurement of evaporation from land surface, an instrument called as *Lysimeters* is used. It consists of tank filled with soil buried under ground with its top almost flush with the ground surface. Knowing the weight of the tank initially and the quantity of water poured into it, the evaporation from the soil surface can be determined.

1.25 TRANSPIRATION

'*Transpiration* is the process by which water absorbed through the roots of the plants is transferred to the atmosphere as water vapour'. It may be noted that transpiration takes place during day light hours only, whereas evaporation continues for all the twenty four hours of a day, the rate of evaporation however differs. Water consumed by the plants is of importance as it forms a large proportion of rainfall.

1.25.1 Factors Affecting Transpiration

The transpiration depends upon the following factors :
- Growth period of the plant,
- Radiation, and
- Moisture present.

- **Growth Period of Plant :** The rate of transpiration is dependent upon the rate of plant growth. The growing season and the stage of plant development affects the transpiration.
- **Radiation :** The incoming solar radiation is another important factor that affects *transpiration* as the entire process of transpiration takes place during day light hours of the day.
- **Moisture Present :** Transpiration is assumed to vary directly with the available moisture present in the soil. The plants extract moisture from the root zone till the wilting point is reached.

1.25.2 Measurement of Transpiration

Of the various methods of measurement of transpiration, the most common method is by the '*phytometer*'.

A phytometer consists of a closed vessel filled with soil in which the plant is grown, the escape of moisture being by transpiration only. The water is added to the plant till it attains the complete growth.

If

W_I = Initial weight of the apparatus in the beginning.

W_F = Final weight of the apparatus at the end of experiment.

W_A = Water added during plant growth.

and W_T = Water lost due to transpiration.

then $W_T = W_I + W_A - W_F$

However, as it is not possible to simulate 'the natural conditions, the results obtained are far from satisfactory.

Transpiration Ratio (T.R.) is defined as the ratio of quantity of water absorbed (by the root system) and transpired to the dry matter produced, excluding the roots'.

i.e. $$\text{T.R.} = \frac{\text{Weight of water absorbed and transpired}}{\text{Weight of dry matter produced}}$$

The value of T.R. varies for different crops from 350 to 750, that for rice being 700.

1.26 EVAPO-TRANSPIRATION

1.26.1 Introduction

In the study of hydrologic balance for an area, the hydrologist is mostly concerned with the *'total evaporation'* rather than *'evaporation'* and *'transpiration'* that takes place independently. The process of *'evaporation'* and *'transpiration'* can be clubbed together under one head called as *'Evapo-transpiration'* or *'Total Evaporation'*.

It includes all the water losses that take place from a given area by *'transpiration'*, evaporation from water bodies, soil surfaces and vegetation etc. The term *'evapo-transpiration'* is synonyms to the *'consumptive use'* of water.

When the plant roots are supplied with unlimited quantity of water covering the soil, that satisfy the entire requirements, it is called *'Potential evapo-transpiration'* (E_{pt}). The actual evapo-transpiration that takes place under specified condition is known as actual evapo-transpiration (E_{At}).

1.26.2 Estimation of Evapo-Transpiration (or Consumptive Use)

The methods commonly adopted for measurement of evapo-transpiration are as follows :
- By Lysimeters,
- From field plots and
- By Evapo-transpiration equations.

1.26.2.1 By Lysimeters (Fig. 1.22)

These are water tight tanks with previous bottoms filled with soil, set into the ground with its top almost flush with the ground surface. Soil used in the tank should simulate field condition and the plant grown should also be same as in its surroundings.

Evapo-transpiration is then determined by measuring the amount of water required to maintain constant moisture conditions within the tank.

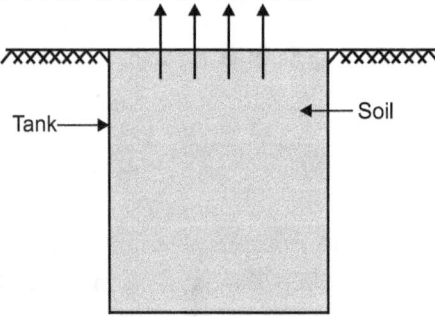

Fig. 1.22 : Lysimeter

Thus, if R_W = Rainfall water

I_W = Irrigation water

Q_D = Quantity of water drained

ΔS = Surface and subsurface changes in storage

E_T = Evapo-transpiration

then, $E_T = R_W + I_W - Q_D \pm \Delta S$

The method is laborious and costly.

1.26.2.2 Field Plot Method

The 'water-budget equation' can be used to determine the 'evapo-transpiration' from a field plot. Thus,

$$\text{Evapo-transpiration} = \begin{pmatrix} \text{Precipitation} \\ \text{surface runoff} \end{pmatrix} - \begin{pmatrix} \text{Irrigation water supplied} \\ \text{Deep percolation to ground water} \end{pmatrix}$$

As it is not possible to determine the exact quantity of 'deep percolation', it is advisable to supply water in small quantities to reduce its effect.

As compared to measurement by lysimeter, this method gives fairly correct results as the determination of evapo-transpiration is carried out under actual natural conditions.

1.26.2.3 By Evapo-Transpiration Equations

The methods commonly adopted are as follows :

(1) Blaney - Criddle Method : As per this method, the monthly evapo-transpiration (or consumptive use) is given by the formula, which is used throughout the world.

$$E_T \text{ (or } C_u) = \frac{K \cdot P}{100}(4.55\, t + 81) \text{ in MKS units}$$

where, K = Monthly consumptive use coefficient for the crop.

P = Monthly percentage of day light hours in a year.

t = Monthly mean temperature °C.

E_T = Evapo-transpiration or consumptive use in cm.

The above equation can be written as –

$$E_T \text{ or } C_u = K \cdot f$$

where, $f = \frac{P}{100}(4.55\, t + 81)$

However, as the value of K obtained was too low, f is replaced by Σf, which indicates summation for all months of the growth period.

i.e. $E_T \text{ or } C_u = K \Sigma f$

(2) Hargreaves Class A Pan Method : By this method the evapo-transpiration is related in terms of pan evaporation by a certain constant say K.

$$\therefore \quad K = \frac{\text{Evapo-transpiration or Consumptive use } (E_T)}{\text{Evaporation from the pan } (E_P)}$$

$$\therefore \quad E_T = K \cdot E_P$$

The value of K differs crop to crop and for the same crop at various places.

The average values of K can be taken from the Hargreaves recommended tables, in which the various crops are divided into different groups as A, B, C, D, E, F and G, ...

1.27 INFILTRATION

1.27.1 Introduction

Infiltration which forms an important phase of the hydrologic cycle was first studied by Horton (1933). Horton defined infiltration as 'the passage of water through the ground surface into the soil, Percolation on the other hand is the passage of water within the soil. (Fig. 1.23).

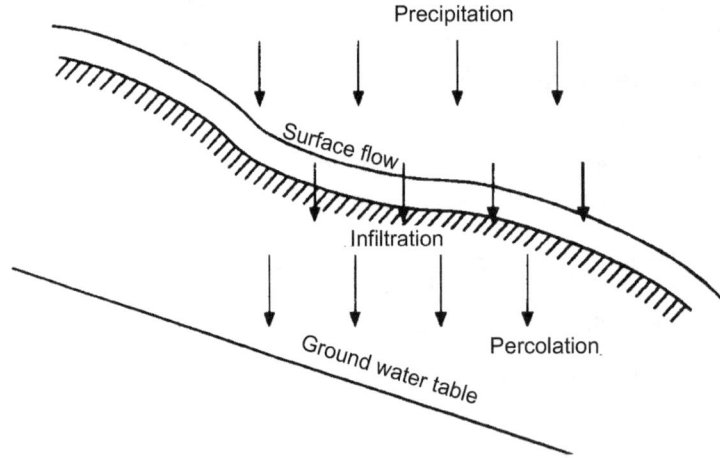

Fig. 1.23 : Infiltration

When precipitation falls on the surface of soil, part of it enters into it and replenishes the deficiency in the soil moisture and remaining flows downward by gravity and joins the ground water. Thus, infiltration which is loss of water from the surface run-off point of view, is a source of ground water recharge.

1.27.2 Infiltration Capacity (f_p)

It is defined as 'the maximum rate at which a particular soil under given conditions can absorb water that falls over it' and is expressed as cm/hour. If the intensity of precipitation

(i) equals or exceeds f_p, the infiltration capacity will be equal to the actual infiltration rate (f_i). Horton expressed the relation between f_p and rainfall duration t as follows :

$$f_p = f_o + (f_o - f_c) e^{-kt}$$

where f_o = Initial rate of infiltration.

f_c = Constant rate of infiltration after the saturation point is reached.

k = Positive constant depending upon type of soil and vegetation.

Thus, if i = Rainfall intensity.

f_p = Maximum rate of infiltration.

and f_a = Actual rate of infiltration.

then, $f_a = f_p$ if i > p

and $f_a = i$ if i > f_p

1.27.3 Factors Affecting Infiltration

The factors affecting infiltration are as follows :

- Soil characteristics, its type, permeability, texture etc. affect the infiltration rate.
- Vegetation cover : Infiltration from a soil covered with grass, vegetation etc. will be less as compared to the uncovered one.
- Quality of water : The turbidity of the water, presence of impurities in water etc. also affect the rate of infiltration.
- Rainfall, its duration and intensity also affect the infiltration.

Thus, it can be stated that knowing the infiltration characteristics of a basin, it may be possible to determine the amount of rainfall excess that is likely to occur from a given storm and the information as regards the resulting flood can be obtained.

1.27.4 Practical Utility of Infiltration

The practical utility of infiltration is that it replenishes the ground water storage, controls the erosion of soil and reduces flood intensity and supplies moisture for the growth of plants.

1.28 METHODS OF DETERMINING INFILTRATION RATE

The methods commonly adopted for determining infiltration rate are as follows :

- By infiltrometers
- Rain (fall) simulators
- By hydrograph analysis.

1.28.1 By Infiltrometers

In this method, actual experiments are carried out on small field plots by supplying the water artificially and the rate of infiltration is determined directly. The infiltrometer may be either of *'flooding type'* or *'artificial rain simulator type'*.

Flooding Type Infiltrometer : The simplest type of infiltrometer (Fig. 1.24) consists of a metallic cylinder, open at both top and bottom, 300 mm diameter and 600 mm in length, sunk into the ground with its top projecting 100 mm above the ground.

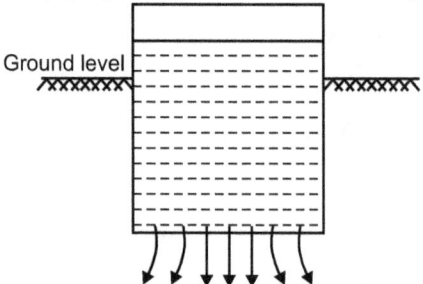

Fig. 1.24 : Single infiltrometer

Water is then poured on its upper part to a depth of 50 mm and is allowed to infiltrate. Water at intervals is added to it to make up loss due to infiltration and a graph of infiltration rate against the time is plotted. The drawback of this method is that water infiltrating through such apparatus may flow at the outlet from the sides and as such the results obtained will be far from satisfactory. To overcome this difficulty, a *double-ring infiltrometer'* (Fig. 1.25) made up of two concentric rings is used.

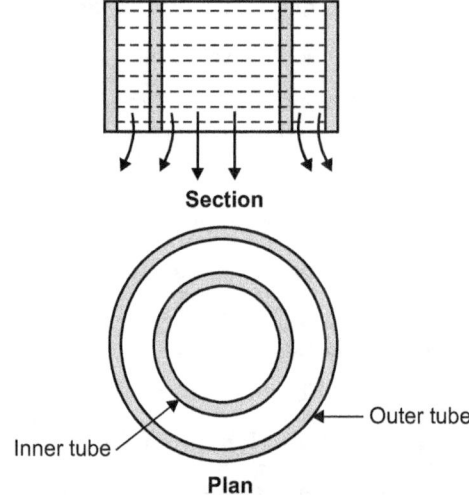

Fig. 1.25 : Double tube infiltrometer

The two rings varying from 225 to 900 mm diameter are driven into the ground and water is maintained at the same level in both the rings. The outer tube prevents the loss of water that takes place from sides of the inner tube. The computations of the infiltration rate is based on the area represented by the inner ring only.

Some of the drawbacks of the measurement of infiltration by infiltrometer are as follows :
- The actual effect of raindrop impact on the soil over which it falls is not considered.
- The natural soil structure of the area gets disturbed when the tube or ring is driven into it.

1.28.2 Rain (Fall) Simulators

The method first adopted by Horton, consists in applying water over an area by sprinkling at a rate which is in excess of infiltration capacity. The apparatus can produce artificial rainfall of various intensities and of desired duration. Knowing the total quantity of rainfall falling over the given area and measuring the rate of resulting surface runoff, the infiltration and also the rate of infiltration can be calculated. The values of infiltration obtained by this method are lower than obtained by the method (1.28.1) explained above due to the consideration of rainfall impact on the soil.

1.28.3 By Hydrograph Analysis

The method consists in determining the infiltration capacity from the knowledge of intensities of rainfall occurring during a storm and measuring the resulting run-off from such storms. The method is superior to all the methods explained above and the infiltration results obtained by this method are helpful for practical purposes.

1.29 INFILTRATION CAPACITY CURVE

It is a plot of infiltration capacity versus the time and indicates the manner in which the infiltration capacity varies with time during and after the storm.

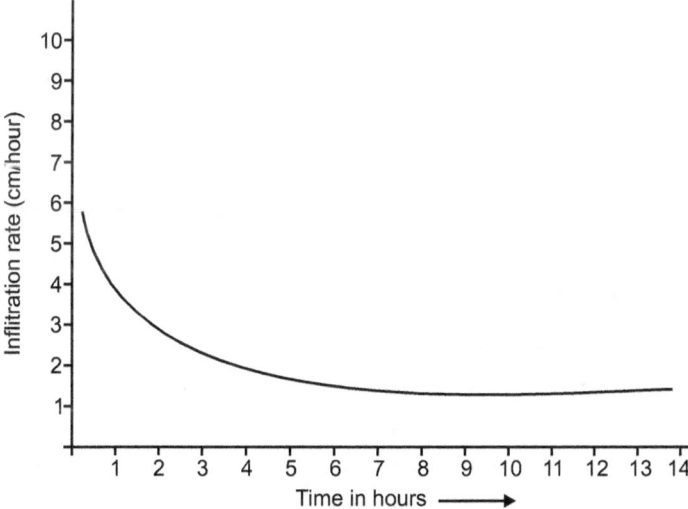

Fig. 1.26 : Infiltration capacity curve

It is obvious that the rate of infiltration will be very high at the commencement of the storm that takes place after a long dry spell. The rate of infiltration thereafter decreases with time and also due to degree of saturation depending upon the type of soil. Ultimately, after a period of about 2 to 3 hours, the rate of infiltration reaches more or less a constant value as shown in Fig. 1.26.

1.30 INFILTRATION INDICES

1.30.1 Introduction

The infiltration concept can be used for computation of surface run-off by making use of simple relation

(Surface run-off) = (Rainfall) + (Losses due to interception, depression storage, evaporation, transpiration and infiltration)

The above relation holds good provided the amount, intensity and duration of rainfall and infiltration and sub-surface storage characteristics of the basin are uniform over the entire area under consideration. However, in practice, this may not be true. Thus, making the rational infiltration approach impractical in the solution of hydrological problems that require a run-off relation. In practice, therefore, the concept of *'infiltration indices'* have been put forth by the hydrologists advocating the infiltration approach. However, as the results obtained from such indices are not based on rational application of infiltration theory, they are considered to be empirical. The two such indices used are known as ϕ-index and W-index.

1.30.2 Infiltration Index

It is defined as 'the average rate of infiltration (i.e. loss) such that the volume of rainfall in excess of that rate will be equal to the volume of observed run-off'. The infiltration indices commonly used are as follows :

- The ϕ-index,
- The average or W-index and
- $W_{minimum}$ index

1.30.2.1 The ϕ-Index

The basic assumption on which this index is based is that, for a specified storm with given initial condition the rate of basin recharge remains constant for the entire storm period. i.e. if a time versus intensity graph of a rainfall is plotted, the ϕ-index is the average rainfall intensity above which the volume of rainfall equals the volume due to observed run-off.

Mathematically, ϕ-index = $\dfrac{\text{Total basin recharge}}{\text{Rainfall duration}}$

provided, the intensity of rainfall is continuously in excess of basin recharge (i.e. ϕ-index). It may be noted that, the concept of ϕ-index assumes excessive run-off at the beginning and too little at the end of storm. The ϕ-index represents combined result of interception, depression storage and infiltration and enables to estimate the amount of run-off.

1.30.2.2 Hyetograph

It is a bar graph that indicates time distribution of rainfall, all losses (due to interception, depression storage and infiltration) and rainfall excess. From the Fig. 1.27 it is obvious that the φ-index divides the rainfall into rainfall excess and the losses due to interception, depression storage and infiltration.

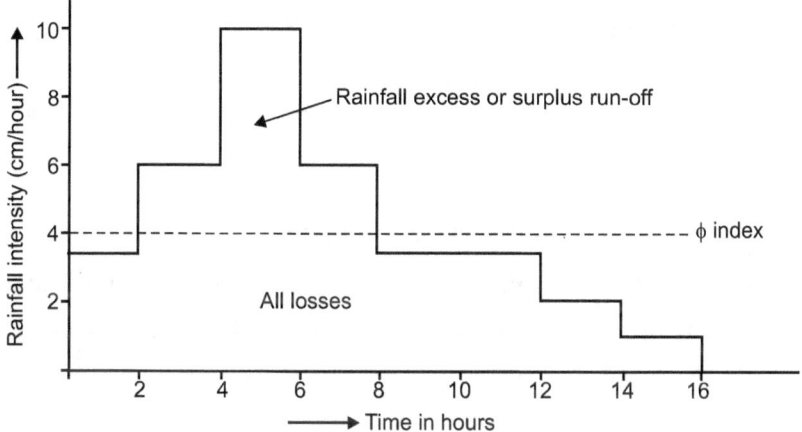

Fig. 1.27 : Hydrograph of a storm

The area under a hyetograph represents the total precipitation received in the period. The time interval used depend on the purpose, in urban drainage problems small durations are used while in flood flow computations in larger catchments the intervals are of about 6 hours.

1.30.2.3 W-Index or Average Index

W-index or Average index is defined as 'the average rate of infiltration during the time the rainfall intensity is in excess of infiltration capacity'.

i.e. $$W_{index} = \frac{F_t}{t_R} = \frac{P - R - S}{t_R} \text{ (cm/hour)}$$

where F_t = Total infiltration

t_R = Time during which rainfall intensity exceeds infiltration capacity
i.e. $i > f_p$

P = Total rainfall (in cm)

R = Total surface run-off (in cm)

S = Effective surface storage (or retention)

Obviously, W-index is equivalent to φ-index minus the average rate of retention by interception, and depression storage.

1.30.2.4 W_{min} ϕ-Index

Under very wet conditions if the infiltration capacity is essentially equal to f_c (i.e. constant rate) and the rate of retention is minimum, the values of both W and ϕ are almost identical and the infiltration capacity attains a minimum constant rate and is called as W_{min} index. This index is very useful for the problem related to maximum flood studies.

1.30.2.5 Supra-Rain Curve

It is technique by means of which the value of ϕ-index applicable to a particular storm can be derived. The rainfall in excess of a particular given value of ϕ-index for the entire pattern of storm rainfall is known as *Supra-rain*. Supra-rain curve will be valid only for the given storm, for different storm, new supra-rain curve is to be drawn.

SOLVED PROBLEMS

Problem 1.1 : Calculate the hourly values of rainfall excess from the following observations :

(i) Hourly rainfall of magnitude 30 mm, 68 mm and 40 mm occurs over an area of 30 hectares as follows :

        8 ha of ϕ = 48 mm/hour

        12 ha of ϕ = 35 mm/hour

        10 ha of ϕ = 12 mm/hour

Solution :

(i) During the first hour rainfall = 30 mm/hour

    Rainfall excess = Rainfall + Infiltration index

$$\text{Rainfall excess during first hour} = \frac{8(0) + 12(0) + 10(30-12)}{30} = \frac{180}{30} = 6 \text{ mm}$$

(ii) Similarly,

$$\text{Rainfall excess during second hour} = \frac{8(68-48) + 12(68-35) + 10(68-12)}{30}$$

$$= \frac{8(20) + 12(33) + 10(56)}{30}$$

$$= \frac{(160 + 396 + 560)}{30}$$

$$= 37.2 \text{ mm}$$

(iii) Similarly,

$$\text{Rainfall excess during the third hour} = \frac{8(0) + 12(40-35) + 10(40-12)}{30}$$

$$= \frac{0 + 60 + 280}{30} = 11.334 \text{ mm}$$

∴ Total of rainfall excess during 3 hours duration

$$= 6 + 37.2 + 11.334 = 54.534 \text{ mm}$$

Problem 1.2: *Calculate the average infiltration index for the catchment from the following data:*

(i) *A 6 hours storm rainfall having the following depths in centimetres occurred over the catchment.*

0.5, 1.2, 5.8, 4, 8, 4.5

(ii) *The equivalent surface run-off that resulted from the above rainfall was found to be 15 cm over the entire catchment.*

Solution :

The total rainfall during a storm of 6 hours

$$= 0.5 + 1.2 + 5.8 + 4 + 8 + 4.5$$
$$= 24.00 \text{ cm}$$

And the equivalent surface run-off in 6 hours

$$= 15 \text{ cm (given)}$$

∴ Total infiltration into the ground in 6 hour duration

$$= \text{(Total rainfall)} - \text{(Total surface runoff)}$$
$$= 24 - 15 = 9 \text{ cm in a period of 6 hours}$$

∴ Average rate of infiltration/hour $= \dfrac{9}{6} = 1.5$ cm/hour

Thus, it can be seen from the average rate of infiltration of 1.5 cm/hour and rainfall during 6 hours, the rainfall during 1st and 2nd hour is less than average rate of infiltration and thus the rate of infiltration will be same as the rainfall. However, in 3rd, 4th, 5th and 6th hours the rainfall exceeds the average rate of infiltration. Therefore, assuming the average rate of infiltration during these four hours as f_a, we may write

$$0.5 + 1.2 + 4(f_a) = \text{(Total infiltration in 6 hours)} = 9 \text{ cm}$$

∴ $\quad 4 f_a = 9 - 1.7 = 7.3$

∴ $\quad f_a = \dfrac{7.3}{4} = 1.825$ cm/hr

∴ Average rate of filtration = 1.825 cm/hr.

Problem 1.3 : *Calculate the value of φ-index from the following data of storm of 8 cm precipitation that resulted in a direct run-off of 4.4 cm.*

Time in Hours	1	2	3	4	5	6
Incremental Rainfall per Hour in cm	0.57	0.58	1.25	3.00	1.4	1.2

Solution :

Given : Storm is of 8 cm precipitation, and run-off = 4.4 cm

∴ Total infiltration during 6 hours = 8 – 4.4 = 3.6 cm

Now, the problem is to be solved by trial and error method.

i.e. Assuming the time of rainfall excess = 6 hours

$$\text{Average infiltration index, } \phi = \frac{\text{Total infiltration}}{\text{No. of hours}}$$

$$\phi = \frac{3.6}{6}$$

$$= 0.6 \text{ cm/hour}$$

However, this value of φ renders the rainfalls of the first hour and second hour as ineffective as their values are less than φ i.e. 0.6 cm/hour.

Modifying the value of time of rainfall excess as say 4 hours (instead of 6 hours in the first trial) for the next trial.

∴ During this period, the infiltration that has taken place

$$= (8 - 0.57 - 0.58 - 4.40)$$

$$= 2.45$$

∴ Average rate of infiltration, $\phi = \frac{2.45}{4}$

$$= 0.6125 \approx 0.6 \text{ cm/hour. This is OK.}$$

The table of rainfall excess will be as follows :

Time in Hours	1	2	3	4	5	6
Rainfall Excess	00	00	0.6375	2.3875	0.7875	0.5875

Check :

Total rainfall excess = 00 + 00 + 0.6375 + 2.3875 + 0.7875 + 0.5875

= 4.4 cm ... (i)

and Direct runoff = 4.4 (given) ... (ii)

As the values of equations (i) and (ii) are same, therefore, OK.

THEORETICAL QUESTIONS

1. Explain with a neat diagram, the entire process and hydrologic cycle.
2. What is 'Hydrology'? Explain its scope and importance in Civil Engineering ?
3. State the various applications of hydrology to (civil) engineering.
4. What is meant by evaporation ? Explain the various factors that affect evaporation.
5. Explain the following methods of measurement of evaporation.

    (i) By Evaporimeters,

    (ii) By Empirical formulae,

    (iii) By Analytical methods.

6. Explain the various methods of reducing evaporation from lakes or reservoirs.
7. State the various factors that affect transpiration. How will you measure transpiration by various methods ?
8. State only various methods to find the evaporation from a reservoir. Explain any one method. What is the importance of estimation of evaporation ?
9. Discuss the factors affecting the evapo-transpiration.
10. Discuss the influence of various factors affecting evaporation and evapo-transpiration. Explain any one method of measuring the evaporation.
11. Briefly discuss the factors affecting the evaporation. What are the methods used to control evaporation from reservoirs.
12. Write a short note on Evapo-transpiration.
13. Define infiltration capacity and state the factors affecting the same.
14. Define and explain in brief W-index.
15. Define infiltration index.
16. What do you understand by *'infiltration indices'* ? Explain their use.
17. What is an infiltration index ? State the different infiltration indices used in practice. Describe briefly how you will derive any one of them for a catchment area.
18. What are 'W' and 'ϕ' indices ? Explain their importance.

NUMERICAL PROBLEMS

1. A storm with 150 mm precipitation produced a direct run-off of 87 mm. If the time distribution of storm is as follows, determine the ϕ-index of the storm.

Time from Start (Hour)	1	2	3	4	5	6	7	8
Incremental Rainfall in each Hour (mm)	6	14	22	36	29	24	15	8

2. Run-off from a catchment area of 500 sq. km is observed to be 20 million cub. m. Rainfall distribution in the area is as given below :

Time from Beginning in Hours	0	1	2	3	4	5	6
Rainfall in mm	0	10	15	38	20	25	13

   Determine the infiltration index.

3. Run-off from a catchments area 150 sq. km was 8.15 Mm³. Rainfall in the area was observed as below. Determine the rate of infiltration.

Time in Hours	0	1	2	3	4	5	6
Rainfall in mm	0	15	18	25	40	20	10

✠ ✠ ✠

UNIT – II

RUN-OFF AND HYDROGRAPH

2.1 INTRODUCTION

When precipitation falls towards the earth, a portion of it is retained by the vegetation as *'interception'*, stored in the depressions of the ground as *'depression storage'* and as *'soil moisture'*.

Part of the precipitation reaches the underground as *'infiltration'*. When all these requirements are satisfied, the excess precipitation spreads and covers the soil surface with a film of water, called as *'surface detention'* and flows over the land surface as *'over land flows'* and enters the (natural) channel and flows as surface *'run-off'*.

The water retained as interception, depression, storage and soil moisture (i.e. capillary water) constitutes *'basin recharge'*.

- The surface run-off may consist of the following two portions.
- Overland flow that flows over the surface (i.e. surface run-off) to join the nearby channel.

Interflow which is the portion of the precipitation that infiltrates into the soil and flows laterally in the surface soil to an adjacent channel. This is further classified as prompt interflow (with minimum time lag) and delayed interflow.

The part of the precipitation that percolates into the ground through the soil to join the *'ground water'* is called as ground water run-off and has been discussed in details in chapter 4 on 'Ground Water Hydrology' of this book.

The overland flow and (prompt) interflow as explained above are usually combined together to form direct run-off.

2.2 RUN-OFF AND ITS CLASSIFICATION

Thus, run-off may be defined as 'that portion of the precipitation as well as any other flow contribution that enters the natural surface stream or channel'. Thus, it is a flow collected i.e. output from the drainage basin in a given unit of time. It is one of the different phases of hydrologic cycle.

The run-off from a catchment in any specified period is the total amount of water that flows into the natural stream and is expressed as :

- Millimetres (or centimeters) of water over the entire catchment area (also called as drainage basin) or

- In hectare-metres or sometimes in cubic metres, of water per unit area of the catchment or drainage basin.

Classification of Runoff :

Depending upon the time delay between the precipitation and the run-off, the run-off may be classified into :

- Direct runoff as explained above and
- Base flow which is a delayed flow from the catchment that joins the natural channel as ground water flow.

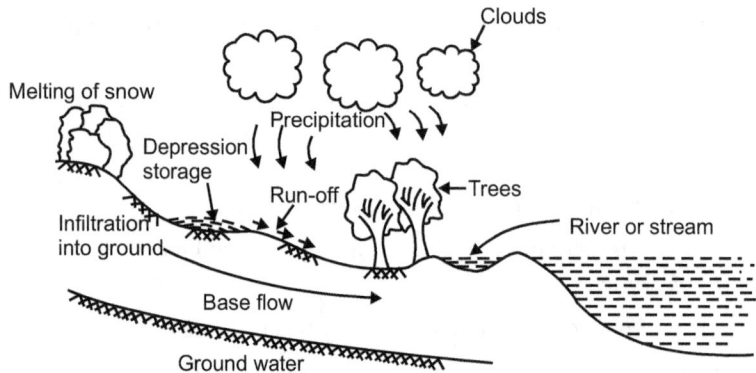

Fig. 2.1 : Different routes of runoff

Direct Run-off : It is part of the runoff which enters the stream immediately after the rainfall. it includes surface runoff, prompt interflow and rainfall on the surface of the stream. In the case of snow-met, the resulting flow entering the stream is also a direct runoff. Sometimes terms such as direct storm runoff and storm runoff are used to designate direct runoff.

Base Flow : The delayed flow that reaches a stream essentially as groundwater flow is called base flow. Many times delayed interflow is also include sunder this category. in the annual hydrograph of a perennial stream the base flow is easily recognized as the slowly decreasing flow of the stream in rainless periods.

2.3 FACTORS AFFECTING THE RUN-OFF

The various factors that affect the run-off from the catchment or drainage basin are as follows :

(1) Precipitation Characteristics : The run-off from a catchment mainly depends upon the type of storm precipitation (i.e. rainfall), its duration, intensity and the extent. The precipitation in the form of rains will immediately contribute to run-off as compared to the snowfall. Run-off also depends upon the intensity of rainfall. A more intense rainfall will contribute more to the surface run-off as compared to the rainfall of less intensity (the infiltration losses in case of intense rainfall will be less as to one with less intense rainfall).

(2) Catchment Characteristics : The shape, size and location of the catchment and its elevation, greatly affect the run-off. Usually intense rainfall occurs over a smaller catchment area and thus results in more run-off from such catchments. As rainfall of uniform intensity is not likely to occur over large catchments, the run-off from the large catchments is likely to be less.

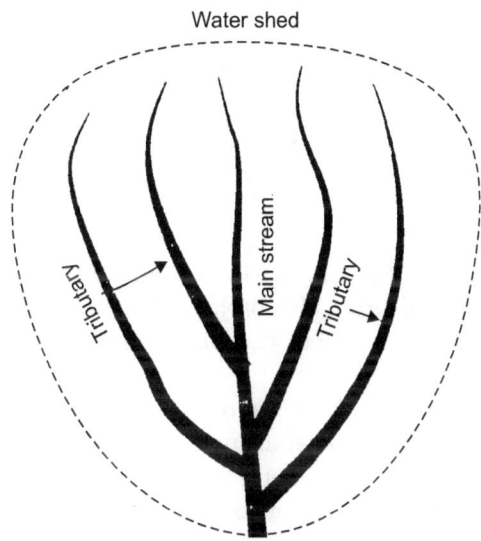

Fig. 2.2 : Fan shaped catchment

The shape of the catchment also affects the run-off. In case of fan shaped (Fig. 2.2) catchment all tributaries are practically of same size and therefore the flows from them are likely to join the main stream at the same time (which is called as time of concentration (t) of the run-off). On the other hand, in case of fern leaf catchment (Fig. 2.3) all tributaries are not of the same length and thus the time of concentration will not be same and the run-off from the main stream will be less.

(3) Geological Characteristics of the Catchment : The run-off also depends upon the geological characteristics such as type of surface and subsoil, its permeability etc. If the soil strata is impervious, the run-off will be more and if it is pervious, the water will percolate and the run-off will be reduced.

(4) Topography of the Catchment : The run-off from the catchment depends upon its inclination i.e. slope of catchment and also upon whether the catchment area is smooth or it is a rugged terrain.

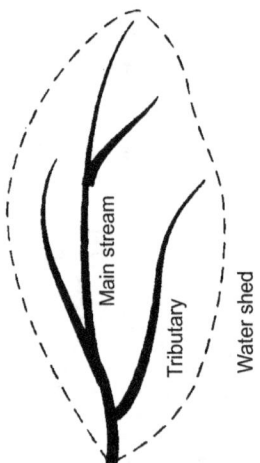

Fig. 2.3 : Fern leaf catchment

(5) Meteorological Characteristics : Meteorological characteristics such as seasonal and annual temperature, humidity and velocity of wind over the catchment affect the run-off appreciably.

(6) Catchment Surface Characteristics : The run-off also depends upon surface condition of the catchment which may be cultivated or natural, with vegetation cover or barren, and well drained or poorly drained, forest land etc.

(7) Characteristics of Storage : The capacity of the reservoir, the flood moderation etc. also affect the run-off from the catchment.

2.4 RAINFALL-RUN-OFF RELATIONSHIP

Run-off (R) forms one phase of hydrologic cycle and is a certain percentage of rainfall (P) i.e. R = kP, where k is constant that depends upon recharge and precipitation.

A simple relation between run-off and rainfall may be expressed as follows :

$$\text{Run-off} = \text{Rainfall} - \text{(all) Losses} \qquad \ldots (2.1)$$

These losses include interception, depression storages, soil moisture, infiltration, evaporation from land and water surfaces, transpiration etc. As it is somewhat difficult to estimate accurately the above losses, the above equation (2.1), even though it appears very simple, cannot be used in practice. At the most, one can correlate the various values of run-off (R) with the rainfall (P) and prepare a best-fit line and use it for approximate estimation of run-off or alternatively, run-off R and rainfall P can be expressed by straight line relation as

$$R = k_1 P + k_2$$

where k_1 and k_2 are the coefficients which can be determined by the number of observation sets of R and P.

However, for large catchment areas the relationship between R and P can be expressed in the exponential form as $R = a(P)^b$, where a and b are constants.

2.5 METHODS OF ESTIMATING RUN-OFF

Run-off of a catchment may be estimated by
- Direct measurement of the river flow.
- By indirect measurements.

The various methods of indirect measurement of run-off may be classified as follows :
- By empirical formulae, tables, curves etc.
- By the infiltration method.
- By rational method.
- By unit hydrograph method.

2.5.1 By Empirical Formulae, Tables, Curves etc.

The various formulae relating run-off to rainfall are as follows :

(1) Binnie's Percentage Method : Sir Alexander Binnie after carrying out experiments on the rivers in the Madhya Pradesh (M.P.) has established relationship of run-off as a certain percentage of rainfall in the area as given below :

Annual Rainfall in mm	500	600	700	800	900	1000	1100
Run-off Expressed as Percentage of Rainfall	15	21	25	29	34	38	40

However as the characteristics of the catchments of other rivers (outside M.P.) may not be similar to those of the rivers in the M.P. from where the above data is collected, the method is quite approximate in its nature.

(2) Run-off Coefficient : As already stated above, run-off is a function of rainfall and as such as equation in the form R = kP may be written where k is a constant which depends upon the type of surface.

Recommended values of k are as follows :

Sr. No.	Types of Surface	Value of Constant (k)
1.	Urban residential	0.20 to 0.30
2.	Commercial and industrial	0.9
3.	Parks, farm etc.	0.05 to 0.30
4.	Concrete or asphalt pavements	0.85 to 1.00

The above method is suitable for urban drainage problems where the impervious area is considerably large. The method is unsuitable for rural regions.

(3) Barlow's Table : T.G. Barlow after carrying out experiments on catchments below 130 square km. area in Uttar Pradesh (U.P.) has recommended the following values of run-off percentages for various types of catchments as follows :

Class	Description of Catchment Area	Percentage of Run-off
A	Flat, cultivated and black cotton (B.C.) soil	10
B	Flat partly cultivated soil	15
C	Average type	20
D	Hills and planes with little cultivation	35
E	Very hilly, steep with practically no cultivation	45

The above values of percentage are for average type of monsoon and are to be suitably modified by multiplying by following coefficient depending upon the season.

Sr. No.	Nature of Season	Class or Type of Catchment				
		A	B	C	D	E
1.	Light rain and no heavy down pour.	0.70	0.80	0.80	0.80	0.80
2.	Average or varying rainfall, no continuous down pour.	1.00	1.00	1.00	1.00	1.00
3.	Continuous down pour	1.5	1.5	1.6	1.7	1.8

(4) Strange's Tables : W.L. Strange after carrying out experiments in Maharashtra has established ratios between rainfall and run-off. Daily run-off and yield table along with run-off curves are as given below. He has classified the catchments as good, average and bad and surface of catchment as dry, damp and wet prior to rainfall.

Daily Run-off Strange's Table

Daily Rainfall in mm	Run-off Percentage and Yield When the Original State of Ground is					
	Dry		Damp		Wet	
	%	Yield in mm	%	Yield in mm	%	Yield in mm
6.25	–	–	–	–	8	0.50
12.50	–	–	6	0.75	12	1.50
18.75	–	–	8	1.50	16	3.00
25.00	3	0.75	11	2.75	18	4.5
31.25	5	1.56	14	4.37	22	6.88
37.50	6	2.25	16	6.00	25	9.375
43.75	8	3.50	19	8.31	30	13.10
50.00	10	5.00	22	11.00	34	17.00
62.5	15	9.375	29	18.15	43	26.87
75.00	20	15	37	27.75	55	41.25
100.00	30	30	50	50.00	70	70.00

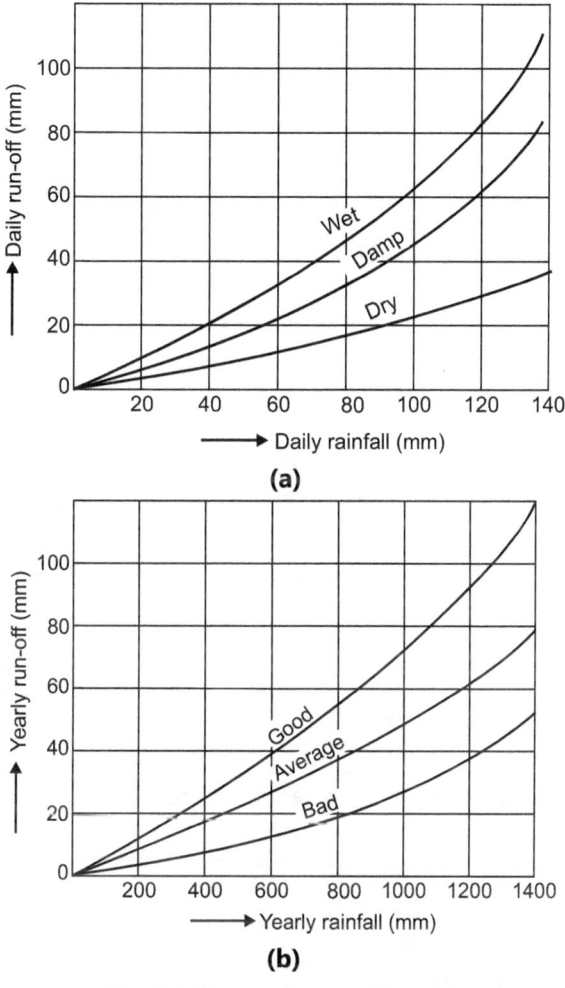

Fig. 2.4 : Strange's run-off curves

(5) Inglis - Desouza Formula : After gauging number of streams in Western India (i.e. Maharashtra) in plain and ghat areas Inglis and Desouza recommended the two formulae as given below :

(a) For plain areas : $R = \dfrac{P}{254}(P - 17.8)$

(b) For ghat areas : $R = 0.85\,P - 30.5$

where R and P represent average annual run-off and rainfall in mm.

(6) Lacey's Formula : Lacey in his formula has introduced monsoon duration factor F and catchment S in addition to run-off and rainfall. According to Lacey,

$$R = \left\{\dfrac{P}{1 + 304.8\left(\dfrac{F}{PS}\right)}\right\}, \text{ where R and P have usual meaning}$$

For the five types of catchments, advocated by Barlow, Lacey has recommended the following values for catchment factor S.

Types or Class of Catchment	Value of S
A	0.25
B	0.60
C	1.00
D	1.70
E	3.45

Lacey has further classified the monsoon on the basis of its duration as 'very short' of 'standard length' and 'very long' and has mentioned the values of monsoon factor F as given below.

Sr. No.	Class or Type of Monsoon	Recommended Value of (F/S) for types of Catchment				
		A	B	C	D	E
1.	Very short	2.00	0.83	0.50	0.23	0.14
2.	Standard length	4.00	1.67	1.00	0.58	0.28
3.	Very long	6.00	2.50	1.50	0.88	0.43

(7) A.N. Khosala's Formulae : A.N. Khosala has introduced mean annual temperature (T) that accounts for losses due to evapo-transpiration, solar radiation and velocity of wind etc.

i.e. $R = P\left(\dfrac{T}{2.08}\right)$, where R and P are in cm and T is in °C.

2.5.2 By the Infiltration Method

Surface run-off from a given storm is equal to that portion of the rainfall which is not lost through interception, depression storage, evaporation and infiltration. Thus, if we can estimate the first three then we have to deal with only rainfall, infiltration and run-off. Thus, if now we can determine infiltration, run-off may be obtained by subtracting infiltration from rainfall.

Infiltration implies the movement of the water through the soil surface and into the soil. The rate of infiltration is maximum in the beginning and it reaches minimum as the soil gets saturated with water. The infiltration capacity of a soil at any given instant is the maximum rate at which water enters the soil. The infiltration rate is defined as 'the rate at which water actually enters the soil during a given storm' and it will always be equal to infiltration capacity or rate of rainfall whichever is less.

The infiltration capacity can be determined experimentally by measurement of (surface) run-off from pre-determined test plot, where precipitation may occur naturally or artificially. The plot will be subjected to rainfall rates, in excess of its infiltration capacity resulting in a surface run-off which can be measured accurately by conventional methods.

Alternatively, if the uniform rate of infiltration of the area is ascertained, then

Surface run-off = (Designed rainfall) – (Infiltration)

Fig. 2.5 shows an infiltration capacity curve plotted by carrying out actual experiments. The run-off may be determined once such infiltration curves are prepared.

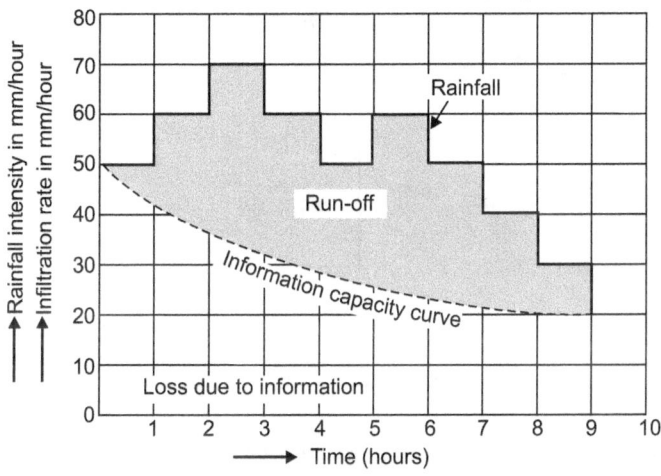

Fig. 2.5 : Run-off determination from infiltration capacity curve

By Infiltration Indices :

If the area under consideration is heterogeneous, then the method of infiltration curve becomes very difficult as the rate of infiltration from the soil will not remain constant and such cases infiltration indices method may be exployed (for the determination surface run-off) e.g. W_{index} (i.e. average rate of infiltration).

$$W_{index} = \frac{P - R - I_a}{t_R} \text{ (in cm/hour)}$$

Where, P = Total storm precipitation in cm

R = Total storm runoff in cm

I_a = Initial loss

t_R = Rainfall duration in hours

Since I_a rates are difficult to obtain, the accurate estimation of W-index is rather difficult. The minimum value of the W-index obtained under very wet soil conditions, representing the constant minimum rate of infiltration of the catchment, is known as W_{min}. it is to be noted that both the φ index and W-index vary from storm to storm. Another index i.e. φ index is defined as 'the rainfall rate above which the rainfall volume equals the run-off volume' as shown in Fig. 2.6. The φ index is derived from the rainfall hyetograph with the knowledge of the resulting runoff volume. The initial loss is also considered as infiltration. The φ value is found by treating it as a constant infiltration capacity. if the rainfall intensity is less than φ, then the infiltration rates is equal to the rainfall intensity; however, if the rainfall intensity is larger than φ the difference between the rainfall and infiltration in an interval of time represents the runoff volume as shown in Fig 2.6. The amount of the rainfall in excess of the index is called rainfall excess. in connection with runoff and flood studies it is also known as effective rainfall. the φ index thus accounts for the total abstraction and enables magnitudes to be estimated for a given hyetograph.

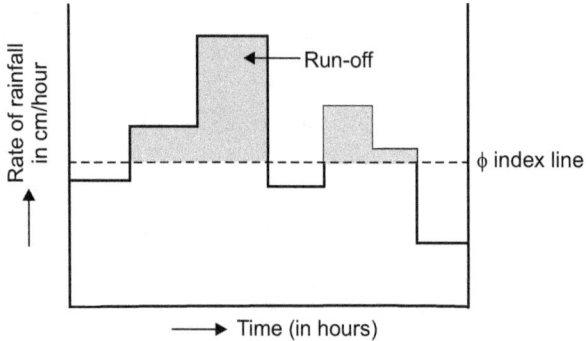

Fig. 2.6 : φ$_{index}$ and run-off volume

2.5.3 By Rational Method

In this method, the run-off and rainfall are correlated by the following equation

$$Q = C i A$$

Where,   Q = Flood flow in cubic metres per second

A = Drainage area that contributes to run-off in hectares

i = Intensity of rainfall in cm per hour

and   C = Coefficient of run-off, which depends upon catchment characteristics such as type of soil, vegetal cover etc.

2.5.4 Unit Hydrograph Method

Hydrograph is a graphical representation of discharge against time. A unit hydrograph is a hydrograph having a volume of 25 mm of direct run-off which results from a storm of specified duration and pattern areal distribution. Hydrographs from other storms of similar duration and pattern are assumed to possess the same time base having ordinates of direct run-off which are proportional to run-off volumes. As volume of flow is obtained by discharge multiplied by time, the area enclosed under hydrograph determines the volume of flow during that period. The accuracy of the flood hydrograph analysis mainly depends upon how accurately the rainfall, infiltration and rate of accumulation of run-off are determined.

After determining the infiltration index and the unit hydrograph from the rainfall-run-off observations, the flood hydrograph for a given rainfall excess can be calculated.

2.6 HYDROGRAPH

(1) Definition : 'Hydrograph is a graphical representation of discharge against time. A typical hydrograph resulting from a given storm is shown in Fig. 2.7.

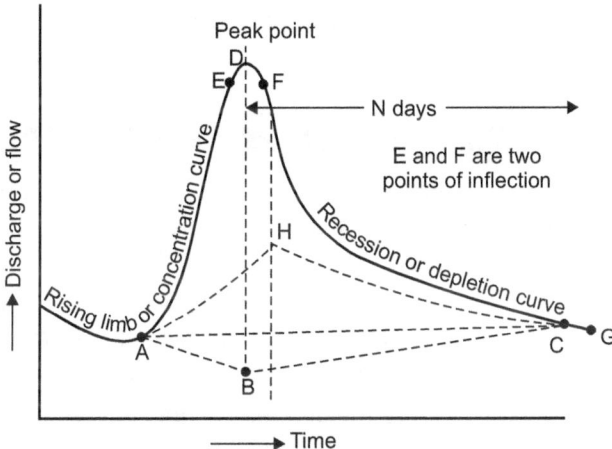

Fig. 2.7 : Flood hydrograph (with single peak)

(2) Components of Hydrograph : It consists of three component parts as follows :

- The concentration curve or rising limb AE that joins the first point of the rising limb A to the point E, the first point of inflection.
- The crest segment EF joining the two points of inflection having peak point D between them, and
- The recession or falling limb (or depletion curve), FC that begins from the second point of inflection. Each of the above three parts have certain peculiar characteristics, that determine the shape of the hydrograph. It incorporates flow in all the three phases of run-off i.e. surface run-off, interflow and the base flow.

Initially i.e. before the storm occurs there is only base flow that contributes to the stream flow shown as point A in the Fig. 2.7. After the storm takes place the initial losses such as interception, depression storages, soil moisture and infiltration etc. are met with and the surface run-off takes place that gradually adds to the stream flow. This is shown as AE, E being the first point of inflection.

The point 'D' on the hydrograph represent the peak flow. The curved portion EF is called as *crest segment* lying between the two points E and F of inflection. After the point F, the stream flow starts receding and the curved portion FC represents the withdrawal of the water stored in the stream during the rising period and the hydrograph starts falling.

Obviously the area under the hydrograph ADC represents the total volume of run-off during the given storm. Sometimes double peaked hydrographs are possible due to complex storms that cause rainfall of different intensities with some time interval. However, for analysis of floods and for the derivation of the unit hydrograph usually single peaked hydrographs are considered.

It may be remembered that the two different storms of a given catchment and also two identical storms in two different catchments will produce two different hydrographs. Thus it can be said that the hydrograph represents the typical response of a given catchment to the rainfall input.

2.7 FACTORS AFFECTING THE SHAPE OF HYDROGRAPH

The shape of the hydrograph is influenced by various factors such as the catchment, the storm characteristics and the initial losses such as interception, depression storages, soil moisture and infiltration and evaporation and transpiration losses.

The shape of the catchment decides the time required for water from the farthest part of the catchment to join the outlet point and thus affects the shape of the hydrograph including its peak. The size of the catchment also considerably affects the run-off characteristics.

The peak discharge is found to vary as the area of catchment raised to certain value say n where n is less than unity. The recession curve of hydrograph which represents the withdrawal from the storage, depends upon the natural slope of the stream. In case of small catchments having predominant overland flow, the steep slope of the catchment will bring large peak flows. The vegetal cover in the catchment will retard the overland flow and also increase the infiltration and thus the peak discharges are reduced.

As regards the storm characteristics, the three important factors that affect the shape of the flood hydrograph are the duration, intensity and variation in the direction of the storm.

2.8 METHODS OF BASE FLOW SEPARATION

As already stated, the three types of flow that contribute to the hydrograph are as follows :

- Surface run-off of the water entering the stream as *'overland flow'*.
- Sub-surface flow which is the water that has infiltrated into the upper layers of soil that reaches the natural stream within a short period, called as *'interflow'*, and
- Ground water flow which is the water that has infiltrated deep and joined the ground water storage and is called as *'base flow'*.

Thus, the total run-off consists of overland flow, interflow and the base flow. As overland flow and interflow occurs as surface run-off the combination of these two is called as *'direct run-off'*. Thus, the total run-off consists of direct run-off and base flow.

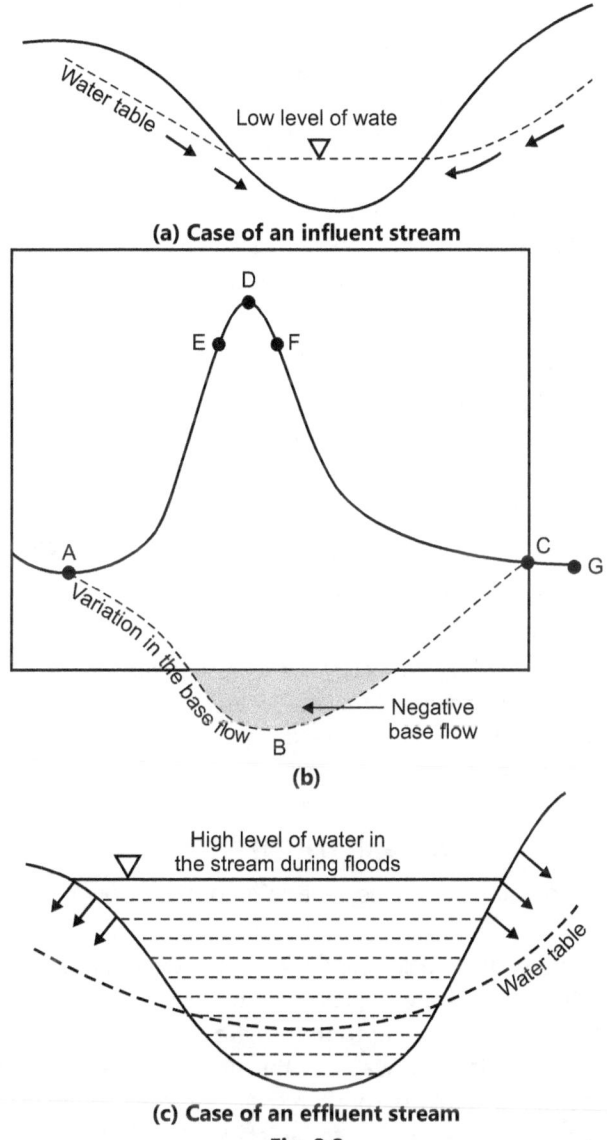

(a) Case of an influent stream

(b)

(c) Case of an effluent stream

Fig. 2.8

In order to derive an unit hydrograph, it is necessary to separate the base flow from the total run-off. The base flow when separated from the total run-off constitutes direct run-off. The three commonly adopted methods for the separation of base flow are as explained below.

2.8.1 By Straight Line Method

This is the simplest method of separating the base flow from the total run-off. The method consists in joining the point A of beginning of the surface run-off to the end point C of the recession curve by a straight line i.e. line AC as shown in Fig. 2.8. The point A where there is a sharp change in the run-off rate, can easily be identified. However, the other point C which marks the end of the direct run-off is somewhat difficult to locate. An empirical formula that assists in determining the time interval in days say N measured from the peak point D to the end of the hydrograph is as follows :

$$N \text{ (in days)} = 0.828 \, A^{0.2}$$

Where, A represents the catchment area in square kilometers. The portion of the hydrograph lying above this line AC represents surface or direct run-off.

2.8.2 By Extension of Base Flow Curve

This method which is widely used, consists in extending the base flow curve that existed before the beginning of the surface run-off to intersect the vertical drawn from the peak point D of the hydrograph, at the point B. This point of intersection B is then joined to the point C at the end of the hydrograph by a straight line. Thus, the lines AB and BC indicate the separation of the base flow from the surface run-off.

2.8.3 By Backward Extension of Base Flow Recession Curve

In cases where there is appreciable contribution from the ground water flow that reaches the stream quickly, this third method is used.

The method consists in extending the base flow recession curve after recession of the flood hydrograph i.e. point G in backward direction so as to intersect it into the vertical drawn from second point of inflection F (on the recession curve) in the point H and joining this point H to the beginning point of the hydrograph A by a free hand smooth curve AH, then the arcs AH and HG of the two curves separate the base flow from the surface run-off.

2.8.4 Direct Run-off Hydrograph (DRH)

The flood hydrograph obtained after the separation of base flow is called as 'direct run-off hydrograph'.

It may be noted that in the above discussion, the level of water in the stream was sufficiently low as compared as the ground water table before the occurrence of storm and hence there was contribution from the ground water to the stream flow and the stream is called **influent stream.** However, when the level of water in the stream during floods is higher than the ground water, the flow will take place from the stream to the ground water and is known as 'negative base flow' and the stream is said to be 'effluent stream' as shown in the Fig. 2.8 (a), (b) and (c). In case of high floods in the stream, as the base flow forms a very small part of the total run-off, it is usual practice to assume a constant value for the base flow for the simplification of the problem.

2.9 UNIT HYDROGRAPH (U.H.G.)

(1) Introduction and Definition (Fig. 2.9) : The concept of unit hydrograph first suggested by Sherman in 1932 is of immense use in the prediction and estimation on of the flood hydrographs of known rain storm from a catchment. The basic assumption of the theory of unit hydrograph states that if two identical storms occur over a catchment with exactly identical conditions prior to the rain, the hydrographs of run-off resulting from these two storms would be expected to be the same.

A unit hydrograph of a catchment is defined as 'a hydrograph of direct run-off (i.e. the difference between the total run-off and base flow) resulting from one centimetre (earlier it was one inch in British System) of effective rainfall (also called as rainfall excess) of a specified interval occurring uniformly over the entire catchment area at a uniform rate'. The important characteristic of unit hydrograph is its specified duration i.e. a 6 hour unit hydrograph implies a unit hydrograph resulting from a rainfall of 6 hours duration i.e. It is a hydrograph obtained by surface run-off from a storm of 6 hours duration that results in a rainfall excess of one centimetre depth. This implies that a storm that results in the rainfall excess of say m centimetre in a unit duration (which may be 2 hours, 3 hours, 4 hours etc.) will produce a hydrograph (of run-off) whose ordinates will be in the multiples of m times, the ordinates of unit hydrograph (i.e. 1 cm rainfall excess) of the same assumed unit duration.

(2) The Basic Assumptions of Unit Hydrograph
- The time base of the hydrograph remains the same irrespective of the rain intensity
- The unit hydrograph is linear
- The unit hydrograph is time invariant

(3) Principles Involved in Unit Hydrograph : The principles on which the theory of unit hydrograph (U.H.G.) is based is as follows :
- The effective rainfall is evenly distributed with its (specified) duration and occurs over the entire area of the drainage basin.
- For all storms of unit duration irrespective of their intensities, the base period of the surface run-off is practically the same.
- The hydrographs resulting from other storms of similar or like duration and pattern are assumed to have the same time base but having ordinates of the direct run-off in proportion to the volumes of run-off.
- The hydrograph of run-off due to a given rainfall period (from the basin) reflects the physical characteristics of the basin.

(4) Practical Difficulties in Derivation of U.H.G. : Some of the practical difficulties that will have to be faced in the derivation of unit hydrograph are the selection of the unit period (of the hydrograph), exact determination of base flow, variation of intensity and non-uniformity of rainstorm over the entire catchment area and the effect of movement of the storm in large catchments.

(5) Utility of Unit Hydrograph : The unit hydrograph serves an important tool in the following two cases :
- It enables to estimate the maximum flood discharge of a given stream.
- It assists in the preparation of a flood hydrograph for any anticipated rainfall in the catchment.

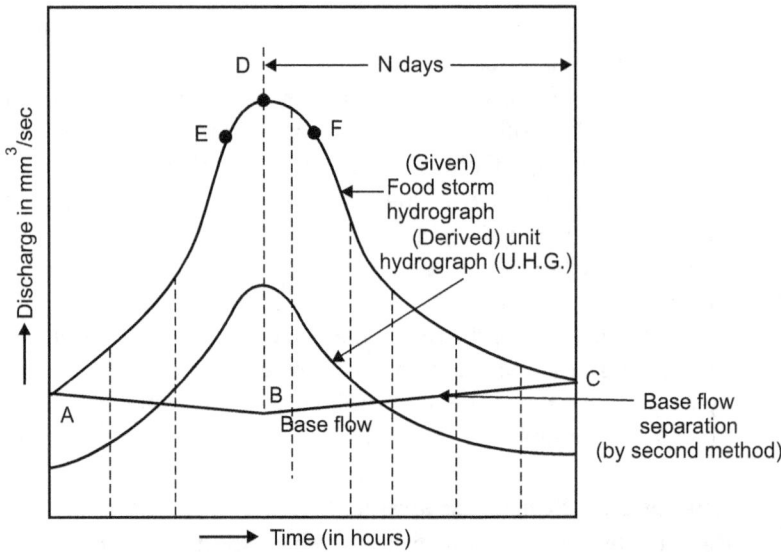

Fig. 2.9 : Derivation of unit hydrograph (from a given storm hydrograph)

(6) Construction of a Unit Hydrograph (Fig. 2.9) : The procedure to be followed in the construction of a unit hydrograph of some specified (unit) duration from a given storm hydrograph of the same duration, is as follows :

(i) For a uniformly distributed isolated intense storm over the entire drainage basin, select the appropriate unit period.

(ii) For the assumed storm, prepare a storm hydrograph from the available records of river flow (i.e. discharge) for that unit duration and draw ordinates at some uniform time interval for the entire hydrograph.

(iii) Separate the base flow from the total run-off indicated by the hydrograph obtained in the step (ii) above.

(iv) Determine the ordinates of *direct run-off* (i.e. total run-off minus the base flow) by subtracting the *base flow ordinates* from the corresponding ordinates of the total run-off as determined in the step (ii) above.

(v) Calculate the volume of direct run-off from the formula

Volume of direct run-off = $(\Sigma 0) \cdot (t) \cdot (60 \times 60)$ cubic metres

Where, ΣO = Summation of ordinates of the direct run-off as obtained in step (iv) above in m³/sec.

and t = Selected interval of time between the consecutive ordinates

(b) Determine the depth of direct run-off by the formula

$$\text{Depth of direct run-off} = \frac{(\Sigma O) \cdot (t) \times (60 \times 60)}{A \times (10^3)^2} \times 100 \text{ (centimetres)}$$

$$= \frac{0.36 \times (\Sigma O) \times t}{A} \text{ (centimetres)}$$

Where, A represents the area of the entire drainage basin in sq. kilometers.

- Now, compute the required ordinates of the unit hydrograph by the relation –

$$\text{Unit hydrograph ordinates} = \left[\frac{\text{Direct runoff ordinates}}{\text{Volume of direct runoff measured in cm}}\right]$$

- Plot the ordinates of the unit hydrograph obtained in step (vi) above at the respective time intervals (to scale) and join them by a smooth free hand curve to represent the (shape of) the required unit hydrograph. This unit hydrographs represents a unit volume (i.e. 1 cm) of run-off.

(7) Use of the Unit Hydrograph : The UHs establish a relationship between the ERH and DRH for a catchment. They are of great use in

- The development of flood hydrographs for extreme rainfall magnitudes (for use in the design of hydraulic structures)
- Extension of flood flow records based on rainfall records
- Development of flood forecasting and warning systems based on rainfall

(8) Limitations of the Unit Hydrograph :

- Unit hydrographs assume uniform distribution of rainfall over the catchment and uniform intensity during the duration of rainfall excess. In practice, these two conditions are never satisfied.
- Under conditions of non-uniform areal distribution and variation of in intensity, the unit hydrograph theory can still be used if the areal distribution is consistent between different storms.
- The size of the catchment imposes an upper limit on the applicability of the unit hydrograph theory (because the centre of the storm can vary from storm to storm and each of these storms can give a different DRH under otherwise identical conditions in very large basins).
- The upper limit for use of the unit hydrograph method is 5000km²
- n the case of very large basins, the flood hydrographs can be studied by dividing it into a number of smaller sub-basins, developing DRHs for these sub-basins by the UH method, and then routing these DRHs through their respective channels to obtain the composite DRH at the catchment outlet

2.10 S-CURVE OR S-HYDROGRAPH (I.E. SUMMATION HYDROGRAPH)

S-curve or S-hydrograph is a hydrograph which is produced by a continuous effective rainfall at constant rate for an infinite period.

It can be derived by summation of the ordinates of an infinite series of unit hydrographs of same unit duration spaced at the same unit duration apart and hence the name summation hydrograph. It is a curve which rise continuously in the form or shape of the letter S, till a constant discharge value i.e. equilibrium is reached.

The discharge of the S-curve at the time of equilibrium

$$= \frac{A \cdot i \times (100 \times 100)}{100 \times 3600} = \frac{A \cdot i}{36} \ (m^3/sec)$$

where $\quad A$ = Area of catchment in hectares

and $\quad i$ = Constant rate of effective rainfall in cm/hour

If A is expressed in sq. km, then the above formula modifies as follows :

$$\text{Discharge of the S-curve} = \frac{A \cdot i \times (1000 \times 1000)}{100 \times 3600} = (2.78 \ A \cdot i) \ m^3/sec$$

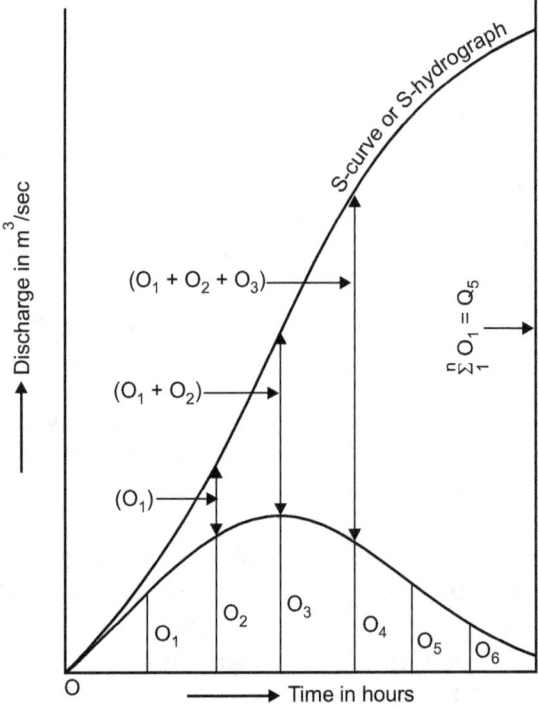

Fig. 2.10 : S-curve or S-hydrograph

Principle of Superposition :

If a unit hydrograph of a specified unit duration is available, then unit hydrographs of any other duration can be derived by the superposition technique. If the other durations are in integral multiples of the specified unit duration, the calculation work becomes comparatively easier e.g. to derive a 9 hours unit hydrograph from a 3 hour unit hydrograph with their starting points separated by 3 hour are added together (i.e. summation) to obtain a hydrograph of 3 centimetre run-off (i.e. 1 cm × 3) during a 9 hour period. If the ordinates of this summation hydrograph are divided by *three*, then a 9 hour unit hydrograph will be available. However, if the required unit hydrograph is not in the exact multiples of the given unit hydrograph, then technique of superposition cannot be applied. In such cases, the above S-curve or S-hydrograph method is to be applied (Fig. 2.10).

It is possible to develop S-curve or S-hydrograph graphically by the addition of series of identical unit hydrographs spaced at intervals which are same as the duration of effective rainfall from which they were obtained. The method of developing S-hydrograph is fully explained in the illustrative problem 2.7.

2.11 SYNTHETIC UNIT HYDROGRAPH

The methods explained above for the development of unit hydrograph are applicable to catchments for which complete information as regards the rainfall and resulting flood hydrograph are available. However, there may be certain catchments for which the above data may not be available and yet the unit hydrograph is to be derived. For the construction of unit hydrographs in such cases, *'synthetic unit hydrograph'* method is adopted. There are several methods adopted for the derivation of synthetic unit hydrograph and are based on the geometric and topographic characteristics of the catchments by direct or indirect analogy with catchments having similar nature or by empirical formulae.

The method commonly adopted is the one advocated by Snyder (1938) and is explained in details as follows.

Synder after analyzing a large number of hydrographs from drainage basins (i.e. catchments) [in the United States of America] of sizes varying from 25 sq. km. to 25000 sq. km., choose the important three elements for the derivation of unit hydrographs as follows :

- The peak flow or discharge (Q_p),
- Time base (T) and
- Time of peak (t_p) (also called as basin lag).

After determining the values of the above three elements for the regional location of the catchment (i.e. drainage basin) Synder proposed the empirical equations as follows :

(1) Time of Peak or Basin lag :

i.e. $$t_p = C_t \left[L \cdot L_{C_a} \right]^{0.3}$$

where t_p is basin lag in hours.

L = Length of the main stream in kilometres measured along the water course from the basin divide to the gauging station and

L_{C_a} = Distance measured from the outlet or gauging stations to a point on the stream nearest to the centroid of the drainage basin.

The centroid of drainage basin is determined by cutting the basin outline on the cardboard and marking the point of intersection by drawing verticals by suspending plumb bob from different corners of the map.

C_t = A coefficient whose value varies from 1.00 to 2.20 depending upon watershed slope, the lower values being adopted for steeper slope water sheds (i.e. drainage basins).

(2) Peak Discharge Q_P :

$$Q_P = \frac{C_p \cdot A}{t_p}$$

Where, Q_P = Peak discharge in cumecs/sq. km.

or q_P i.e. discharge per unit area of the drainage basin

$$\therefore \quad q_P = \frac{C_p \cdot A}{t_p} \times \frac{1}{A} = \frac{C_p}{t_p}$$

Where,   A = Drainage basin area measured in sq. km.

C_p = Coefficient whose value varies from 4.0 to 5.0.

(3) Base Time (in days) i.e. T :

$$T = 3 + 3\frac{t_p}{24}$$

Synder further used a standard duration (i.e. in hours) t_r of effective rainfall given by the following equation :

$$t_r = \frac{t_p}{5.5}$$

But for any other duration (in hours) t_r' (other than adopted standard duration t_r) the basin lag time (i.e. time required from midpoint of duration t_r to the unit hydrograph peak). Synder has given the modified basin lag equation $t_p' = t_p + \frac{(t_r' - t_r)}{4}$ and this new value of t_p' is to be used in the above empirical equation for obtaining solution.

SOLVED PROBLEMS

Problem 2.1 : Computation of Direct-run-off from the Rainfall Excess from a given storm Hydrograph of following data. The area of drainage basin is 50 sq. km.

Time of Observation	Ordinates of Hydrographs of Total Run-off (m³/sec)	Base (m³/sec)	Ordinates of Direct Run-off (m³/sec)
(1)	(2)	(3)	(2) – (3) = (4)
4 AM	16	16	00
6 AM	30	14	16
8 AM	62	14	48
10 AM	70	15	55
12 PM	60	13	47
2 PM	32	12	20
4 PM	16	16	00
			∴ Σ ordinates = 186

Solution :

- Calculate the ordinates of the direct run-off by subtracting the base flows from the corresponding ordinates of the hydrograph of total run-off and enter them in the column 4 in the table given above (i.e. separation of base flow).

- Using the formula already derived in the Article 2.9 calculate the depths of the direct run-off in cm as follows :

$$\text{Depth of direct run-off in cm} = \left[\frac{(0.36)(\Sigma O)(t)}{A}\right]$$

where   t = Common time interval between the successive ordinates in hours

= 2 hours

A = Catchment area or area of drainage basin in sq. km.

and   ΣO = 186 from the above table.

∴   Depth of direct run-off in cm = $\frac{(0.36 \times 186) \times (2)}{50}$ = 2.678 cm

Problem 2.2 : Development of Unit Hydrograph (U.H.G.) : The table below gives ordinates of a 6 hour flood hydrograph of a storm over a catchment area of 250 sq. km. The constant base flow is 10 m³/sec. Compute the ordinates of the 6 hour unit hydrograph and find the depth of the direct run-off.

Time in Hours (1)	Ordinates of 6 hr. Flood Hydrograph (m³/sec) (2)	Base Flow (m³/sec) (3)	Ordinates of D.R.H. (m³/sec) (2) – (3) = (4)	Ordinates of 6 Hour U.H.G. (m³/sec) (5) (4) / (Ordinate of D.R. in cm)
00	10	10	00	00
06	110	10	100	11.57
12	260	10	250	28.83
18	210	10	200	23.14
24	160	10	150	17.35
30	110	10	100	11.57
36	80	10	70	8.10
42	60	10	50	5.78
48	45	10	35	4.05
54	35	10	25	2.89
60	25	10	15	1.73
66	15	10	05	0.58
72	10	10	00	00
			$\Sigma 0 = 1000$	

Procedure :

- Subtract the base flow from the ordinates of 6 hr. flood hydrograph to obtain the ordinates of the direct run-off and enter them in the column (4) under ordinates of D.R.H.
- Compute the direct run-off volume in centimetres by the equation

$$\text{Depth of direct run-off in cm} = \frac{(0.36)(\Sigma 0) \times t \text{ (in hour)}}{\text{Area of catchment}}$$

$$= \frac{0.36 \times 1000 \times 6}{250} = 8.64 \text{ cm}$$

- Compute the ordinates of the 6 hr. unit hydrograph by dividing the ordinates of direct run-off by the volume of direct run-off in cm and enter them in the column (5).
- Plot the 6 hr. unit hydrograph to a convenient scale i.e. time in hours (x-axis) versus the ordinates of 6 hr. U.H.G. along y-axis to obtain the plot of 6 hr. U.H.G.

WATER RESOURCES ENGINEERING - I (TE CIVIL SU) — RUN-OFF AND HYDROGRAPH

Problem 2.3 : Development of flood hydrograph n hours duration from the given unit Hydrograph of n hours duration. The following table gives the ordinates of a 4 hour unit hydrograph and the base flow. Calculate the ordinates of the 4 hour flood hydrograph of 5 cm of rainfall excess and plot it to convenient scale.

Time in Hours (1)	Ordinates of 4 hr. U.H.G. (m^3/sec) (2)	Base Flow (m^3/sec) (3)	Ordinates of Direct Run-off (m^3/sec) col. (2) × n_{cm} of Excess Rainfall (2) − (3) = (4) Here n = 5 cm (given)	Ordinates of 4 Hour Flood Hydrograph (m^3/sec) (5) col (3) + col (4)
04	00	3.50	00	3.50
08	0.15	3.00	0.75	3.75
12	0.40	2.50	2.00	4.50
16	0.90	2.00	4.50	6.50
20	1.60	1.50	8.00	9.50
24	2.90	1.9	14.50	16.40
28	3.10	2.2	15.5	17.7
32	2.80	2.5	14.00	16.50
36	2.10	3.00	10.5	13.50
40	1.5	3.20	7.5	10.75
44	0.80	3.40	4.00	7.40
48	0.40	3.50	2.00	5.50
52	0.15	3.80	0.75	4.55
56	00	3.50	00	3.50

Procedure :

- Calculate the ordinates of the direct run-off of 5 cm rainfall excess by multiplying the given ordinates of 4 hour unit hydrograph written in column (2), and enter them in the column (4) above as shown.
- Add the base flow from column (3) to the ordinates of the direct run-off of column (4) to obtain the ordinates of 4 hour flood hydrograph and enter them in the column (5) above.
- Plot the 4 hour flood hydrograph on the graph paper to suitable scale with time in hour on x-axis at interval of 4 hours versus the ordinates of the 4 hour flood hydrograph entered in the column (5) above to obtain a 4 hour flood hydrograph.

WATER RESOURCES ENGINEERING - I (TE CIVIL SU)   RUN-OFF AND HYDROGRAPH

Development of a flood hydrograph resulting from two (or more) rainfall periods by the use of unit hydrograph of specified duration.

Assumption : The storm pattern (of the flood hydrograph) should be similar to the given unit hydrograph. e.g. Given a 2 hour unit hydrograph and it is desired to obtain the flood hydrograph that results from a rainfall of 6 hour duration with the intensity of rainfall changing as follows :

n_1 cm for 2 hours for the first 2 hours duration.

n_2 cm for 2 hours for the next 2 hours duration and

n_3 cm for 2 hours for the next-next i.e. last 2 hours duration.

Procedure : Divide the given rain storm into 3 distinct sections each of 2 hours duration and calculate the ordinates of the flood hydrograph of each section separately and add them up to obtain the ordinates of the total storm of 6 hours duration as shown in the example below.

It is to be remembered that the second section of the storm hydrograph will commence 2 hours later then the first section. Also the storm hydrograph of the last (i.e. third) section will commence 2 hours later than that of the second i.e. 4 hours later than that of the first section.

Problem 2.4 : *From the ordinates of 2 hour unit hydrograph calculate the ordinates of storm hydrograph that results from 2 hours duration having rainfall of 2.5 cm, 5.6 cm and 2.60 cm at an interval of 2 hours.*

Data given :

Time in Hours	02	04	06	08	10	12	14	16	18	20	22	24	26
Ordinates of 2 hr. Unit Hydrograph m^3/sec	00	120	400	550	420	350	300	180	120	100	70	30	00

Given : Constant base flow of 12 m³/sec and initial loss of 10 mm; an infiltration index of 3 mm/hour.

Solution :

Given : Rainfall during first 2 hour duration = 2.5 cm

The initial loss = 10 cm = 1 cm

and infiltration index = 3 mm/hour

∴ Infiltration index during first 2 hours = 2 × 3 = 6 mm = 0.6 cm

∴ Rainfall excess during the first 2 hour duration

$$= \text{(Rainfall)} - \text{(Initial loss)} - \text{(Infiltration loss)}$$
$$= 2.5 - 1 - 0.6$$
$$= 0.9 \text{ cm}$$

Similarly rainfall excess during the next 2 hours duration

$$= \begin{bmatrix} \text{Rainfall during} \\ \text{that period} \end{bmatrix} - \text{(Infiltration loss)}$$
$$= 5.6 - 0.6$$
$$= 5 \text{ cm}$$

Similarly rainfall excess during the next i.e. last 2 hours duration

$$= 2.60 - 0.60$$
$$= 2 \text{ cm}$$

Notes :

- As the rainfall excess of 2 hour unit hydrograph by definition is 1 cm, the ratios of rainfall excesses during the subsequent 2 hours interval are $\frac{0.90}{1.00}$; $\frac{5}{1}$ and $\frac{2}{1}$ i.e. 0.90, 5 and 2 cm respectively.
- Thus the ordinates for such excess rainfalls will be obtained by simply multiplying the ordinates of 2 hr. unit hydrograph by 0.90, 5 and 2 respectively and are to be entered in the appropriate column as shown in the tabular form.
- The calculations of run-off due to rainfall excess due to 0.90 cm will commence from 2 hours.
- The calculations of run-off due to rainfall excess of 5 cm will commence from (2 hours + 2 hours) i.e. 4 hours.
- The calculations of run-off due to 2 cm rainfall excess will commence from (2 hours + 2 hours + 2 hours) i.e. 6 hours.

WATER RESOURCES ENGINEERING - I (TE CIVIL SU) — RUN-OFF AND HYDROGRAPH

(Solution of the problem in a Tabular form see on the next page.)
Solution of the Problem 2.4 in a tabular form :

Time in hours	Given 2 hour U.H.G. ordinates (m³/sec)	Rainfall excess in cm in 2 hours duration	Direct runoff ordinates from rainfall excess during successive 2 hours duration			Total of col. (4), (5) & (6)	(Given) Base flow (m³/sec)	Ordinates of total runoff i.e. Flood hydrograph (m³/sec)
			for 0.90 cm	for 5.00 cm	for 2.00 cm			
			(4) col (2) × 0.9	(5) col (2) × (5)	(6) col (2) × (2)			col. (7) + col. (8)
(1)	(2)	(3)	(4)	(5)	(6)	(7)	(8)	(9)
02	00	0.90	00	00	00	00	12	12
04	120	5.00	108	00	00	108	12	120
06	400	2.00	360	600	00	960	12	972
08	550		495	2000	240	2735	12	2747
10	420		378	2750	800	3928	12	3940
12	350		315	2100	1100	3515	12	3527
14	300		270	1750	840	2860	12	2872
16	180		162	1500	700	2362	12	2374
18	120		108	900	600	1608	12	1620
20	100		90	600	360	1050	12	1062
22	70		63	500	240	803	12	815
24	30		27	350	200	577	12	589
26	00		00	150	140	290	12	302
28				00	60	60	12	71
30					00	00	12	12

Problem 2.5 : Given unit hydrograph ordinates for Bhatgar Dam Project. To derive the U.H.G. ordinates for 1 hour duration. Plot the flood hydrograph of the storm as under.

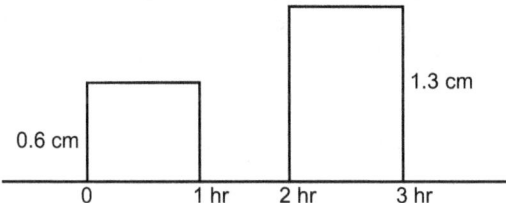

Fig. 2.11

Hours (1)	Q (cumecs)
0	0
1.375	14.147
2.750	54.231
4.125	99.031
5.500	126.147
6.875	112.00
8.250	82.526
9.625	56.599
11.00	40.084
12.375	28.295
13.750	20.042
15.125	15.326
16.500	11.789
17.875	9.432
19.25	8.253
20.625	5.895
22.00	4.176
23.375	3.906
24.750	2.358
26.125	1.170
27.50	0.610
28.875	0

(1)	(2)	(3)	(4)	(5)	(6)	(7)
Time (Hours)	U.H.G. Ordinates	1st Storm $E_1 = 0.6$ cm (2) × 0.6	IInd Storm $E_2 = 0$ cm (2) × 0	IIIrd Storm $E_3 = 1.3$ cm (2) × 1.3	Base Flow (Cumecs)	Flood Hydrograph (Cumecs) (3) + (4) + (5) + (6)
0	0	0	–	–	20	20
1	9	5.4	0	–	20	25.4
2	25	15.0	0	0	20	35.0
3	58	34.8	0	11.7	20	66.5
4	93	55.8	0	32.5	20	108.3
5	121	72.6	0	75.4	20	168.0
6	124	74.4	0	120.9	20	215.3
7	108	64.8	0	157.3	20	242.1
8	85	51.0	0	161.2	20	232.0
9	65	39.0	0	140.2	20	199.2
10	52	31.2	0	110.5	20	161.7
11	40	24.0	0	84.5	20	128.5
12	32	19.2	0	67.6	20	106.8
13	25	15.0	0	52.0	20	87
14	20	12.0	0	41.6	20	73.6
15	16	9.6	0	32.5	20	62.1
16	12.5	7.5	0	26	20	53.5
17	9.5	5.7	0	20.8	20	46.5
18	8	4.8	0	16.25	20	41.05
19	7	4.2	0	12.35	20	36.55
20	6.5	3.9	0	10.4	20	34.30
21	5.5	3.3	0	9.10	20	32.20
22	5	3.0	0	8.45	20	31.45
23	4	2.4	0	7.15	20	29.55
24	3.5	2.1	0	6.5	20	28.6
25	2.5	1.5	0	5.2	20	26.7
26	2	1.2	0	4.55	20	25.75
27	1	0.6	0	3.25	20	23.85
28	0.5	0.3	0	2.6	20	22.90
29	–	–	0	1.3	20	21.30
30	–	–	–	0.65	20	20.65

Conclusion : Peak Discharge occurs at 7 hrs and its value is 242.1 cumecs. Time base has increased from 28 hrs to 30 hrs., hence there is a two hr. increase in the time base.

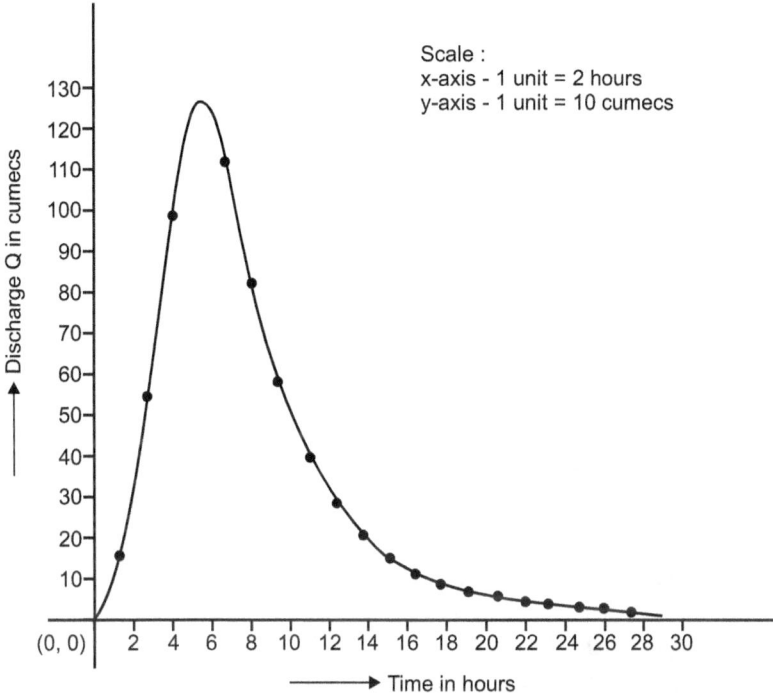

Fig. 2.12 : Flood hydrograph of storm for problem 2.5

For Fig. 2.12, computation of flood hydrograph from unit hydrograph for problem 2.5 refer Fig. 2.13.

Development of Unit hydrograph of desired duration from Unit hydrograph of specified unit duration.

Sometimes a unit hydrograph of desired unit duration may not be available, then in such cases it can be developed from known unit hydrograph of specified unit duration. Here two cases may arise as follows :

Case (i) : Development of a unit hydrograph of longer period from a given unit hydrograph of specified duration.

If the unit hydrograph of unit duration t hours be given and it is required to develop unit hydrograph of unit duration t_1 hours, where t_1 is larger than t and t_1 is equal to nt, where n is a positive integer, then the *principle of superposition* can be adopted. e.g. if it is required to construct a unit hydrograph of 6 hours unit duration (i.e. t_1 = 6 hours) from the known unit hydrograph of 2 hours duration (i.e. t = 2 hours), then the following procedure is to be followed.

- In the tabular form as shown in below enter the given data of 2 hour unit hydrograph (i.e. time in hours and ordinates of a 2 hour unit hydrograph) in the first two respective columns.

- Enter the ordinates of next two unit hydrograph of 2 hours duration, each lagging from the previous one by 2 hours interval in the columns (3) and (4) respectively.

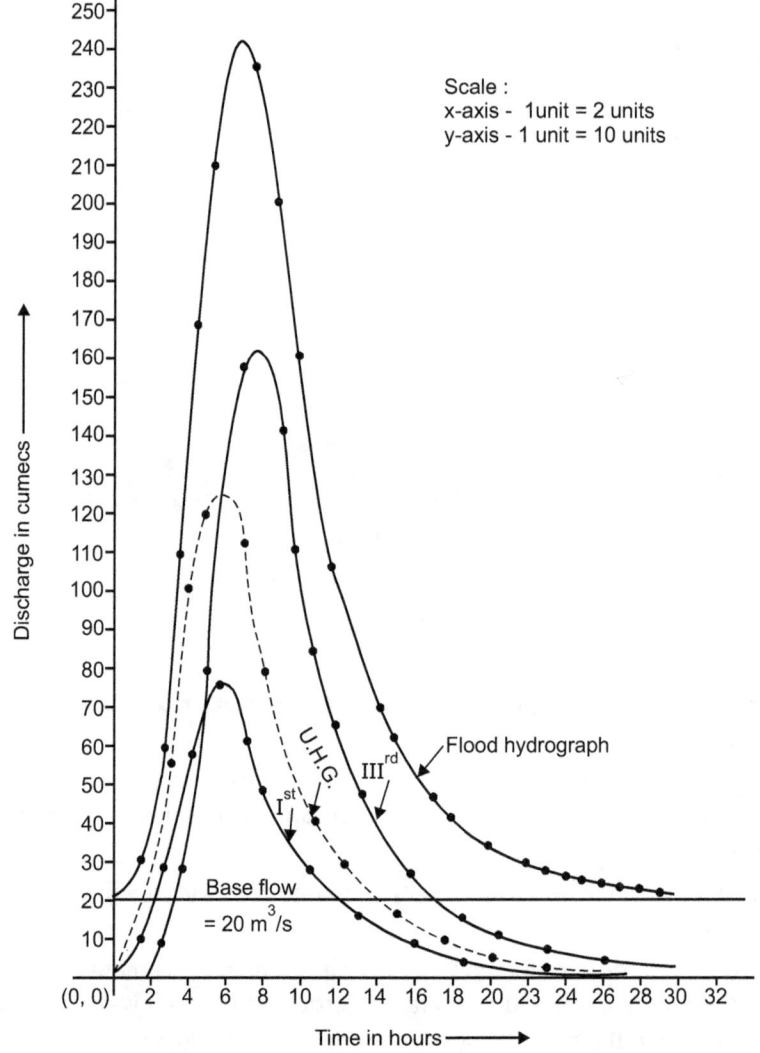

Fig. 2.13 : Computation of flood hydrograph from unit hydrograph for problem 2.5

- Enter the sum of the ordinates of three successive 2 hour unit hydrograph of each horizontal row into the next 5th column.
- Divide the above sum entered in the column (5) by three and enter the result in the next column 6 which represents the ordinates of 6 hour unit hydrograph. The illustrative problem below explain the entire process.

Problem 2.6 : Development of 6 hour unit hydrograph from the known 2 hour unit hydrograph i.e. $t = 2$ hour, $t_1 = 6$ hour, $t_1 = nt = 3 \times 2$.

Time in hrs.	Ordinates of 2 hr. U.H.G. (m³/sec)	Ordinates of 2 hr. U.H.G. with 2 hr. Lag Period (m³/sec)	Ordinates of 2 hr. U.H.G. with 4 hr. Lag Period (m³/sec)	Summation of Ordinates of Columns (2), (3) & (4) (m³/sec)	Required Ordinates of 6 hrs. U.H.G. $\frac{col.\ 5}{3}$ (m³/sec)
(1)	(2)	(3)	(4)	(5)	(6)
0	00	–	–	00	00.0
2	15	00	–	15	05.0
4	70	15	00	85	28.3
6	120	70	15	205	68.3
8	140	120	70	310	103.3
10	120	140	120	380	126.7
12	80	120	140	340	113.3
14	50	80	120	250	83.3
16	25	50	80	155	51.7
18	15	25	50	90	30.00
20	05	15	25	45	15.00
22	00	05	15	20	6.67
24	–	00	05	05	1.67
26	–	–	00	00	0.00

Case (ii) : Development of unit hydrograph of shorter unit duration from the known unit hydrograph.

In this case it is required to develop a unit hydrograph of t_1 unit duration from a known unit hydrograph of t hour duration in which $t_1 > t$ or $t_1 < t$ and where t_1 is not exactly in the integral multiples of t. The method of S-curve or S-hydrograph is to be adopted as illustrated below in Problem 2.7.

Problem 2.7 : Aim : *To develop the S-curve hydrograph.*

Theory : *The S-curve hydrograph is also called the summation hydrograph.*

When a unit hydrograph of a desired duration t_1 is neither available nor can be developed by the analysis of rainfall run-off data, then there is no alternative but to somehow or the other derive this unknown hydrograph from the known hydrograph. The problem is simple when the duration of the unknown hydrograph is an integral multiple of the known hydrograph.

Say if a 6 hrs. U.H.G. is to be obtained from a 3 hr. U.H.G., then it can be obtained by superimposing the 3 hrs. U.H.G. over another 3 hrs. U.H.G. with a time lag of 3 hrs. and then dividing the results by 2.

The problem however becomes complex when the duration of unknown hydrograph is shorter and/or not an integral multiple of the known hydrograph. In such cases, use of the 'S' hydrograph can be made, which is based on the principle of superposition. Once the 'S' hydrograph is constructed, then the hydrograph of any desired duration can be obtained.

Procedure for Problem 2.7 :

The S-curve hydrograph is essentially a hydrograph produced by a continuous effective rainfall at a constant rate for an infinite period. Each of the readings of the first storm is lagged by 4 hrs. and readings for 6 such storms is obtained.

The summation of all these ordinates gives the S-curve ordinates. This is a steeply rising curve which attains a constant value when equilibrium discharge is reached.

(Please see 'S' hydrograph table on the next page.)

Problem 2.8 : 'S' Hydrograph

Hrs.	Ist storm	IInd storm	IIIrd storm	IVth storm	Vth storm	VIth storm	'S'	'S' smoothened	S' 2 hr. lag	S – S'	$\frac{4}{2}$(S–S') = 2 hr. U.H.G.	2 Hr U.H.G. smoothened
0	0	–	–	–			0	0	–	0	0	0
1	2.25	–	–	–			2.25	2.25	–	2.25	4.5	4.5
2	8.5	–	–	–			8.5	8.5	0	8.5	17.0	17.0
3	23.0	0.00	–	–			23.0	23.0	2.25	20.75	41.5	41.5
4	46.25	2.25	–	–			46.25	46.5	8.5	38.0	76.0	76.0
5	74.25	8.5	–	–			76.5	76.5	23.0	53.5	107.0	107.0
6	99.0	23.0	–	–			107.5	110.0	46.5	63.5	127.0	127.0
7	111.5	46.25	–	–			134.5	134.5	76.5	58.0	116.0	116.0
8	109.5	74.25	0.00	–			155.75	155.75	110.0	45.75	96.0	96.0
9	95.5	99.0	2.25	–			172.0	174.0	134.5	39.5	79.0	74.0
10	77.5	111.5	8.5	–			185.0	185.0	155.75	29.25	58.5	58.5
11	60.5	109.5	23.0	–			195.0	195.0	174.0	21.0	42.0	46.0
12	47.25	95.5	46.25	0.00			203.0	203.0	185.0	18.0	36.0	36.0
13	37.25	77.5	74.25	2.25			209.25	208.0	195.0	13.0	26.0	26.0
14	29.25	60.5	99.0	8.5			214.25	214.25	203.0	11.25	22.5	20.0
15	23.25	60.5	60.5	23.0			218.25	218.25	208.0	10.25	20.5	16.0

... Continued

Hrs.	Ist storm	IInd storm	IIIrd storm	IVth storm	Vth storm	VIth storm	'S'	'S' smoothened	S' 2 hr. lag	S – S'	$\frac{4}{2}(S-S')$ = 2 hr. U.H.G.	2 Hr U.H.G. smoothened
16	18.375	47.25	109.5	46.25	0	—	221.375	221.375	214.25	7.125	14.25	14.0
17	14.5	37.25	95.5	74.25	2.25	—	223.75	223.75	218.25	5.5	11.0	11.0
18	11.5	29.25	77.5	99.0	8.5	—	225.75	226.0	221.375	4.625	9.25	9.25
19	9.25	23.25	60.5	111.5	23.0	—	227.5	228.0	223.75	4.25	8.5	8.5
20	7.75	18.375	47.25	109.5	46.25	0	229.125	228.0	226.0	2.00	4.0	4.0
21	6.75	14.5	37.25	95.5	74.25	2.25	230.5	230.0	228.0	2.0	4.0	4.0
22	6.0	11.5	29.25	77.5	99.0	8.5	231.75	232.0	228.0	4.0	8.0	8.0
23	5.25	9.25	23.25	60.5	111.5	23.0	232.75	232.0	230.0	2.0	4.0	4.0
24	4.5	7.75	18.375	47.25	109.5	46.25	233.57	232.0	232.0	0.0	0.0	0.0
25	3.75	6.75	14.5	37.25	95.5	74.25	232.0	232.0	232.0	—	—	—
26	3.0	6.0	11.5	29.25	77.5	99.0	226.25	232.0	232.0	—	—	—
27	2.25	5.25	9.25	23.25	60.5	111.5	212.0	232.0	232.0	—	—	—
28	1.5	4.5	7.75	18.375	47.25	109.5	188.62	232.0	232.0	—	—	—
29	0.875	3.75	6.75	14.5	37.25	95.5	158.62	—	232.0	—	—	—
30	0.375	3.0	6.0	11.5	21.25	77.5	127.42	—	232.0	—	—	—
31	0.125	2.25	5.25	9.25	23.25	60.5	100.62	—	—	—	—	—
32	—	1.5	4.5	7.75	18.375	47.25	78.87	—	—	—	—	—

...Continued

Hrs.	Ist storm	IInd storm	IIIrd storm	IVth storm	Vth storm	VIth storm	'S'	'S' smoothened	S' 2 hr. lag	S – S'	$\frac{4}{2}$(S–S') = 2 hr. U.H.G.	2 Hr U.H.G. smoothened
33	–	0.875	3.75	6.75	14.5	37.25	63.25					
34	–	0.375	3.0	6.0	11.5	29.25	50.125					
35	–	0.125	2.25	5.25	9.25	23.25	40.125					
36	–	–	1.5	4.5	7.75	18.375	31.62					
37	–	–	0.875	3.75	6.75	14.50	25.875					
38	–	–	0.375	3.0	6.0	11.50	14.875					
39	–	–	0.125	2.25	5.25	9.25	16.75					
40	–	–	–	1.5	4.5	7.75	13.25					
41	–	–	–	0.675	3.75	6.75	11.375					
42	–	–	–	0.375	3.0	6.0	8.375					
43	–	–	–	0.125	2.25	5.25	7.625					
44	–	–	–	–	1.5	4.5	6.00					
45	–	–	–	–	0.875	3.75	4.625					
46	–	–	–	–	0.375	3.0	2.375					
47	–	–	–	–	0.125	2.25	2.375					
48	–	–	–	–	–	1.5	1.5					
49	–	–	–	–	–	0.875	0.875					
50	–	–	–	–	–	0.375	0.375					
51	–	–	–	–	–	0.125	0.125					

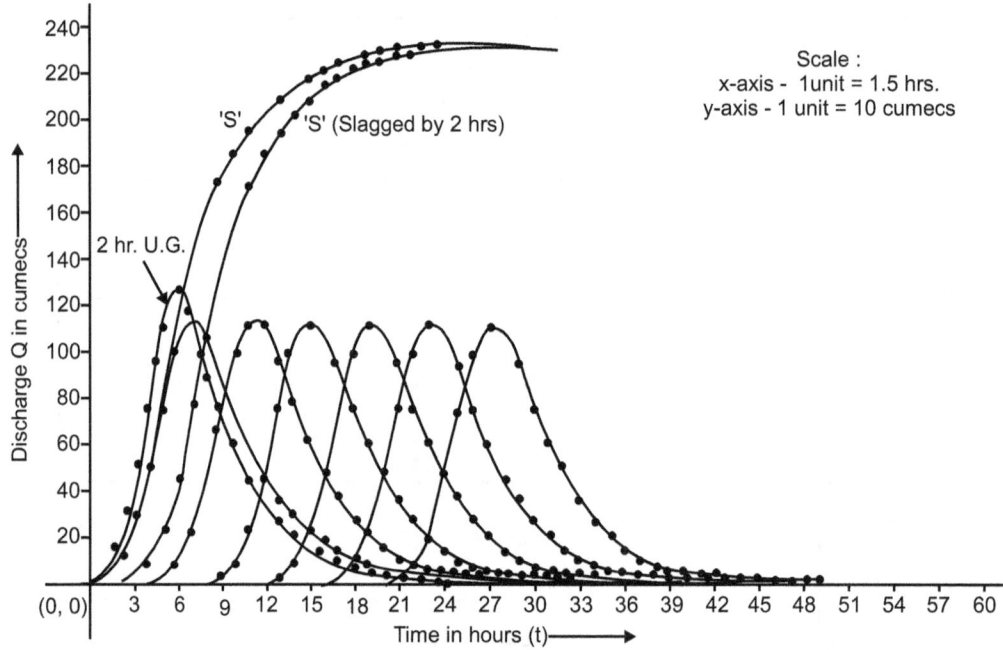

Fig. 2.14 : S-hydrograph for problem 2.8

Conclusion :

In cases where a U.H.G. of a desired duration is to be obtained, when it is not available nor can it be developed from the analysis of rainfall run-off data, then the 'S' curve hydrograph provides the necessary result.

The problem becomes however complex when the duration of the unknown hydrograph is shorter or is not an integral multiple of the duration of the known hydrograph.

Hence, in such cases, firstly the 'S' curve is constructed and then it can be used to compute the hydrograph of any desired duration.

Problem 2.9 : Study of S-curve :

Title : *Study of S-curve and its use.*

Object : *(i) To determine the ordinates of a summation curve or S-curve.*

(ii) To determine the ordination of 2 hr. unit hydrograph.

Data : *The ordination of 4 hr. unit hydrograph is as given below :*

Time in Hours	Ordinates of 4 h Unit Hydrograph in (m³/sec)
0	0
1	40
2	250
3	440
4	600
5	700
6	610
7	520
8	450
9	380
10	320
11	270
12	220
13	180
14	140
15	110
16	80
17	60
18	40
19	20
20	10
21	0

Solution : Results entered in a tabular form as shown below.

(1)	(2)	(3)	(4)	(5)	(6)	(7)
Time (Hours)	4H - UH Ordinates (m³/sec)	S-curve Ordinates Lagged by 4 hrs.	S-curve Ordinates (m³/sec)	Ordinates of S-curve Lagged by 2 hrs.	Column 4 – Column 5	Ordinates of 2h Unit Hydrograph = Column (6) $\times \frac{4}{2}$
0	0	–	0	–	0	0
1	40	–	40	–	40	80
2	250	–	250	0	250	500
3	440	–	440	40	400	800
4	600	0	600	250	350	700
5	700	40	740	440	300	600
6	610	250	860	600	260	520
7	520	440	960	740	220	440
8	450	600	1050	860	190	380
9	380	740	1120	960	160	320
10	320	860	1180	1050	130	260
11	270	960	1230	1120	110	220
12	220	1050	1270	1180	90	180
13	180	1120	1300	1230	70	140
14	140	1180	1320	1270	50	100
15	110	1230	1340	1300	40	80
16	80	1270	1350	1320	30	60
17	60	1300	1360	1340	20	40
18	40	1320	1360	1350	10	20
19	20	1340	1360	1360	0	0
20	10	1350	1360	1360	0	0
21	0	1360	1360	1360	0	0

Procedure :

To calculate the ordinates of 2h - U.H. from 4h - U.H. ordinates.
- First from the ordinates of 4h - U.H. calculate the S-curve ordinates lagged by 4 hrs.
- From this we will get the ordination of S-curve by adding the ordination of 4h - U.H. and S-curve ordinates lagged by 4 hrs.
- Then from this, find the ordinates of S-curve lagged by 2 hrs.
- In observation table, (column 4 – column 5) $\times \dfrac{4}{2}$ will give the ordinates of 2h - U hydrograph.

The equilibrium discharge can be calculated by the formula

$$Q_E = A \times 10^6 \times i \times 10^{-2} \times \dfrac{1}{3600}$$

$$= A \times i \times \dfrac{10^4}{3600}$$

$$= 2.78 \times A \times i$$

Where
$\quad A = $ sq. km.
$\quad i = $ cm/hr
$\quad \Sigma Q = 1360 \ m^3/sec$
$\quad \Delta t = 4$ hrs.

$\therefore \quad A \text{ (sq. km)} \times \dfrac{1}{100} = \Delta t \times \Sigma Q \times 60 \times 60$

$\therefore \quad \dfrac{A \times 10^6}{100} = \Delta t \times \Sigma Q \times 3600$

$\therefore \quad A = \dfrac{\Delta t \times \Sigma Q \times 3600}{10^4}$

$\quad = 0.36 \times \Delta t \times \Sigma Q$
$\quad = 0.36 \times 4 \times 1360$

$\therefore \quad A = 1958.4$ sq. km.
$\therefore \quad Q_E = 2.78 \times A \times i$

$\quad = 2.78 \times 1958.4 \times \dfrac{1}{4}$

$\quad = 1361.008 \ m^3/sec$

$\therefore$ The equilibrium discharge occurs at
$\quad T - D = 17$ hours

Where $\quad T = $ base time.

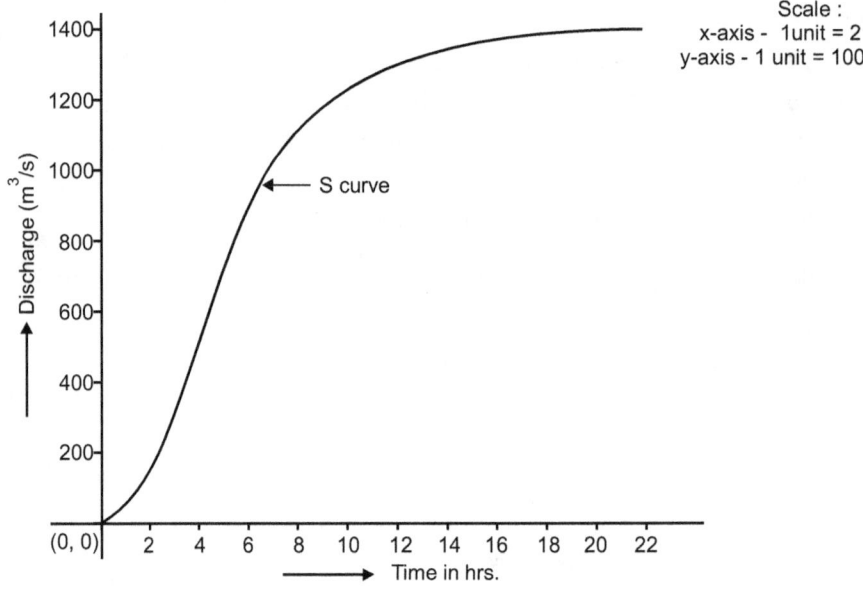

Fig. 2.15 : For problem 2.9

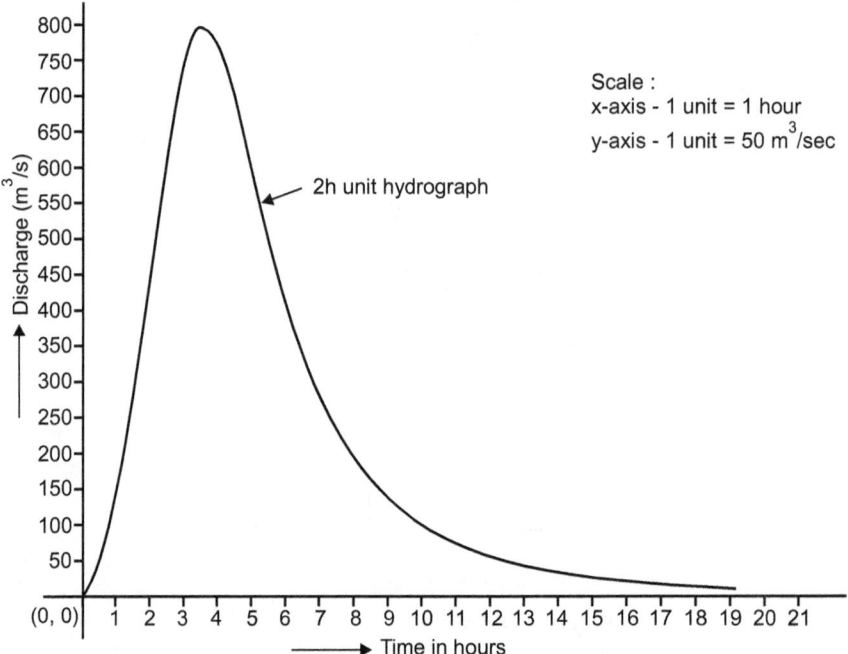

Fig. 2.16 : For problem 2.9

WATER RESOURCES ENGINEERING - I (TE CIVIL SU)   RUN-OFF AND HYDROGRAPH

Problem 2.10 : *Construction of Synthetic Unit Hydrograph by Snyder's method.*
Aim : *To draw the synthetic unit hydrograph by Snyder's method.*
Theory : *The three parameters of the unit hydrograph are :*
  (1) Unit storm
  (2) Time
  (3) Area of catchment.

Procedure :
- From the storm hydrograph, the unit storm is noted.
- Trace the area with the main valley on a sufficiently thick cardboard and calculate the C.G. by appropriate method.
- Measure length of the stream along the main stream (L).
- Measure length of stream from C.G. to the point of concentration or outlet point. Let this be (L_C).
- Calculate the peak discharge and time of peak flow. Also the base width by the formulae.

Solution :

(1) t_P (hours) = $1.2 (L \cdot L_C)^{0.3}$ ... L and L_C in kms

Scale :   1 in = 1 mile
         2.54 cm = 1.6093 km

∴   1 cm = $\dfrac{1.6093}{2.54}$ km

∴   1 cm = 0.6336 km

Multiplying by factor (16/11),
     1 cm = 0.9216 km

∴   1 cm² = 0.8493 km²
     L = 23.8 cm

∴   L = 23.8 × 0.9216 = 21.77 km
     L_C = 11.5 cm

∴ L_C = 11.5 × 0.9216 = 10.521 km

(2) ∴ t_P (hours) = $1.2 (21.77 \times 10.521)^{0.3}$
           = 6.1255 hrs

(3) t_r (hours) = $\dfrac{t_P}{5.5}$

           = $\dfrac{6.1255}{5.5}$

           = 1.1137 hrs

(4) q_P (m³/km² area) = $\dfrac{2.78 \times C_P}{t_P}$ or $\dfrac{C_P}{t_P}$ (4)

∴ q_P = $\dfrac{4}{6.1255}$

(5)	Q_P (m³/s)	$= 0.653$ m³/area $= q_P \times A$ (where A = catchment area in km²) $= 0.653 \times 130 \times 0.8493$ $= 71.03$ m³/s
(6)	T (hours)	$= (72 + 3t_P)$ $= 72 + 3(6.1255)$ $= 90.376$ hrs
(7)	W_{50}	$= \dfrac{5.6}{(q_P)^{1.08}} = \dfrac{5.6}{(0.653)^{1.08}}$
∴	W_{50}	$= 8.873$ hrs
(8)	W_{75}	$= \dfrac{3.21}{(q_P)^{1.08}} = \dfrac{3.21}{(0.653)^{1.08}}$
∴	W_{75}	$= 5.068$ hrs

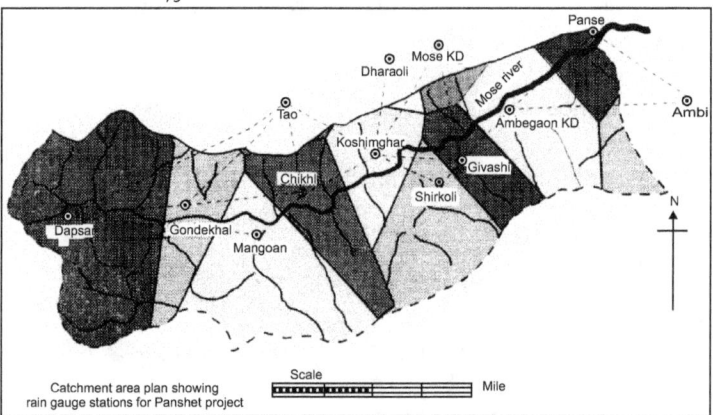

Fig. 2.17 : For problem 2.10

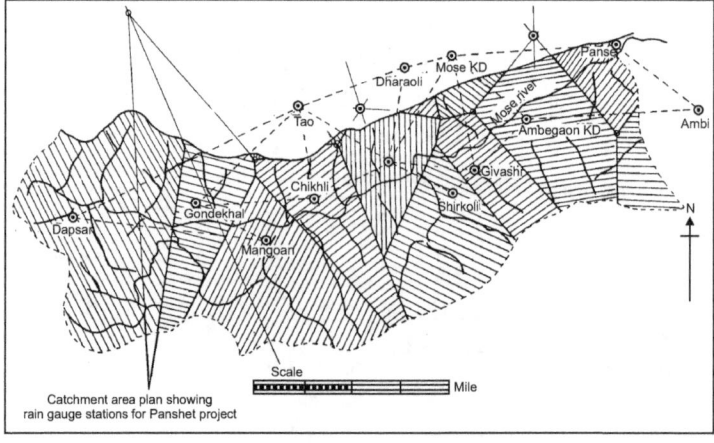

Fig. 2.18 : For problem 2.10

(9) Check for depth $= \dfrac{0.36 \Sigma o \times t}{A}$

where A = km², t = interval in hrs., o = ordinates in m³/s.

∴ Check for depth $= \dfrac{0.36 \times 154.5 \times 5}{130 \times 0.8493}$

∴ d = 2.51 cm

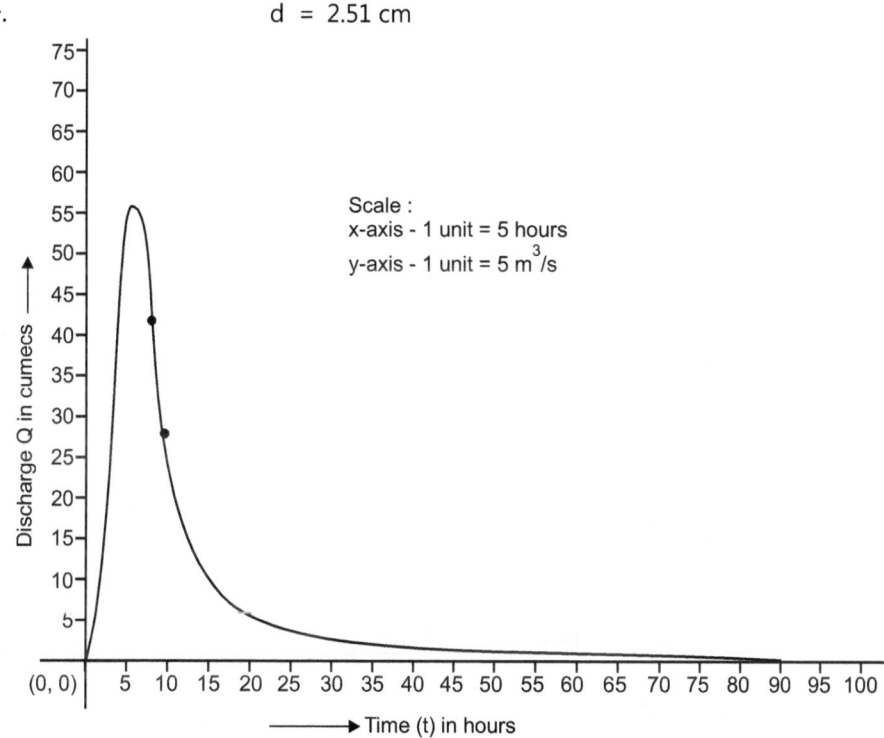

Fig. 2.19 : Synthetic unit hydrograph by Snyder's method for problem 2.10

Problem 2.11 : *Construction of hydrograph.*

Object :

(1) To draw total flood hydrograph.

(2) To derive direct run-off hydrograph.

(3) To construct unit hydrograph.

Data : *Isolated storm of one hour duration occurs over a basin of 150 km² in area. Flow data at one hour interval is given as follows.*

Sr. No.	Time in Hours	Total Flood in Cumecs	Base Flow in Cumecs
1.	8 a.m.	15	15
2.	9 a.m.	25	16
3.	10 a.m.	90	14
4.	11 a.m.	147	19
5.	12 noon	181	19
6.	1 p.m.	193	20
7.	2 p.m.	192	20
8.	3 p.m.	180	22
9.	4 p.m.	162	23
10.	5 p.m.	136	24
11.	6 p.m.	115	27
12.	7 p.m.	96	26
13.	8 p.m.	80	26
14.	9 p.m.	67	27
15.	10 p.m.	56	28
16.	11 p.m.	46	30
17.	12 p.m.	38	30
18.	1 a.m.	32	32

Procedure :
- Draw the total flood hydrograph of total flood v/s time.
- On the same graph draw the graph of base flow v/s time.
- Find the difference between total flood and base flow. Plot the graph of difference of the base flow and total flood v/s time.
- The above graph is plotted and is known as *'Direct Run-off Hydrograph'*. Find the area below this graph.
- Equating the above area as the volume of water in whose period, the depth is found out by dividing the volume by area of basin.
- The unit flood at various base floods are calculated by dividing depth of run-off to base flood. From this plot the unit flood hydrograph.

Calculations :

Area below direct run-off hydrograph = 143.7 m³/hr

Depth of run-off = $\dfrac{143.7 \times 60 \times 60}{150 \times 10^6}$ = 3.45 cm = 34.5 mm

The base flow is divided by this depth and the unit flood is obtained.

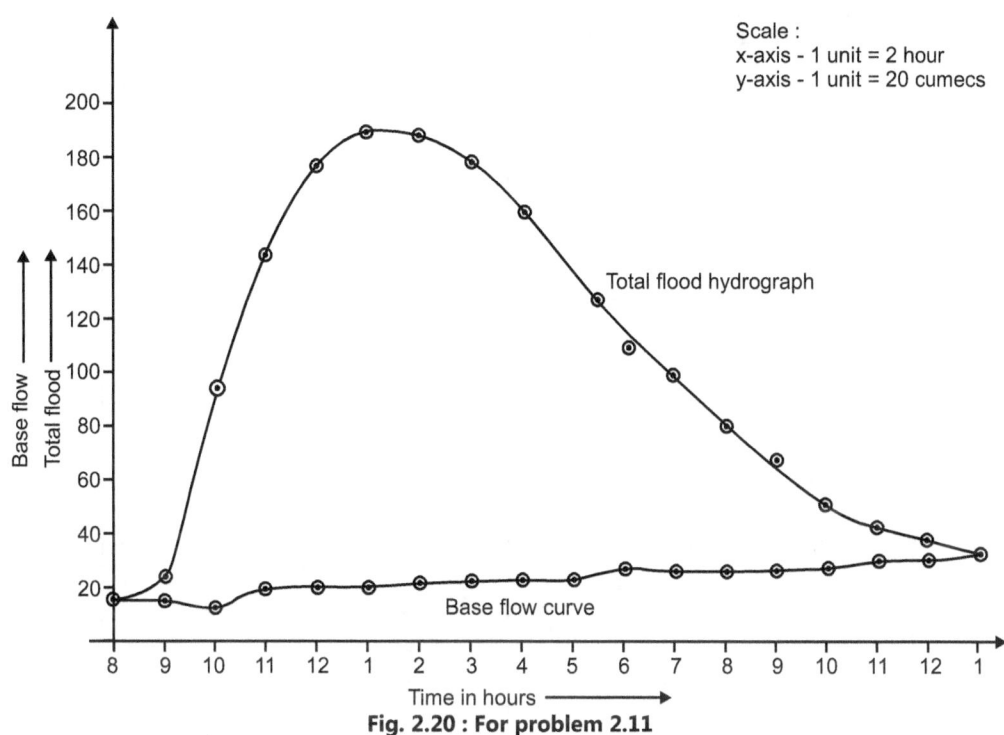

Fig. 2.20 : For problem 2.11

Fig. 2.21 : For problem 2.11

Results entered in Tabular form for Problem 2.11 :

Total Flood in Cumecs	Base Flow (B.F.)	T.F. – B.F. (cumecs)	(T.F. – B.F.) / 3.45
15	15	00	00.00
25	16	09	02.61
90	14	76	22.00
147	19	128	37.1
181	19	162	46.96
193	20	173	50.1
192	20	172	49.86
180	22	158	45.8
162	23	139	40.3
136	24	112	32.5
115	27	88	25.51
96	26	70	20.3
80	26	54	15.65
67	27	40	11.6
56	28	28	08.12
46	30	16	04.64
38	30	08	02.32
32	32	00	00.00

THEORETICAL QUESTIONS

1. What is meant by run-off ? How the run-off is classified ?
2. Discuss the various factors affecting run-off from catchment.
3. State how run-off and rainfall are interrelated.
4. Explain the following methods of estimating run-off.

    (i) By empirical formulae,

    (ii) By rational method,

    (iii) By infiltration method,

    (iv) By unit hydrograph method.

5. What is meant by single peak flood hydrograph ? Explain the various component parts of hydrograph.
6. State the factors that affect the shape of the hydrograph.
7. Define a unit hydrograph and state the basic principles (or assumptions) involved in its construction.

8. Describe clearly the procedure of deriving (or constructing) a unit hydrograph from an isolated storm.
9. Explain the following terms :
   (i) Total run-off or flood hydrograph,
   (ii) Direct run-off hydrograph,
   (iii) Base flow.
10. Explain the various methods of separating base flow from the flood hydrograph. Compare the merits and demerits of these methods.
11. State the practical utility of unit hydrograph.
12. Define S-curve or S-hydrograph and explain how will you develop it. What is its use ?
13. What is synthetic hydrograph ? Explain Snyder's method of synthetic hydrograph.
14. Discuss the points that are to be considered in deriving a unit hydrograph for a given catchment.
15. Explain with the help of neat sketches how you will obtain a 4 hour unit hydrograph from a 2 hour unit hydrograph.
16. Distinguish between S-curve hydrograph and Synthetic unit hydrograph.
17. 'All the physical characteristics of a basin are reflected in the unit hydrograph.' Discuss the above statement.

NUMERICAL PROBLEMS

1. Ordinates of a one day hydrograph from a catchment area of 400 sq. km. are given below. Derive a one day unit hydrograph.

Time (Days)	0	1	2	3	4	5	6	7	8
Discharge (Cumecs)	0	10	40	75	125	60	30	10	0

2. Given below are the ordinates of a 6 hour unit hydrograph.

Time (Hours)	0	3	6	9	12	18	24	30	36	42	48	54	60	66
6 hr unit H Ordinates m^3/s	0	15	25	45	60	80	70	60	45	32	20	10	50	0

A storm gave the rainfall excess of 4 cm, 6 cm and 5 cm in three successive intervals of 6 hours each. Compute the flood hydrograph using a unit hydrograph given above. Assume a constant base flow of 20 m³/sec. Plot the resulting hydrograph and estimate the peak flow and time of its occurrence.

3. The ordinates of a 2 hour unit hydrograph are as follows (unit rainfall = 1 cm)

Time in Hours	0	2	4	6	8	10	12	14	16	18
Discharge (m³/sec)	0	60	180	330	280	180	110	60	20	0

(i) Plot the S-hydrograph.

(ii) Estimate approximately the area of the catchment basin.

4. The ordinates of a 4 hour unit hydrograph of a basin of area 300 km² measured at 1.00 hour intervals are;

   6, 36, 66, 91, 106, 93, 79, 68, 58, 49, 41, 34, 27, 23, 17, 13, 9, 6, 3, 1.5 m²/s

   Obtain the ordinates of a 3.00 hour unit hydrograph for the basin unsing the S-curve technique.

5. The ordinates of a 4 hour unit hydrograph are given below calculate the ordinate of 2-h unit hydrograph for the same catchment :

Time (Hours)	0	4	8	12	16	20	24	28	32	36	40	44
Ordinates of 4-h - UH in m³/sec	0	20	80	1300	1500	130	90	52	27	15	5	0

UNIT – III

STREAM GAUGING AND FLOODS

3.1 INTRODUCTION

The important phases of hydrological cycle are *'precipitation'*, *'evaporation'*, *'transpiration'*, *'infiltration'* and *'surface run-off'*. The most accepted method of measurement of *'run-off'* from a catchment is by the measurement of discharge of the stream draining it and is known as *'stream gauging'*.

'Stream gauging' is an important branch of hydrometry and aims at determining the velocity of flow and the discharge passing through the stream. The stream flow which represents *'run-off'* includes both surface run-off as well as ground water flow. Thus measurement, analysis and interpretation of stream flow data form an important phase of hydrology. Of all the phases of hydrological cycle, *'run-off'* i.e. stream flow is the only phase that can be measured with reasonable accuracy.

3.2 PRELIMINARY SURVEY AND SELECTION OF SITE

3.2.1 Preliminary Survey

A preliminary survey should be made to ensure that the physical and hydraulic features of the proposed site conform to the requirements for the application of the methods of flow measurement which it is intended to use.

3.2.2 Selection of Gauge Site

A site should be selected so that it is possible to measures that whole range of flows which may be encountered or which are to be measured. The whole range of flows which may be encountered or which are to be measured. The whole range of measurement, referred to one reference gauge, may be made at a single section or for certain range of discharge at two or more sections. Similarly, different methods of measurement may be employed for separate parts of the range.

The flowing additional requirements should be complied with for the establishment of stage discharge relationship.

- It is desirable to select a site where the relationship between stage and discharge is substantially consistent and stable.
- There should be no eddied or other abnormality in the flow.
- A significant change in discharge at the gauging site should be accompanied by a significant change in stage.
- There should not br any variable back water effect.
- As far as possible, sites where weed growth is prevalent should be avoided.
- Access to the site at all stages and at all times should be available.

3.3 DETERMINATION OF RIVER STAGE

The 'river stage' is defined as the elevation of the water surface in a river measured above the mean sea level or any arbitrary assumed datum. If a relation between stage and discharge can be established, the stream flow can be determined from a known stage-discharge curve. The various methods adapted for the determination of a stage of a river are as follows :

3.3.1 Staff Gauge (Fig. 3.1)

The simplest type of river stage measurement is by installing a vertical graduated staff at a point along the river course where some portion of it will be under water at all stages of river.

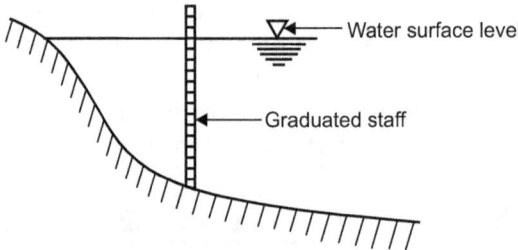

Fig. 3.1 : Vertical staff gauge

It should be fixed permanently to a structure such as a bridge, abutment or pier etc. and the graduations should be distinctive so as to read from a distance. Sometimes graduations may be painted directly on piers, abutments etc.

Sometimes inclined staff gauges specially graduated to read the stages directly can also be used.

3.3.2 Suspended Weight Wire Gauge

As shown in Fig. 3.2, it consists of a stainless steel cable wound on a drum with a weight attached at its end. In order to measure the stage of a river a weight is lowered from the bridge etc. so that it just touches the level of water.

The counter of the 'wire weight gauge' measures the number of rotations of the drum. Knowing the length of one turn of cable round the drum, the elevation or stage of stream can be determined from the known elevation of the bridge structure over it. The drawback of such gauges is that these gauges are subject to damages from floating matter in the stream and an observer is required to record the staff gauge readings at frequent intervals.

Even though such gauges are simple and economical initially, a constant attendance is required for its efficient functioning. In the absence of frequent stage readings, large scale changes in the stage may get unnoticed.

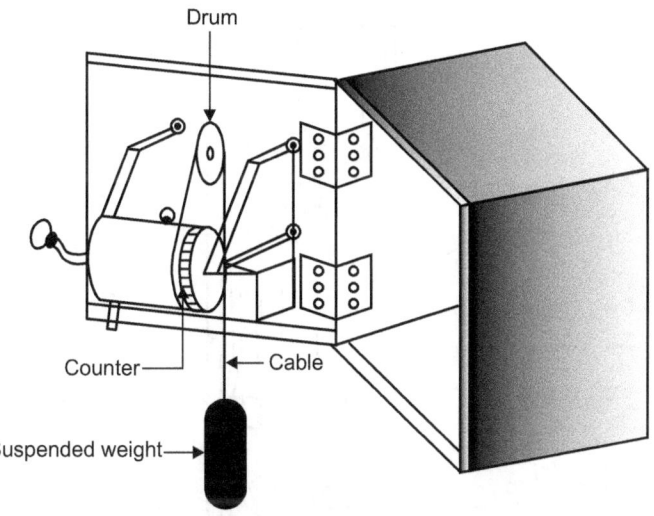

Fig. 3.2 : (Suspended weight) wire gauge

3.3.3 Automatic Recording Gauges (Fig. 3.3 (a) and (b))

The drawbacks in case of manual gauges as stated above are overcome to certain extent by installation of automatic recording gauges. The float actuated continuous water stage recording gauge mostly used (Fig. 3.3 (a) and (b)) consists of a vertical float moving up or down in a stilling well according to the rise or fall in the level of water. The motion of the float is transferred to a pen holder that records the level of water continuously across a long chart by a clockwork mechanism. The float is balanced by a counter weight passing over the pulley of a recorder. The provision of stilling well protects the gauge from floating debris and wave action.

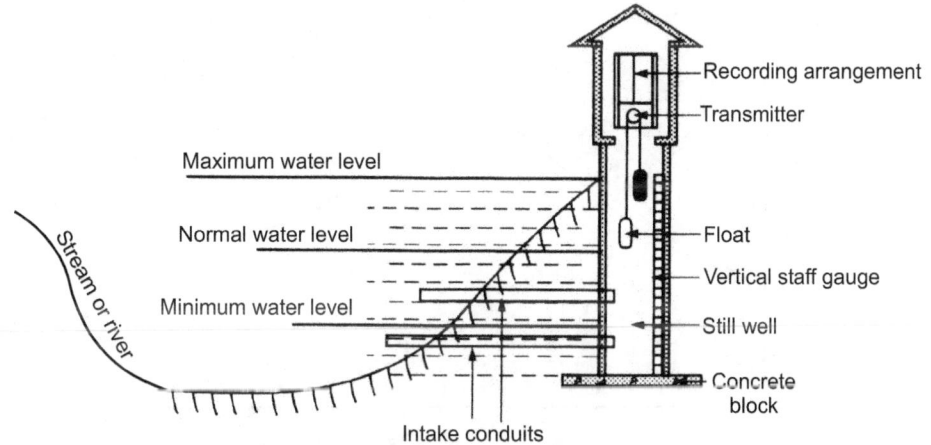

Fig. 3.3 (a) : Automatic gauge or stage recorder

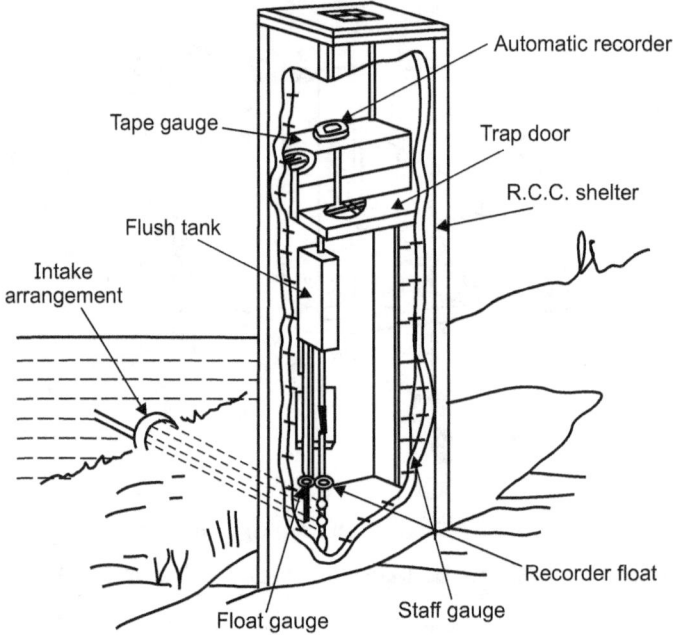

Fig. 3.3 (b) : Float type gauge installed in R.C.C. shelter (U.S.G.S.)

Due care should be taken to install the gauge at such elevation, that it will not be submerged during floods. Even though automatic recording gauge furnish accurate results, they are found to be expensive.

3.3.4 Stage-Hydrograph (Fig. 3.4)

It is a graphical presentation of stage versus chronological time. It is very useful in determining the stream flow and also in flood warning.

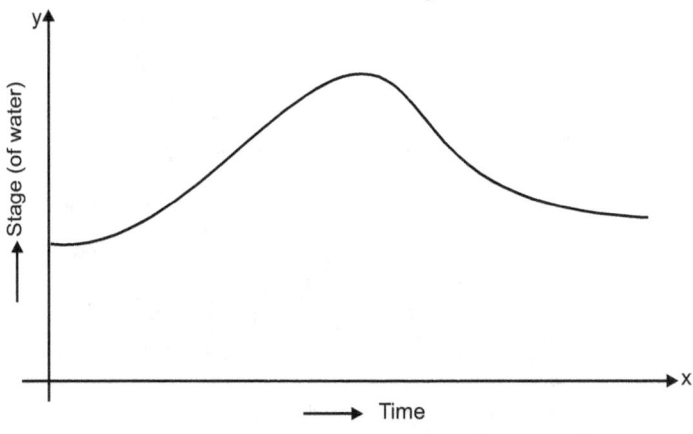

Fig. 3.4 : Stage-hydrograph

3.4 STREAM FLOW MEASUREMENT

Some of the usual methods of stream flow measurements (i.e. stream gauging) can be classified as :

- Direct measurement methods and
- Indirect measurement methods.

3.4.1 Direct Measurement Methods

3.4.1.1 Area-Velocity Method

In this method the measurement of flow is determined directly i.e. knowing the cross-sectional area (a) and the mean velocity of flow (V_a), the discharge passing through it will be equal to (aV_a). The entire cross-section of a stream is plotted by observing soundings and a relation between stage and area of cross-section is established. The next stage is the determination of mean velocity of flow of the stream. As the velocity of flow along the cross-section of the steam varies, it is usual practice to sub-divide the stream into sub-sections and measure the velocity of flow at each such sub-sections by surface floats, velocity rods or current meters.

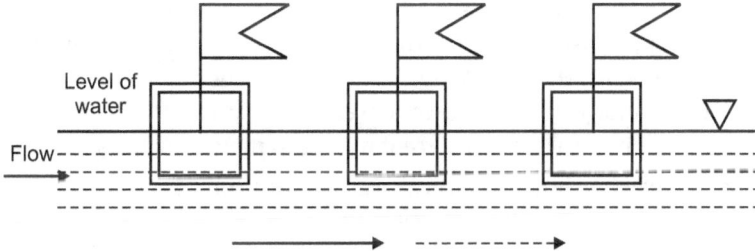

Fig. 3.5 : Surface floats

A surface float (Fig. 3.5) made of wooden disc of about 100 to 150 mm diameter, is allowed to float over the surface of water a distance 'D' and the time required for the float to travel this distance is noted.

The surface velocity, $\quad V_s = \dfrac{D}{t}$

From which the average velocity,

$$V_a = 0.85\, V_s$$

However, as the travel of float is obstructed by debris, wind, waves etc. the method is less accurate.

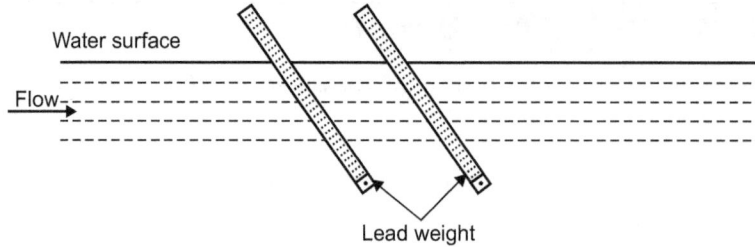

Fig. 3.6 : Velocity rods

Velocity rods (Fig. 3.6) are made of wooden circular section 30 to 40 mm in diameter, with a lead weight attached at its bottom so that it gets immersed upto depth of 0.95 times the depth of water in the stream to give the average velocity of flow. Knowing the distance travelled (D) and the time required for its travel 't', the velocity of stream is obtained by the relation,

$$V_a = \frac{D}{t}$$

Current Meter : It is an instrument which is commonly used for the measurement of velocity of stream flow.

It consists of an element that rotates, due to the stream current, the number of rotations being proportional to the velocity of stream flow. Every revolution of the element causes a click in a set of head phones and the operator has to just count the number of clicks that occur in a given time interval. The velocity is then determined from the rating curve of the current meter. The Central Water and Power Research Station (C.W. and P.R.S.), Khadakwasla, Pune undertakes the job of calibrating current meters in their laboratory.

The current meters may be either of 'vertical axis' or 'horizontal axis' type.

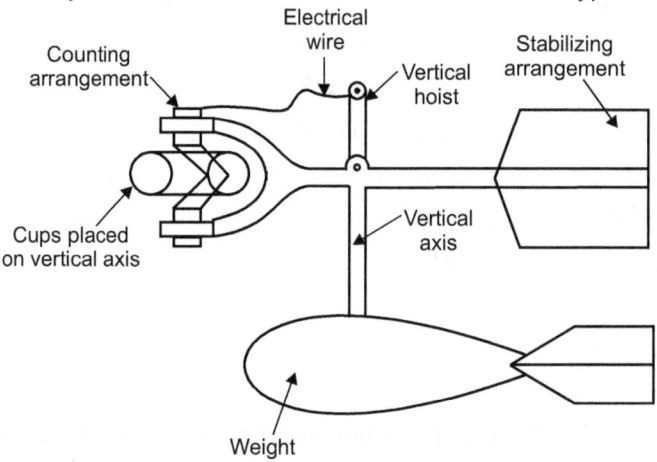

Fig. 3.7 : Current meter (vertical axis)

In the vertical axis (Fig. 3.7) the cups mounted on the vertical axis rotate in horizontal plane. The modern Price meters or Gurley meters belong to this type and are usually used for measurement of velocities of flow 0.1 to 4 m/sec.

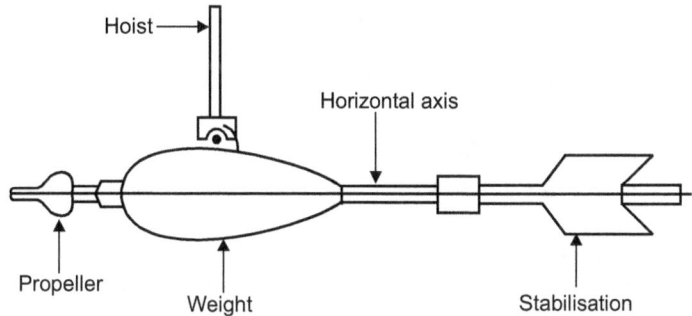

Fig. 3.8 : Horizontal axis propeller - current meter

In case of horizontal axis current meter (Fig. 3.8) a propeller is fixed to one end of the horizontal shaft. The performance of current meter of this type is found to be better than the vertical axis current meter.

Calibration of Current Meter : The establishment of relationship between revolution or rotations per second of the meter and the velocity of stream flow is known as 'rating of current meter' and the procedure of determining its rating being called as its 'calibration'.

As the meter is designed to have its rotational speed directly proportional to the velocity of stream flow, an equation can be written as

$$V = aN + b$$

where
V = Velocity of stream flow in m/sec
N = Rotations or revolutions of meter per second

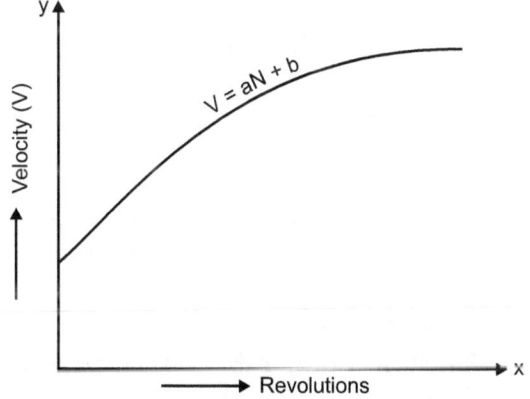

Fig. 3.9 : Graphs of velocity versus revolutions

'a' and 'b' are the constants of the meter to be determined by its calibration in a specially constructed masonry tank 90 m in length, 2.4 m wide having a depth of 2.1 m. The meter which is suspended on a trolley is moved through the tank at a known speed. The number of clicks or ticks at one second interval are recorded. The time and distance travelled by the trolley for a fixed number of rotations of the meter is also recorded. The procedure is then repeated for different velocities of the trolley and a graph of velocity versus the revolutions per second (Fig. 3.9) is plotted and the values of constants 'a' and 'b' of the meter are determined. Once, the values of 'a' and 'b' are determined, the unknown speed can be determined from the known number of revolutions per second by referring the calibration chart.

Knowing the area of each sub-section and its corresponding velocity of flow, the flow passing through each sub-section is determined. Summation of all such discharges through sub-sections is the total required discharge (i.e. stream flow) passing through the section. The accuracy of the estimation of discharge increases with the increased number of sub-sections and vice-a-versa.

3.4.1.2 Moving Boat Method (Fig. 3.10)

The method described above is, however, inconvenient in case of large alluvial rivers in floods due to the difficulty of keeping the boat stationary during observations. In such cases moving boat method may be adopted with advantage. The method consists of a moving boat mounted with the propeller type current meter at right angles to the direction of stream flow.

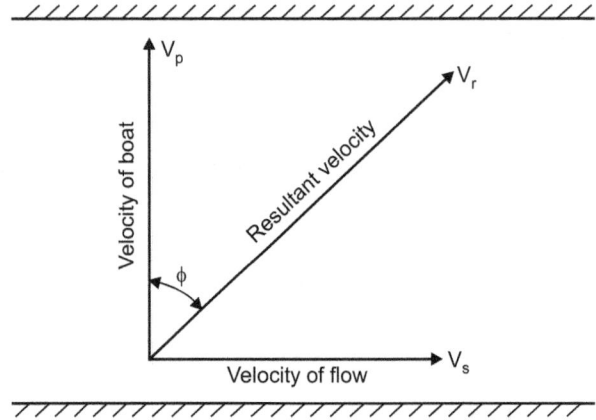

Fig. 3.10 : By moving boat method

Thus, if V_P = Velocity of boat moving at right angles to stream flow
            V_S = Velocity of stream flow
and V_r = Resultant velocity making an angle ϕ with the direction of boat
then, $V_P = V_r \cos \phi$
and $V_S = V_r \sin \phi$

Further, if the time required for travel between two vertical sub-sections is say dt, then the horizontal distance between the two sub-sections will be V_P dt.

∴ The discharge dQ passing between two consecutive vertical sub-sections with depths of flow as d_i and d_{i+1} will be

$$dQ = \frac{(d_i + d_{i+1})}{2} \times (W_{i+1}) \times (V_S)$$

$$= \frac{(d_i + d_{i+1})}{2} (V_r \cos\phi \cdot V_r \sin\phi) \times dt$$

$$= \left(\frac{d_i + d_{i+1}}{2}\right) (V_r^2 \sin\phi \cos\phi) \, dt$$

Thus, the total discharge passing = $Q = \Sigma \, dQ$

3.4.1.3 Salt Concentration (or Dilution Technique) Method

The method based upon the continuity equation principle, makes use of a chemical, mostly common salt, for the determination of discharge. The chemical of concentration C_1 is injected at a constant rate Q_1, at a particular section into the stream flow (Q) of concentration C. After thorough mixing of chemical with the stream flow, at a sufficient distant down stream let its concentration be C_2.

Applying the equation of continuity,

$$Q_1 C_1 + QC = (Q_1 + Q) C_2$$

∴ $$Q(C_2 - C) = Q_1 (C_1 - C_2)$$

∴ $$Q = \frac{Q_1 (C_1 - C_2)}{(C_2 - C)}$$

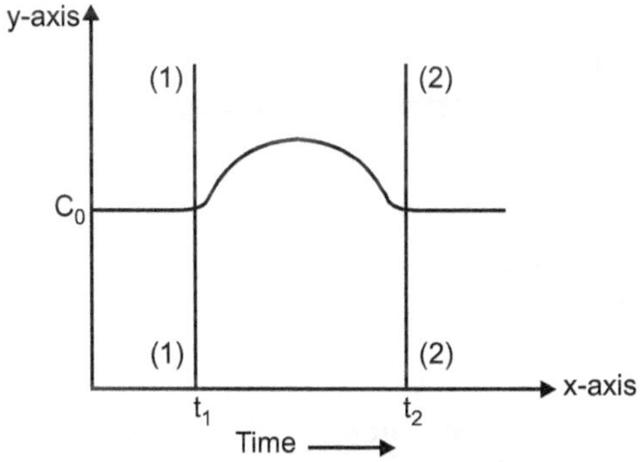

Fig. 3.11 : Concentration method (By sudden injection process)

The method is a convenient for turbulent stream flows as thorough mixing of chemicals is achieved due to turbulence. The chemical used should not be toxic, and not lost in the stream flow. It should be easily detectable on the downstream side and also it should be less expensive. Instead of common salt, radioactive elements such as bromine, iodine or sodium can also be used.

3.4.2 Indirect Measurement Methods

As the name suggests, the discharge passing through the stream is not measured directly, but is obtained from stage-discharge relationship. Once a stage-discharge relationship for a stream at a particular location is established, it is only necessary to measure the depth of flow (i.e. stage) in the stream at that particular section and by referring to the stage-discharge curve, the discharge is computed.

The indirect methods commonly adopted are as follows :

3.4.2.1 By Notches, Weirs, Venturi Flumes and Spillways

(1) Notches and Weirs : (Sharp-crested) : The general form of equation for measurement of discharge (Q) through notches and weirs is

$$Q = C_d L H^n$$

Where C_d = Coefficient of discharge of the notch or weir

L = Length of the notch or weir

and H = Head of water measured above the crest of the notch or weir

(2) For Broad Crested Weirs :

$$Q = C_d \sqrt{2g} \cdot L (Hh^2 - h^3)^{1/2}$$

and for Q_{max},

$$h = \frac{2}{3} H$$

∴ $$Q_{max} = C_d\, 1.7\, LH^{3/2}$$

(3) Venturi Flumes : In venturi flume a control or critical section is created by construction of the width of the channel whose discharge is to be measured. Alternatively, the bottom of the channel can be raised by providing hump to produce control section.

Venturi flumes or control meters are used for channels having large discharge carrying capacity.

(4) Spillways : Spillway i.e. overflow section of a dam is usually used to measure the discharge passing through large streams.

3.4.2.2 Slope-Area Method

This is another indirect method of measurement of discharge passing through a stream. The discharge

$$Q = (\text{Area of cross-section}) \times (\text{Velocity of flow})$$

The area of cross-section of the stream is determined by taking soundings (i.e. measurement of depth of water below the water surface) at suitable intervals and plotting the profile to a suitable scale. The required area of cross-section will be the area enclosed between bed-level of the channel and the high flood level (H.F.L.) line.

For the determination of slope of the channel the difference in elevation of water surface at two sections say Δh is divided by the length of the channel (l) between the two sections.

i.e. Slope of channel $= S = \dfrac{\Delta h}{l}$

Once the slope of the channel is determined, then the velocity of flow is calculated either by Chezy's or Manning's formula

i.e. $V = C\,(RS)^{1/2}$ (Chezy's formula)

or $V = \dfrac{1}{n} R^{2/3} S^{1/2}$ (Manning's formula)

where C = Chezy's constant

$= \dfrac{1}{n} R^{1/6}$

and R = Mean hydraulic radius

$= \dfrac{A}{P}$

A = Area of cross-section of channel flow

P = Wetted perimeter

and S = Slope of water surface

Appropriate values of Chezy's constant 'C' and Manning 'n' should be selected from the known bed, banks and vegetation, etc. in the channel.

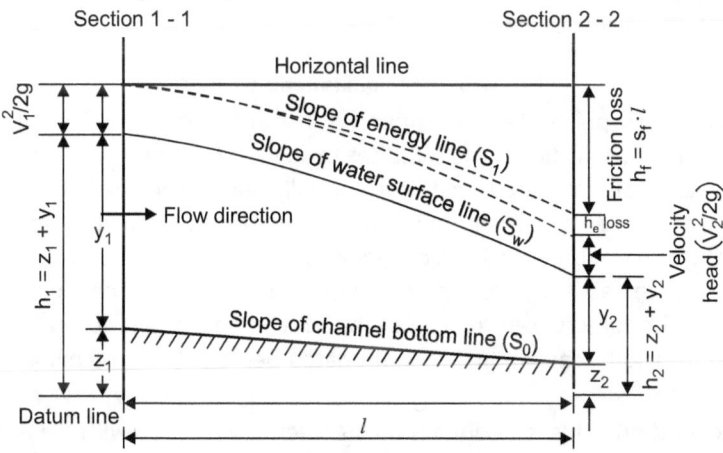

Fig. 3.12 : By slope-area method

3.4.3 Advance Techniques Used in Gauge Discharge

(1) Electromagnetic Method : The electromagnetic principle similar to that of an emf is induced in the conductor (water in the present case) when it cuts a normal magnetic field. Large coils buried at the bottom of the channel carry a current I to produce a controlled vertical magnetic field (Fig. 3.13).

Electrodes provided at the sides of the channel section measure the small voltage produced due to flow of water in the channel. It has been found that the signal output E will be of the order of millivolts and is related to the discharge Q as

$$Q = K_1 \left(\frac{E_d}{1} + K_2 \right)^n$$

where d = Depth of flow, I = Current in the coil, and n, K, and K_2 are system constants.

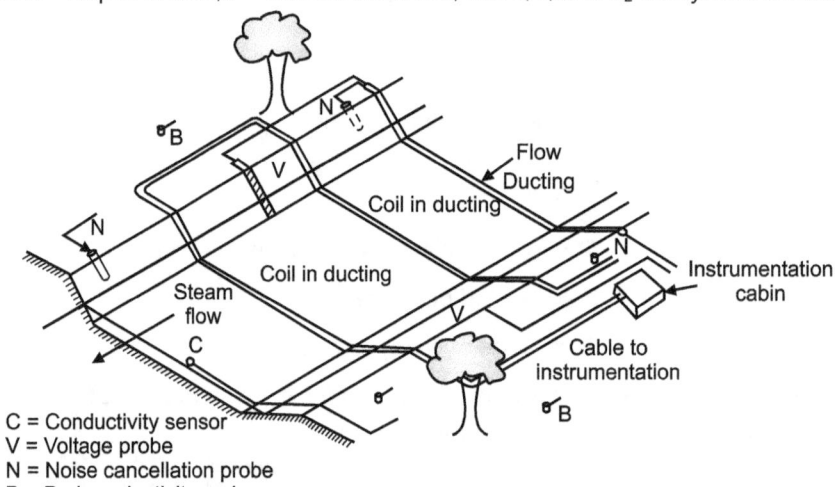

C = Conductivity sensor
V = Voltage probe
N = Noise cancellation probe
B = Bed conductivity probe

Fig. 3.13 : Electromagnetic method

The method involves sophisticated and expensive instrumentation and has been successfully tried in a number of installations. The fact that this kind of set-up gives the total discharge when once it has been calibrated, makes it specially suited for field situations where the cross-sectional properties can change with time due to wood growth, sedimentation, etc. Another specific application is in tidal channels where the flow undergoes rapid changes both in magnitude as well as in direction. Present, day commercially available electromagnetic flowmeters can measure the discharge to an accuracy of ±3%, the maximum channel width that can be accommodated being 100 m. The minimum detectable velocity is 0.005 m/s.

(2) Ultrasonic Method : This is essentially an area-velocity method with the average velocity being measured by using ultrasonic signals. The method was first reported by Swengel (1955), since then it has been perfected and complete systems are available commercially.

Consider a channel carrying a flow with two transducers A and B fixed at the same level h above the bed and on either side of the channel (Fig. 3.14). These transducers can receive as well as send ultrasonic signals. Let A send an ultrasonic signal to be received at B after an elapse time t, Similarly, let B send a signal to be received at A after an elapse time t_2. If C = velocity of sound in water,

$$t_1 = L/(C + v_p)$$

where L = Length of path from A to B and v_p = component of the flow velocity in the sound path = $v \cos \theta$. Similarly, from Fig. 3.14 it is easy to see that

$$t_2 = \frac{L}{(C - v_p)}$$

Thus
$$\frac{1}{t_1} - \frac{1}{t_1} = \frac{2v_p}{L} = \frac{2v \cos \theta}{L}$$

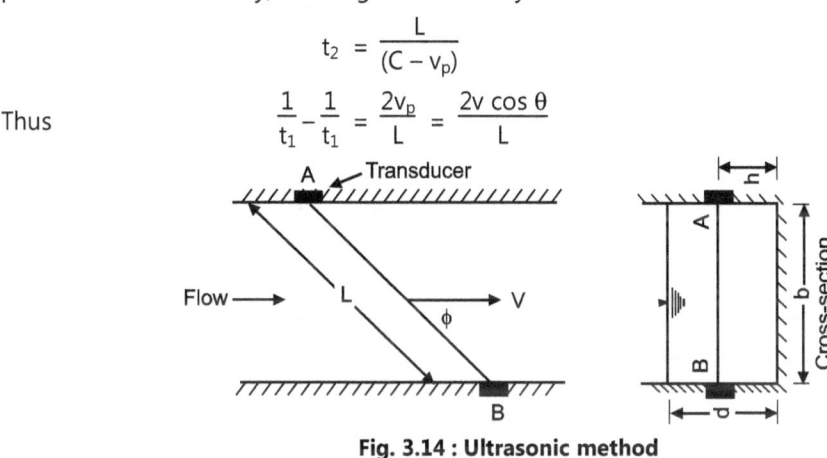

Fig. 3.14 : Ultrasonic method

$$v = \frac{L}{2 \cos \theta}\left(\frac{1}{t_1} - \frac{1}{t_2}\right)$$

Thus for a given L and θ, by knowing t_1 and t_2, the average velocity along the path AB, i.e., v can be determined. It may be noted that v is the average velocity at a height h above the bed and is not the average velocity V for the whole cross-section. However, for a given channel cross-section v can be related to V and by calibration a relation between W V and h can be obtained. For a given set-up, as the area of cross-section is fixed, the discharge is obtained as a product of area and mean velocity V Estimation of discharge by using one signal path as above is called *single-path gauging*. Alternatively, for a given depth of flow, multiple single paths can be used to obtain v for different h values. Mean velocity of flow through the cross-section is obtained by averaging these v values. This techniques is known as *multi-path gauging*.

Ultrasonic flowmeters using the above principal have frequencies of the order of 500 kHz. Sophisticated electronics are involved to transmit, detect and evaluate the mean velocity of flow along the path. In a given installation a calibration (usually performed by the current-meter method) is needed to determine the system constants. Currently available commercial systems have accuracies of about 2% for the single-path method and 1% for the multipath method. The systems are currently available for fivers up to 500 m width.

The specific advantages of the ultrasonic system of river gauging are :

- It is rapid and gives high accuracy.
- It is suitable for automatic recording of data.
- It can handle rapid changes in the magnitude and direction of flow, as in tidal rivers. ,
- The cost of installation is independent of the size of rivers.

The accuracy of this method is limited by the factors that affect the signal velo-city and averaging of flow velocity, such as (i) unstable cross-section, (ii) fluctuating weed growth, (iii) high loads of suspended solids, (iv) air entrainment, and (v) salinity and temperature changes.

3.4.3.1 Discharge Measuring Radar Level Gauge

Radar is emerging technology used to measure water depth in river stream. Radar instruments are a promising new tool for measuring water levels. Radar water-level sensors require less construction to install than traditional contact water-level sensors. The antenna on a radar level gauge generates millions of very short 1 nano second microwave pulses every second. Each pulse is directed and transmitted to and reflected from a product surface. The elapsed time period between transmission and reception of the signal at the speed of light is measured and calculated as a distance. This continuous stream of pulses gives real time level information updated and is evaluated many times a second. Radar level sensors work with safe, low emitted power in the C and K-band frequency range. The proven ECHOFOX signal processing selects the correct level echo reliably. Adjustment by filling and emptying the vessel is not necessary; it can normally be done with simple input of vessel dimensions. Two different emitting frequencies are available for these applications. The compact, high frequency sensors are particularly suitable for applications for which high accuracy is required. Even with small antenna sizes, an excellent signal focusing is reached. Low frequency C-band sensors can penetrate foam and strong condensation and are thus particularly suitable for arduous process conditions. Unaffected by steam, gas composition, pressure and temperature changes the sensors detect the product surface of different products reliably.

3.4.3.2 Shaft Encoders

There are several different method used to measure streams and river and these method will be summarized below. The measurement of rainfalls is often associated with river measurement stations as local rainfall is a key factor especially in hills by mountainous areas.

Regular reporting of river levels to a central server allows authorities to monitor stream and river flows across a country or region and use that date for immediate use purpose short encodes method is very useful.

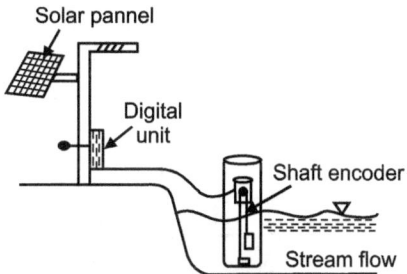

Fig. 3.15 : Shaft encodes

In shaft encoder method a still well of still pipe with a shaft encoder and control / beaded floot system shown in above Fig. 3.15.

While there are many methods / technologies available the most common and the most stroke method is the shaft encoder floot and wheel system. This method required a large well or a smaller pipe to be installed on the stream or rivers bank or on a bridge structure to provide a stroke flow or wind measurement environment. For a small float, a float line and a counter weight so the movement in stream / river level can be measured by rotation or the shaft of a wheel. Typically the shaft rotation is measured very accurately by light or laser encoder and the data is shown on the display and is recorded in the data lagger within the instrument working of shaft encode method is same as automatic recording gauges described in detailed in 3.3.3.

3.4.3.3 Bubblers System

Bubbler systems are ideal for level measurement discharge in river where debris, foam, steam, or surface turbulence makes standard methods of level measurement impractical. Most bubbler systems require an independent pressure transmitter, a display, and a control system.

The bubbler system supplies a constant rate of air flow through a small diameter tube anchored near the bottom of the tank. The amount of pressure required to force the air bubble out of the bottom of the tube is equal to the hydrostatic pressure at that point (i.e. the deepest point in the tank). This is calculated using the formula.

$$H = \frac{P}{Sg}$$

Where,

P = Pressure in inches or centimeters of water.

H = Fluid level in inches or centimeters.

Sg = Specific gravity of the liquid

Fig. 3.15 shows the gauging arrangement by using bubbler gauge.

The air pressure output from the bubble tube must be approximately 3.5 psi (24 kPa) above the maximum hydrostatic pressure in the liquid (i.e. the pressure at the bottom of the tank).

The air bleed valve is adjusted to achieve a bubble rate of approximately 60 bubbles / minute by bleeding off excess air pressure to atmosphere. A solenoid valve is installed between the air bleed valve and the bubble outlet and is closed to purge the bubble tube of debris.

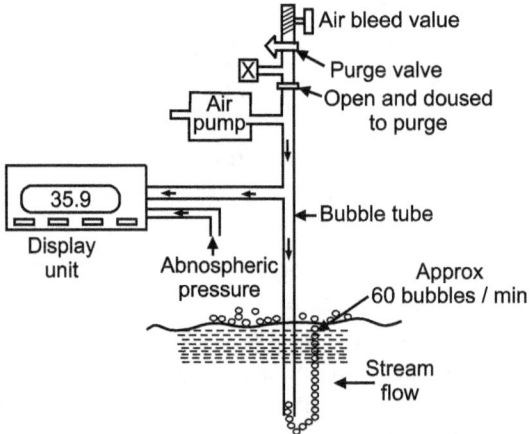

Fig. 3.16 : Bubbler gauge

Fig. 3.16 shows the gauging arrangement by using bubbler gauge. The advantages of such bubbler gauge system is that is does not need a costly stilling arrangement like the one needed foe float operated gauge.

3.4.3.4 Acoustic Doppler Current Meter

Acoustic Doppler Current Meter Profiler technology has revolutionized the river flow gauging at low flows and in shallow rivers. This technology is quite accurate and very cost effective. Further it is very quick and saves time - This technology takes about 10% of the time that is required for conventional method. The equipment could be deployed from a manned boat or a cableway or any other floating device either from a bridge or across a small river. A two men team can deploy an ADCP fitted to a boat by attaching a rope to each bank.

The advantages of ADCP technology, in general are given below :

- Reduction in river gauging time by a factor of about 10.
- Measurement of velocity and bed profile simultaneously from the free surface.
- Instantaneous detailed profiling of the bed.
- Reduction in the uncertainty in velocity measurement.

This could be used for deriving or verifying stage-discharge ratings, checking weir or flume calibrations, velocity profiling in channels, scour around bridge piers, velocity and bed profiling for river models, safe measurement of peak floods. In addition to this the measurements could be linked to GPS (Geographical Position System) and the entire river reach could be surveyed and real time data could be obtained for using in the model.

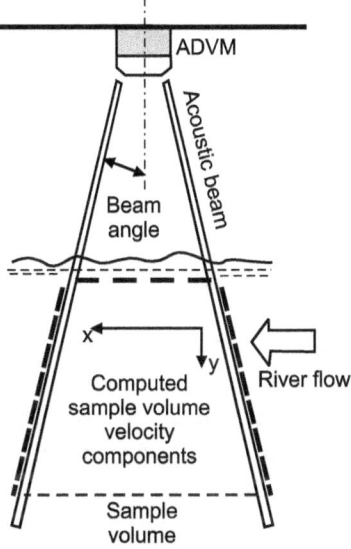

Fig. 3.17 : ADVM schematic

3.5 STAGE-DISCHARGE CURVE

In order to adopt the direct method of measurement for discharge, it is first essential to establish a relationship between the stage (i.e. depths of water in the river) and the corresponding discharge flowing through it. In order to prepare a stage discharge curve, the measured i.e. known quantities of discharges are released and the corresponding stages of water are recorded and then a graph is prepared of stage versus the discharge. Such a stage discharge curve is also called as rating curve. (Fig. 3.18). Once such a stage-discharge curve is prepared, then to calculate the unknown discharge, only its stage is observed and for this observed or recorded value, the corresponding value of the discharge is obtained by referring the above stage-discharge curve.

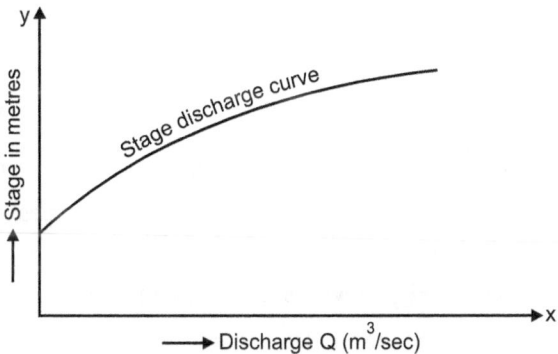

Fig. 3.18 : Stage-discharge curve

3.6 STUDY OF STAGE-DISCHARGE RELATIONSHIP AND EXTENSION OF THE STAGE DISCHARGE CURVE

(a) By logarithmic method,

(b) By Steven's extrapolation method.

3.6.1 Introduction

Stage-discharge relationship method or the velocity-area method is a direct method for computing discharge in a stream by measuring its velocity and area of flow. The entire stream cross-section is divided into a number of parts and area of each part and velocity of flow through it is determined and multiplied to get various values of discharge (partial). Summation of these partial discharges gives the total discharge. Corresponding gauge heights are plotted against discharges. The curve so obtained is known as the *discharge curve*. This curve gives a relationship between the stage of a river at a given time and the corresponding discharge and hence it is known as the stage-discharge curve. With the observed set of gauge discharge measurements, it is generally not possible to draw a complete curve, for very low discharges and for very high discharges, and hence the curve is to be extended. Hence for this two methods are adopted.

3.6.2 Methods of Extension of Stage-Discharge Curve

(1) Logarithmic Method : If the river cross-section under consideration is uniform one, then this method can be easily adopted. The stage-discharge curve for a stream can be expressed as,

$$Q = K(g + g_0)^m$$

where g is gauge height and g_0 is a constant.

$$\therefore \quad Q = K \cdot G^m$$

where K and m are constants.

Taking logs on both sides,

$$\log Q = \log K + m \log G$$

i.e. $\log Q = \log K + m \log G$ is of the form $y = mx + c$

After plotting the points for known values of discharges and stages, the straight line thus obtained can be easily extended so as to get discharge for a higher or lower gauge readings.

(2) Determination of Discharge by Steven's Method of Extrapolation :

Theory : This method is applicable for wider and shallower streams. For such streams, the wetted perimeter P (i.e. P = B + 2y) is approximated to be equal to B.   ($\because$ y <<<< B)

Hence in such cases, the hydraulic radius (D_m) can be approximately equal to 'y'. $\left(\because \dfrac{A}{P} = \dfrac{B \times y}{B} = y\right)$. But 'A' and 'y' are both dependent on the gauge height (stage) and hence the graph of stage versus $A\sqrt{D_m}$ can be easily plotted. Also a graph of stage Q versus $A\sqrt{D_m}$ is plotted on the same graph. 'Q' is found out from the observed values of gauge height for each stage. The graph of Q Vs. $A\sqrt{D_m}$ follows a straight line if $C\sqrt{S}$ (C = Chezy's constant and S = bed slope) remains constant. This straight line can be extended to evaluate discharge for higher values of gauge height.

Procedure :

- From the profile of the river bed, select suitable stages.
- For each stage find out the corresponding area and perimeter and hence hydraulic radius. Also find the corresponding gauge height.
- For this gauge height, find out the discharge from the stage-discharge relationship already obtained.
- Plot the graphs of stage Vs. $A\sqrt{D_m}$ and Q Vs. $A\sqrt{D_m}$ on the same graph paper. The two curves will intersect each other.
- Choose any value of stage and find corresponding to it, the discharge from discharge Vs. $A\sqrt{D_m}$ curve.

3.7 FLOODS

Floods are extreme events/actions of nature, in which the flow of water cannot be contained within the banks of rivers and/or retention areas. As a result it overflows into areas with human settlements, infrastructure facilities and economic activities. Floods become a Disaster when such areas become exposed to the hazard without adequate warning and/or without means of taking defensive actions and the community suffers loss of life, assets, livelihood, and environmental security.

3.7.1 Causes of Flooding

1. Meteorological
2. Hydrological
3. Anthropogenic

(1) Meteorological Cause : Most flood damages are the result of extreme, intense and long duration floods caused by meteorological phenomena such as : Prolonged and intense rainfall, Cyclones, Typhoons, storms and tidal surges.

(2) Hydrological Cause : Flooding can also be caused by increased run off due to : Ice and snow melt, Impermeable surfaces, saturated land, Poor fill infiltration rates, Land erosion.

(3) Anthropogenic Cause : Mankind plays a very important role in the magnitude and frequency of floods in many different ways. Actually, it is the human activities in water catchments, which drastically intensify floods. In this connection, human actions associated with land use change are the most important. Population growth, Land use change, deforestation, intensive agriculture, unplanned flood control measures, Socio economic and development activities, Urbanization, Climate change ,Global Warming.

3.7.2 Types of Floods

Floods are prevalent throughout Asia presenting great challenges for disaster risk managers due to their recurring nature, complex contributing factors and wide ranging consequences. Three types of flood hazards confront the physical planners.

I. River floods
II. Flash floods
III. Coastal floods/Storm surges

3.7.3 Effects of Flooding

Flooding can be very dangerous – only 15 cms of fast-flowing water are needed to knock you off your feet! Floodwater can seriously disrupt public and personal transport by cutting off roads and railway lines, as well as communication links when telephone lines are damaged. Floods disrupt normal drainage systems in cities, and sewage spills are common, which represents a serious health hazard, along with standing water and wet materials in the home. Bacteria, mould and viruses, cause disease, trigger allergic reactions, and continue to damage materials long after a flood.

Floods can distribute large amounts of water and suspended sediment over vast areas, restocking valuable soil nutrients to agricultural lands. In contrast, soil can be eroded by large amounts of fast flowing water, ruining crops, destroying agricultural land / buildings and drowning farm animals. Severe floods not only ruin homes / businesses and destroy personal property, but the water left behind cause's further damage to property and contents. The environment and wildlife is also at risk when damage when damage to businesses causes the accidental release of toxic materials like paints, pesticides, gasoline etc. Floodwater can severely disrupt public and personal transport by cutting off roads and railway lines, as well as communication links when telephone lines are damaged.

Unfortunately, flooding not only disrupts many people's lives each year, but it frequently creates personal tragedies when people are swept away and drowned.

3.8 ESTIMATION OF PEAK FLOOD (MAXIMUM FLOOD)

In case of planning and designing of storage reservoirs and dams, it is necessary to ascertain the peak or maximum flood that is likely to occur so that necessary arrangement for the disposal of excess water can be arranged by the suitable provision of spillways etc. The various methods commonly adopted for estimation for such peak (or maximum) floods are as follows :

- The past flood records,

- Rational method
- Empirical methods,
- Flood frequency studies,
- Unit hydrograph technique.

The use of particular method depends upon
- The desired objective,
- The available data, and
- The importance of the project.

Flood peak values are required in the design bridges, culvert waterways, spillways for dams, and estimation of scour at a hydraulic structure.

3.8.1 The Past Flood Records

Enquiries from the local old people in the area will help in ascertaining the maximum flood marks in the past 35 years that have been left on the permanent objects situated on banks of the river. After knowing such high flood marks, the cross-section of the river, will be plotted and the highest flood level line will be shown on it. Such cross-section of the river assists in determining the wetted perimeter, the area of water flow and the slope of water line etc. The velocity of flow can then be determined either by Manning's or Chezy's formula, by assuming suitable values of n (for Manning's formula) and C (for Chezy's formula). The maximum or peak flood is then can be computed by multiplying the above area of cross-section of the river by the velocity of flow.

3.8.2 Rational Method

The rational method is found to be suitable for peak flow prediction in small size (< 50 km^2) catchments. It finds considerable application in urban drainage designs and in the design of small culverts and bridges. At the start of a rainfall event, the portions nearest the outlet contribute runoff first. As rain continues, farther and farther portions contribute runoff, until flow eventually arrives from all points on the watershed, "concentrating" at the outlet. An isochrone is a line on the catchment joining points having equal time of travel of surface runoff from the point to the catchment outlet. A catchment can have infinite number of isochrones but time of concentration isochrone is the last isochrone on the catchment. For a rainfall of uniform intensity and very long duration over a catchment the runoff increases as more and more flow from remote areas of the catchment reach the outlet. If the rainfall continues beyond the time of concentration (t > t_c), the runoff will be constant and at the peak value (Q_p) equal to

$$Q_P = CiA$$

where,

i = Rainfall intensity;
A = Catchment area;
C = Runoff coefficient = runoff/rainfall.

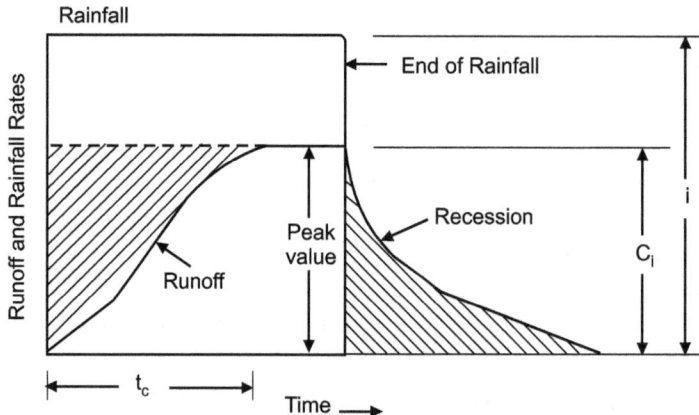

Fig. 3.19 : Runoff hydrograph due to uniform rainfall

The runoff coefficient represents the integrated effect of the catchment losses and hence depends upon the nature of the surface, surface slope and rainfall intensity. The rational formula assumes a homogeneous catchment surface.

If the catchment is non-homogeneous but can be divided into distinct sub areas each having a different C, then the runoff from each sub area is calculated separately and merged in proper time sequence.

If the rainfall is uniformly distributed over such a non-homogeneous catchment for $t > t_c$ then a weighted equivalent runoff coefficient C_e can be determined and used.

$$C_e = \Sigma\, C_j\, A_j / A$$

Time of concentration is assumed to be independent of rainfall intensity. Watershed parameters that may affect t_c are :

- Length of channel and overland flow plane,
- Average slope of channel or watershed, and
- Roughness characteristics of the watershed.

3.8.3 Empirical Methods

Most of the empirical formulae for the determination of maximum discharge express the discharge as a function of catchment area.

 i.e. $Q_{max} \propto A$

 or $Q_{max} = CA^n$

Where, Q_{max} = Maximum flood discharge,

    C = Coefficient, the value of which depends upon the catchment characteristics,

    n = Index, depending upon the type of catchment,

 and   A = Area of catchment in sq. km.

The common formulae used for the determination of Q_{max} are as follows :

(1) Dicken's Formula (1865) :

$$Q_{max} = CA^{3/4}$$

where Q_{max}, C and A have the meanings as stated above.

The values of constant C recommended for the various regions in our country are as follows :

Sr. No.	Name of the Region	Value of C
1.	Northern India	11.4
2.	Central India	13.9 to 19.5
3.	Western Ghats	22.5 to 25 (upto maximum of 35)

(2) Ryve's Formula (1884) :

$$Q = CA^{2/3}$$

The formula was developed for catchment areas in Madras state (Now, Tamil Nadu).

The recommended values of C are as follows :

Sr. No.	Particulars of Catchment Location	Value of C
1.	Catchment lying within 24 km from coast	6.78
2.	Catchment lying between 24 km to 161 km from coast	8.45
3.	Limited places near hills	10.00

(3) Inglis Formula :

$$Q_{max} = \left(\frac{124\,A}{\sqrt{A + 10.4}}\right)$$

If 10.4 is very small as compared to the area of catchment, then neglecting it,

$$Q_{max} \approx \frac{124\,A}{\sqrt{A}} = 124\sqrt{A} \text{ (approximate)}$$

(4) Ali Nawab Jung Bahadur's Formula (Originally Adopted for Old Hyderabad State) :

$$Q_{max} = C\,\{0.385\,A\}^{(0.93 - \frac{1}{4}\log 0.386\,A)}$$

The value of C in the above formula varies from 48 to 60.

(5) Fuller's Formula (for USA Catchments) :

$$Q_{max} = CA^{0.8}\,(1 + 0.8 \log T) \text{ (approximate)}$$

Where, C varies from 0.18 to 1.9 and T = number of year after which such a flood is likely to occur again.

3.9 FLOOD FREQUENCY STUDIES

Introduction :

The method essentially consists in predicting the future maximum flood discharge by the careful study of maximum flood discharges that have occurred in the past, by the theory of probability.

The *Flood frequency (F)* indicates the possibility of a flood of given magnitude being equalled or exceeded in an year and is expressed as percentage i.e. a 5% frequency (F) of a flood denotes that there are 5 out of 100 chances of the flood of a given magnitude being equalled or exceeded.

Recurrence Interval (also called as Return Period) :

It indicates the number of years in which a flood (of specified magnitude) can be expected once and is denoted by a letter T_r which is obtained by,

$$T_r = \left(\frac{100}{F}\right)$$

The flood may be thus be designated by its recurrence interval or return period i.e. 50 years flood means the flood (of specified magnitude) that is likely to occur in 50 years.

Procedure of Determining Recurrence Interval :

Data : The data required is the records of annual maximum flood discharges in N number of years.

Procedure : Arrange the given flood discharges in the decreasing order of their magnitude and mention their serial order i.e. the highest flood must be written at the top and given serial number 1, the next highest being placed second should be given serial number 2 and the lowest flood placed at the bottom will have serial number n.

Then the recurrence interval of a flood having serial number m in the above series can be obtained by any one of the methods mentioned below.

(1) California Method (U.S.A.) :

$$T_r = \frac{N}{m}$$

(2) A. Hazen's Method :

$$T_r = \left(\frac{2N}{2m - 1}\right)$$

(3) Gumbel's Method :

$$T_r = \left(\frac{N}{m + C - 1}\right)$$

where C is the value of Gumbel's correction which depends upon the ratio of (m/n) and can be obtained from the table given below.

m/n Ratio	1	0.90	0.80	0.70	0.60	0.50	0.40	0.30	0.20	0.10	0.08	0.04
Value of C	1	0.95	0.88	0.845	0.78	0.73	0.66	0.59	0.52	0.4	0.38	0.28

Note : In order to obtain the flood of desired frequency it is necessary to plot Q versus T_r (or F) on a probability paper. From such a plot the flood discharge for any value of T_r (or F) can be obtained immediately. However, the method is not suitable for determining the values of higher discharges for such values of recurrence interval that exceed the number of years of records available.

(4) Weibull's Formula :

$$T_r = \frac{N+1}{m}$$

Note : Only in case of larger floods where m is very small, there will be more disagreement between the results obtained by the above formulae. For values of m equal to or above 5, the values of T_r calculated by the above methods, practically remain same. For an event having recurrence interval of T_r (years) the probability P indicating that it will be equal or exceeded in any one year is given by,

$$P = \frac{1}{T_r}$$

∴ The probability that it will not occur in a given year $= 1 - P$.

∴ The probability $\bar{P}$ that at least one event that equals or exceeds the T_r year event will occur in N number of years is given by

$$\bar{P} = 1 - (1-p)^N \quad \text{(from the principles of probability)}$$

3.10 UNIT HYDROGRAPH METHOD

The method of unit hydrograph for determining the peak floods has been already described in previous chapter.

Estimation of Frequency of Floods by Statistical Method :

The data mostly adopted for probability studies is the annual flood series which consists of maximum flood rate at the specified gauge station for each year of recorded flow. After arranging these data in class interval, the entire information can be represented in a graphical form and is known as 'frequency histogram' (Fig. 3.20). It is a graphical plot of number of peaks in selected class interval (along y-axis) versus the peak flow (m³/sec) along x-axis. Such a histogram enables to understand the distribution of the magnitude of the flood.

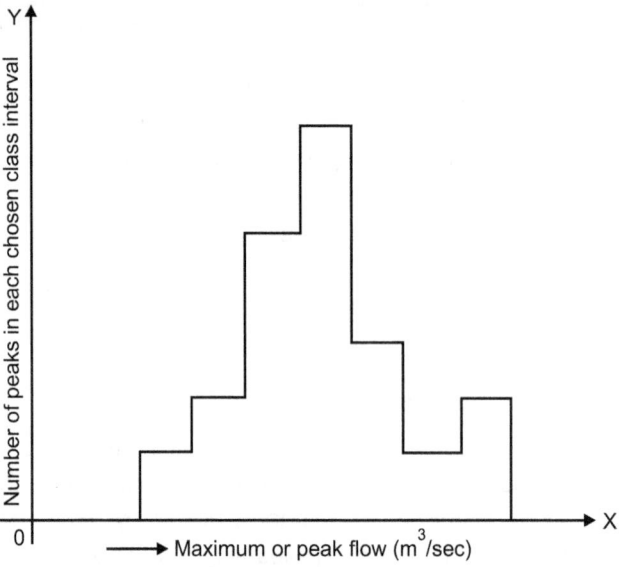

Fig. 3.20 : Frequency histogram

An 'integrated histogram' which is a modified form of frequency histogram (Fig. 3.20) indicates a graphical representation of the total number of floods that have occurred above the lower limit of class interval and is more illustrative.

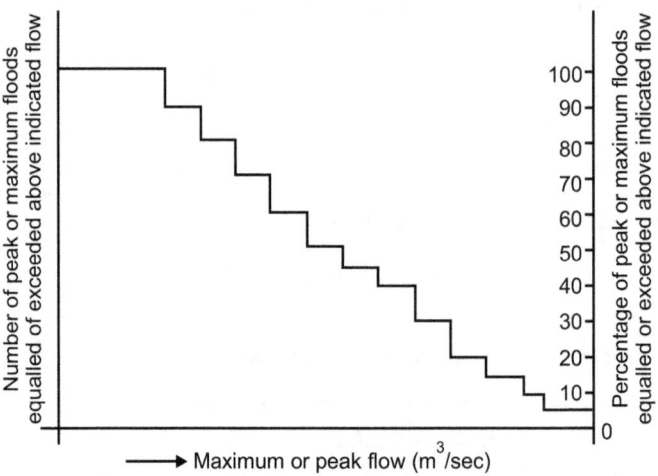

Fig. 3.21 : Integrated histogram of flood peaks (yearly)

Moreover with small class of interval with a long period of available record, the graph of Fig. 3.21 approaches a smooth frequency distribution as shown in the Fig. 3.22. In this plot the y-axis represents the probability density plotted against the flood magnitude in m³/sec along x-axis.

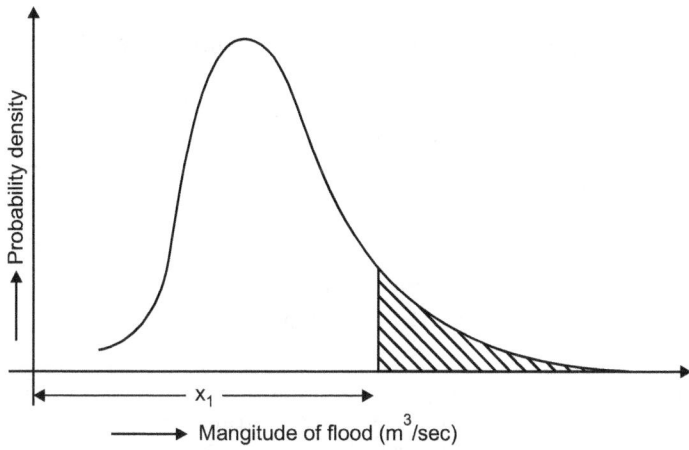

Fig. 3.22 : Flood frequency distribution (Idealized)

From such a plot, the ratio of the area under the curve above any chosen magnitude say x_1, to the area enclosed by the entire curve represents the probability that the flood of the magnitude x_1, may be equalled or even exceeded in any specified year.

It may be noted that several flood frequency distributions have been advocated as the best fitting for the stream flow under consideration, however, their validity cannot be checked in the absence of the real proof of their theory.

3.11 GUMBEL'S METHOD

As per Gumbel's suggestion, the distribution of the floods being unlimited in nature, no physical limit can be imposed to the peak or maximum floods. Thus, Gumbel advocated that the possibility i.e. probability (P) of the occurrence of a flood of value or magnitude that will be equal or exceed than any specified value x, can be expressed by the following expression.

$$P = 1 - e^{-e^{-a}}$$

In which, e = Base of natural logarithms and 'a' which is a reduced variate is given by the following equation.

$$a = \left(\frac{1}{0.78}\right)\left(\frac{1}{\sigma}\right)(x - \bar{x}\ 0.45\ \sigma)$$

Where, x = Magnitude of the flood of probability P,

$\bar{x}$ = Arithmetic mean or average of the floods in the assumed series

and σ = Standard deviation for the flood series

$$\sigma = \sqrt{\left[\frac{\Sigma\ (x - \bar{x})^2}{N\ 1}\right]}$$

Where, N = Total number of items in the flood series
i.e. number of years for which the record exists.

The recurrence interval (T_P) can then be found by making use of the relation $T_P = \dfrac{1}{P}$.

The various values of reduced variates b corresponding to the values of return period (T_P) and also probability of exceedance are given in the standard tables.

3.12 DEFINING THE DESIGN

The Design Flood for a hydraulic structure may also be defined in a number of ways, like :

- The maximum flood that any structure can safely pass.
- The flood considered for the design of a structure corresponding to a maximum tolerable risk.
- The flood which a project (involving a hydraulic structure) can sustain without any substantial damage, either to the objects which it protects or to its own structures.
- The largest flood that may be selected for design as safety evaluation of a structure.

Design Flood is also known as the Inflow Design Flood (IDF). It is the flood adopted for design purpose, and could be :

- The entire flood hydrograph, that is, the possible values of discharge as a function of time.
- The peak discharge of the flood hydrograph.

3.13 CHOICE OF DESIGN FLOOD

The Bureau of Indian standard guidelines IS : 5477 (Part IV) recommends that the Inflow Design Flood (IDF) of a structure, depending on its importance or risk involved, may be chosen from either one of the following :

Probable Maximum Flood (PMF) :

This is the flood resulting from the most severe combination of critical meteorological and hydrological conditions that rare reasonably possible in the region. The PMF is computed by using the Probable Maximum Storm (PMS) which is an estimate of the physical upper limit to storm rainfall over the catchment. This is obtained from the studies of all the storms that have occurred over the region and maximizing them for the most critical atmospheric conditions.

Standard Project Flood (SPF) :

This is the flood resulting from the most sever combination of meteorological and hydrological conditions considered reasonably characteristic of the region. The SPF is computed from the Standard Project Storm (SPS) over the watershed considered and may be taken as the largest storm observed in the region of the watershed. It is not maximized for the most critical atmospheric conditions but it may be transposed from an adjacent region to the watershed under consideration.

3.14 DESIGN FLOOD FOR STORAGE DAMS

Dams are important hydraulic structures which are constructed to serve a variety of purpose. Most dams have a capacity to store substantial amount of water in the reservoir, and a portion of the inflow flood gets stored and the excess overflows through the spillways. According to Bureau of Indian Standard guidelines IS : 11223-1985, "Guidelines for fixing spillway capacity", the IDF to be considered for different requirements.

IDF for the Safety of the Dam :

It is the flood for which, when used with standard specifications, the performance of the dam should be safe against overtopping, structural failures, and the spillway and its energy dissipation arrangement, if provided for a lower flood, should function reasonable well.

- For large dams (defined as those with gross storage greater than 60 million m^3 or hydraulic head greater than 30 m), IDF should be based on PMF.
- For intermediate dams (gross storage between 10 and 60 million m^3 or hydraulic head between 12 m and 30 m), IDF should be based on SPF.
- For small dams (gross storage between 0.5 to 10 million m^3 or hydraulic head between 7.5 m to 12 m), IDF may be taken as 100 years return period flood.
- Floods of larger or smaller magnitude may be used if the hazard involved in the eventuality of a failure is particularly high or low. The relevant parameters to be considered in judging the hazard in addition to the size would be :
- Distance to and location of the human habitations on the downstream after considering the likely future developments; and
- Maximum hydraulic capacity of the downstream channel at a level at which catastrophic damage is not expected.

IDF for Efficient Operation of Energy Dissipation System :

It is a flood which may be lower than the IDF for the safety of the dam. When this flood is used with standard specifications or other factors affecting the performance, the energy dissipation arrangements are expected to work most efficiently.

IDF for Checking Extent of Upstream Submergence :

This depends upon local conditions, type of property and effects of the submergence for very important structures upstream like power house, mines etc. Levels corresponding to SPF or PMF may be used to determine submergence effects. For other structures consideration of smaller design floods and corresponding levels attained may suffice. In general, a 25 year flood for land acquisition of 50 year flood for built-up property acquisition may be adopted.

IDF for Checking Extent of Downstream Damage in the Valley :

This depends on local conditions, the type of property and effects of its submergence. For very important facilities like powerhouse, outflows corresponding to the inflow design flood for safety of the dam, with all spillway gates operative or of that order may be relevant. Normally, damage due to physical flooding may not be allowed under this condition, but disruption of operation may be allowed.

3.15 DESIGN FLOOD FOR BARRAGES AND WEIRS

Weirs and barrages, which are diversion structures, have usually small storage capacities, and the risk of loss of life and property would rarely be enhanced by failure of the structure. Apart from damage/loss of structure the failure would cause disruption of irrigation and communications that are dependent on the barrage. According to the bureau of Indian Standard guidelines IS : 6966 (Part – I) – 1989, "Hydraulic design of barrages and weirs-guidelines for alluvial reaches", the following data are recommended.

- SPF or 500 year return period flood for designing **Free Board**.
- 50 year return period flood for designing of items other than free board.

3.16 DESIGN FLOOD FOR DIVERSION WORKS AND COFFERDAM

Whenever a hydraulic structure like a dam or a barrage is constructed across a river, a temporary structure called a cofferdam is built first for obstructing the river flow and the water diverted through a diversion channel or tunnel. The Bureau of Indian Standards in its guideline IS : 10084 (Part I) – 1982, "Criteria for design of diversion works – Part I : Cofferdams" recommends for the following :

"The cofferdam being a temporary structure is formally designed for a flood with frequency less than that for the design of the main structure. The choice of a particular frequency shall be made on practical judgment keeping in view the construction period and the stage of construction of the main structure and its importance. Accordingly, the design flood is chosen.

For seasonal cofferdams (those which are constructed every year and washed out during the flood season), and the initial construction stages of the main structure, a flood frequency of 20 years or more can be adopted. For cofferdams to be retained for more than one season and for the advanced construction stage of the main structure, a flood of 100 years frequency may be adopted".

3.17 FLOOD FOR CROSS DRAINAGE WORKS

Cross drainage works are normally encountered in irrigation canal network system. Generally canals flow under gravity and often are required to cross local streams and rivers. This is done by either conveying the canal water over the stream by overhead aqueducts or by passing below the stream though siphon aqueducts. These structures are called cross drainage works and according to the Bureau of Indian Standard guidelines IS : 7784 (Part I) – 1993, "Code of practice for design of cross drainage works" the following is recommended.

"Design flood for drainage channel to be adopted for cross drainage works should depends upon the size of the canal, size of the drainage channel and location of the cross drainage. A very long canal, crossing drainage channels in the initial reach, damage to which is likely to affect the canal supplies over a large area and for a long period, should be given proper importance.

Cross drainage structures are divided into four categories depending upon the canal discharge and drainage discharge. Design flood to be adopted for these four categories of cross drainage structures is given as in the following table :

Category of Structure	Canal Discharge (m³/s)	Estimated Drainage Discharge Note* (m³/s)	Frequency of Design Flood
A	0 – 0.5	All discharges	1 in 25 years
B	0.5 – 15	0 – 150	1 in 50 years
		>150	1 in 100 years
C	15 – 30	0 – 100	1 in 50 years
		>100	1 in 100 years
D	>30	0 – 150	1 in 100 years
		>150	Note**

Notes :

* This refers to the discharge estimated on the basis of river parameters corresponding to maximum observed flood level.

** In case of very large cross drainage structures where estimated drainage discharge is above 150 m³/s and canal discharge greater than 30 m³/s, the hydrology should be examined in detail and appropriate design flood adopted, which in no case shall be less than 1 in 100 years flood.

3.18 METHODS FOR DESIGN FLOOD COMPUTATIONS

The criteria for choosing the design flood for various types of hydraulic structures were discussed. For each one of these, any of the following three methods are suggested :

- Probable Maximum Flood (PMF)
- Standard Project Flood (SPF)
- Floor of a Specific Return Period

The methods for evaluating PMF and SPF fall under the hydro-meteorological approach, using the unit hydrograph theory. Flood of a given frequency (or return period) is obtained using the statistical approach, commonly known as flood frequency analysis. In every method, adequate data for carrying out the calculations are required. The data which are required include long term and short term rainfall and runoff values, annual flood peaks series, catchment physiographic characteristics etc.

Within the vast areal extent of our country, it is not always possible to have observations measured on every stream. There are a large number of such ungauged catchments in India which ahs to rely on synthetically generated flood formulae. The Central Water Commission in association with the Indian Meteorological Department and Research Design and Standard Organization unit of the Indian Railways have classified the country into 7 zones and 26 **Hydro-Meteorologically Homogeneous Sub-Zones**, for each one of which flood estimation guidelines have been published. These reports contain ready to use chart and formulae for computing floods of 25, 50 and 100 year return period of ungauged basins in the respective regions. In the subsequent section, we look into some detail about the calculations followed for the computation of,

- PMF and SPF by the hydro-meteorological approach.
- Evaluation of a flood of a given frequency by statistical approach.

It is not required here to explain then in detail.

3.19 THE HYDRO-METEOROLOGICAL APPROACH

The Probable Maximum Flood (PMF) or the Standard Project Flood (SPF) is estimated using the hydro-meteorological approach. For the PMF calculations the worst Possible Maximum Storm (PMS) pattern is estimated. This is then applied to the unit hydrograph of the catchment to obtain the PMF. For the calculation so the SPF, the worst observed rainfall pattern (called the Standard Project Storm or SPF) is applied to the unit hydrograph derived for the catchment.

For the estimation of the PMS or the SPS, which falls under the hydro-meteorological approach, an attempt is made to analyze the causative factors responsible for the production of severe floods. The computations mainly involve estimation of a design storm hyetograph (from past long-term rainfall data within the catchment) and derivation of the catchment response function used which can either be a lumped model or a distributed-lumped model. In the former, a unit hydrograph is assumed to represent the entire catchment area. In the distributed-lumped model, the catchment is divided into smaller sub-regions or sub-catchment and the unit and the unit hydrographs of each sub-region are applied together with **Channel Routing** and sometimes **Reservoir Routing** to produce the catchment response.

PMF/SPF calculation method by the hydro-meteorological approach involves the following steps :

- Data requirement for PMF/SPF studies.
- Steps for evaluating PMF/SPF.
- Limitation of PMF/SPF calculations.

It is not required here to explain them in detail.

3.20 THE STATISTICAL APPROACH

The statistical approach for design flood estimation, otherwise also called flood frequency analysis, may be performed on the past recorded data of annual flood peak discharges either directly observed at the site or estimated by a suitable method. Alternatively, frequency analysis may be carried out on the available record of annual rainfall events of the region. The probability of occurrence of event (say, the maximum flood discharge observed or likely to occur in a year at a location on a river), whose magnitude is equal to or in excess of a specified magnitude X is denoted by P. A related term, the recurrence interval (also known as the return period) is defined as T = 1/P. This represents the average interval between the occurrence of a flood peak of magnitude equal to or greater than X. Flood frequency analysis studies interpret past record of events to predict the future probabilities of occurrence and estimate the magnitude of an event corresponding to a specific return period. For the estimation of flood flows of large return periods, it is often necessary to extrapolate the magnitude outside the observed range of data. Though a limited extrapolation to about twice the length of the record (that is, the number of years of data that is available) expected to yield reasonable accuracy, often water resources engineers are required to project much more than that.

3.21 FLOOD FREQUENCY ANALYSIS

Basic to all frequency analyses, is the concept that there is a collection of data, called the 'population'. For flood frequency studies, this population is taken as the annual maximum flood occurring at a location on a river (called the site). Since the river has flooded during the past years and is likely to go on flooding over the coming years (unless something exceptional like drying up of the river happens !), the recorded flood peak values which have been observed for a finite number of years are only a sample of the total population. Here, *flood peak* means the highest recorded discharge value for the river at any year.

The following assumptions are generally made for the data :

- The sample is representative of the population. Thus, it is assumed that though only a finite years' data of peak flow has been recorded, the same type of trend was always there are would continue to be so in future.
- The data are independent. That is, the peak flow data which has been collected are independent of each other. Thus, the data set is assumed to be random. In a random process, the value of the variant does not depend on previous or next values.

Flood frequency analysis starts by checking the consistency of the data and finding the presence of features such as trend, jump etc. Trend is the gradual shift in the sample data, either in the increasing or decreasing directions. This may occurs due to human interference, like afforestation or deforestation of the watershed. Jump means that one or a few of the data have exceptional values – high or low, due to certain factors, like forest fire, earthquake, landslide etc. which may change the river's flow characteristics temporarily.

The next step is to apply a convenient probability distribution curve to fit the data set. Here, it is assumed that yearly observed peak flow values are random numbers and which are also representative of the population, which includes all flood peak values, even these which have not been recorded or such floods which are likely to happen in future. Each data of the set is termed as a variate, usually represented by 'x' and is a particular value of the entire data range 'x'.

The probability of a variable is defined as 'the number of occurrences of a variate divided by the total number of occurrences', and is usually designated by 'P'. The total probability for all variates should be equal to unity, that is, $\Sigma p = 1$.

Distribution of probabilities of all variates is called Probability Distribution, and is usually denoted a f(x) as shown in Fig. 3.23.

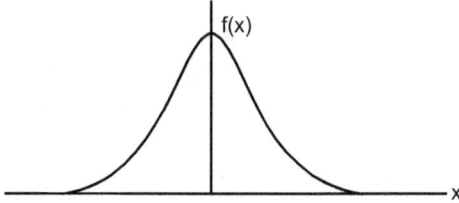

Fig. 3.23 : A typical probability distribution

The cumulative probability curve, F(x) is of the type as shown in Fig. 3.24.

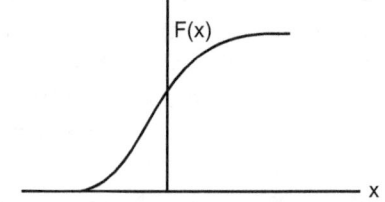

Fig. 3.24 : Cumulative probability curve

The cumulative probability, designated as $P(X \leq x)$, represents the probability that the random variable has a value equal to or less than certain assigned value x is equal to $1 - P(X \leq x)$, or $P(X \geq x)$.

In the context of flood frequency analysis, we may use the above concepts by assuming the recorded yearly flood peaks as the variety 'X'. Then, if the functions f(x) or F(x) becomes known, then it is possible to find out the probability with which certain high flood peak is likely to occur. This idea may be used to recalculate the high flood peak that is likely to be equaled or exceeded corresponding to a given frequency (say, 1 in 100 years). There are a number of probability distributions f(x), which has been suggested by many statisticians. Of these, the more common are :

- Normal
- Log-normal
- Pearson Type III
- Gumbel

Which one of these fits a given data set has to be checked using certain standard statistical tests. Once a particular distribution is found best, it is adopted for calculation of floods likely to occur corresponding to specific return periods. It is not required to explain them in detail here.

3.22 PLOTTING POSITIONS

So far we talked about extrapolation of the sample data. However, if probability is to be assigned to a data point itself, then the 'plotting position' method is used. Here, the sample data (consisting of, say, N values) is arranged in a decreasing order. Each data (say the event X) of the ordered list in then given a rank 'm' starting with 1 for the highest up to N for the lowest of the order. The probability of excedence of X over a certain value x, that is $P(X \geq x)$ is given differently by different researchers, the most common of which are as given in the table below :

Sr. No.	Name of Formula	$P(X \geq x)$
1	California	m/N
2	Hazen	(m – 0.5)/N
3	Weibull	m/(N + 1)

Of these, the Weibull formula is most commonly used to determine the probability that is to be assigned to data sheet.

Example Showing Application for Plotting Positions :

The application of the method of plotting may be explained better with an example. Assume that the yearly peak flood flows of a hypothetical river measured at a particular location over the years 1981 to 2000 is given as in the following table. The data is to used to calculate the flood peak flow that is likely to occur once every 10 years, and once every 50 years.

Year	Peak Flood (m³/s)
1981	700
1982	810
1983	470
1984	300
1985	440
1986	600
1987	350
1988	290
1989	330
1990	670

Contd...

1991	540
1992	430
1993	320
1994	420
1995	690
1996	400
1997	360
1998	510
1999	910
2000	100

Rearranging table according to decreasing magnitude, designate a plotting position and calculate the probability of excedence by, say, the Weibull formula shown in the following table which also gives the Return Period T = (1/P).

m	Peak Flood (m³/s)	Probability $P = \dfrac{m}{N+1}$	Return Period T = 1/P Years
1	910	0.048	21.000
2	810	0.095	10.500
3	700	0.143	7.000
4	690	0.190	5.250
5	670	0.238	4.200
6	600	0.286	3.500
7	540	0.333	3.000
8	510	0.381	2.625
9	470	0.429	2.333
10	440	0.476	2.100
11	430	0.524	1.909
12	420	0.571	1.750
13	400	0.619	1.615
14	360	0.667	1.500
15	350	0.714	1.400

Contd...

16	330	0.762	1.313
17	320	0.810	1.235
18	300	0.857	1.167
19	290	0.905	1.105
20	100	0.952	1.050

SOLVED PROBLEMS

Problem 3.1 : *Construction of hydrograph.*

Solution : Object : (1) To draw total flood hydrograph.

(2) To derive direct run-off hydrograph.

(3) To construct unit hydrograph.

Data : Isolated storm of one hour duration occurs over a basin of 150 km^2 in area. Flow data at one hour interval is given as follows.

Sr. No.	Time in Hours	Total Flood in cumecs	Base Flow in cumecs
1.	8 a.m.	15	15
2.	9 a.m.	25	16
3.	10 a.m.	90	14
4.	11 a.m.	147	19
5.	12 noon	181	19
6.	1 p.m.	193	20
7.	2 p.m.	192	20
8.	3 p.m.	180	22
9.	4 p.m.	162	23
10.	5 p.m.	136	24
11.	6 p.m.	115	27
12.	7 p.m.	96	26
13.	8 p.m.	80	26
14.	9 p.m.	67	27
15.	10 p.m.	56	28
16.	11 p.m.	46	30
17.	12 p.m.	38	30
18.	1 a.m.	32	32

Procedure:

(1) Draw the total flood hydrograph of total flood v/s time.

(2) On the same graph draw the graph of base flow v/s time.

(3) Find the difference between total flood and base flow. Plot the graph of difference of the base flow and total flood v/s time.

(4) The above graph is plotted and is known as *'Direct Run-off Hydrograph'*. Find the area below this graph.

(5) Equating the above area as the volume of water in whose period, the depth is found out by dividing the volume by area of basin.

(6) The unit flood at various base floods are calculated by dividing depth of run-off to base flood. From this plot the unit flood hydrograph.

Calculations:

Area below direct run-off hydrograph = 143.7 m³/hr

$$\text{Depth of run-off} = \frac{143.7 \times 60 \times 60}{150 \times 10^6} = 3.45 \text{ cm} = 34.5 \text{ mm}$$

The base flow is divided by this depth and the unit flood is obtained.

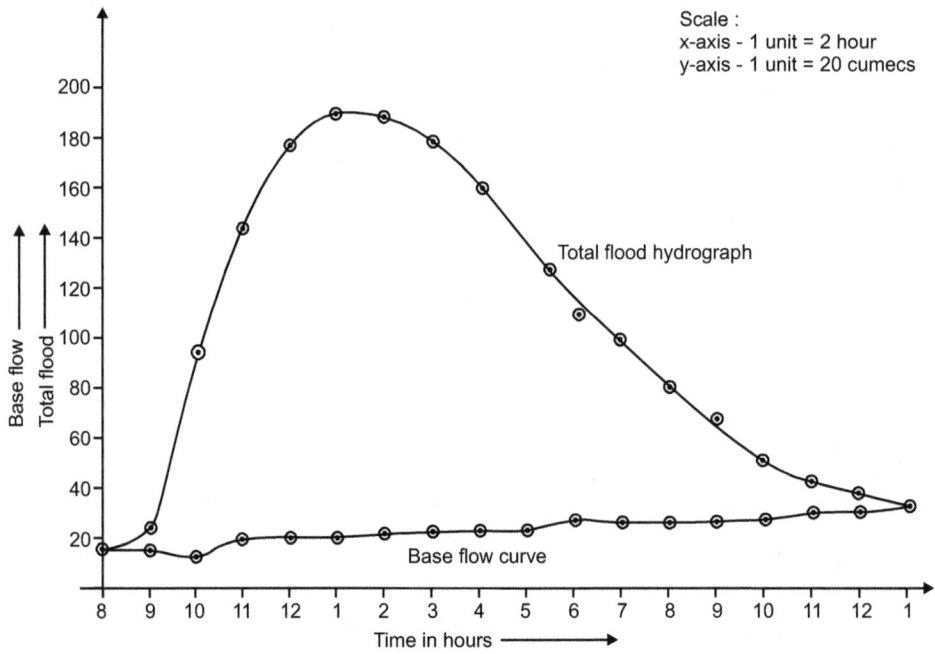

Fig. 3.25 : For problem 3.1

Results entered in tabular form for problem 3.1 :

Total Flood in Cumecs	Base Flow (B.F.)	T.F. – B.F. (Cumecs)	(T.F. – B.F.) 3.45
15	15	00	00.00
25	16	09	02.61
90	14	76	22.00
147	19	128	37.1
181	19	162	46.96
193	20	173	50.1
192	20	172	49.86
180	22	158	45.8
162	23	139	40.3
136	24	112	32.5
115	27	88	25.51
96	26	70	20.3
80	26	54	15.65
67	27	40	11.6
56	28	28	08.12
46	30	16	04.64
38	30	08	02.32
32	32	00	00.00

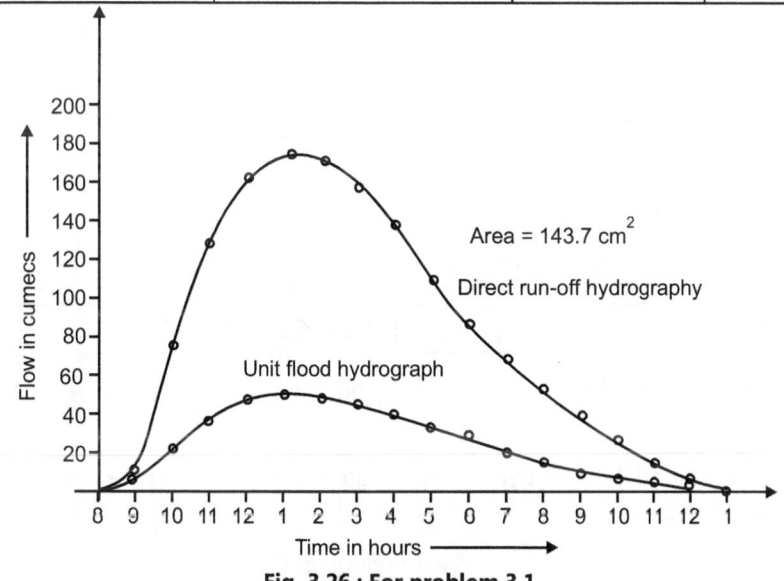

Fig. 3.26 : For problem 3.1

Problem 3.2 : Estimate the maximum flood flow for the catchment having area $A_1 = 40.5 \text{ Km}^2$ by using an appropriate empirical formula. What is the peak discharge for $A_1 = 40.5 \text{ Km}^2$ by maximum world flood experience?

Solution :

(a) By Inglis formula

$$Q_{max} = \left(\frac{124 A}{\sqrt{A + 10.4}}\right)$$

$$Q_{max} = \left(\frac{124 \times 40.5}{\sqrt{40.5 + 10.4}}\right)$$

$$Q_{max} = 704 \text{ m}^3/\text{s}$$

(b) By Dickens formula

$$Q_{max} = CA^{3/4}$$

$$Q_{max} = 6.0 \times (40.5)^{3/4}$$

$$Q_{max} = 96.3 \text{ m}^3/\text{s}$$

(c) Ryve's formula

$$Q = CA^{2/3}$$

$$Q = 6.8 \times (40.5)^{2/3}$$

$$Q = 80.2 \text{ m}^3/\text{s}$$

(d) Maximum Peak Discharge Based on World Experience

$$Q_{mp} = \frac{3025 \times 40.5}{(278 + 40.5)^{0.78}}$$

$$Q_{mp} = 1367 \text{ m}^3/\text{s}$$

THEORETICAL QUESTIONS

1. What are different methods of stream gauging ? Explain the dilution technique of flow measurement in a river.

2. Describe any one method that you would suggest for estimating the discharge in a river when it is in floods.

3. Explain in short the importance of stream gauging. Describe any one method of stream gauging.

WATER RESOURCES ENGINEERING - I (TE CIVIL SU) — STREAM GAUGING AND FLOODS

4. Enumerate various methods of stream gauging and explain with neat sketches area-velocity method.

5. Explain the slope-area method of stream gauging.

6. Write short notes on :

    (i) Moving boat method,

    (ii) Area-velocity method,

    (iii) Automatic recording gauge,

    (iv) Current meter,

    (v) Wire-weight gauge,

    (vi) Staff gauge.

7. Explain the following methods of estimating Flood

    (i) By empirical formulae,

    (ii) By rational method,

    (iii) By infiltration method,

    (iv) By unit hydrograph method.

8. Write a brief note on frequency factor and its estimation in Gumbel's method.

9. What are limitations of flood frequency studies?

10. Explain briefly the following terms :

    (i) Design flood

    (ii) Standard project flood

    (iii) Probable maximum flood

    (iv) design storm

11. Describe any one method that you would suggest for estimating the discharge in a river when it is in floods.

12. Enumerate briefly the various methods used for deforming floods. Explain any one of the methods that is commonly used.

NUMERICAL PROBLEM

Information on the 50-year storm is given below.

Duration (minutes)	15	30	45	60	180
Rainfall (mm)	40	60	75	100	120

A culvert has to drain 25 ha of land with a maximum length of travel of 1.25 km. the general slope of the catchment is 0.001 and its runoff coefficient is 0.20. Estimate the peak flow by the rational method for designing the culvert for a 50-year flood.

UNIT – IV

GROUND WATER HYDROLOGY

4.1 INTRODUCTION

'**Ground Water Hydrology**' is defined as 'the science of occurrence, distribution and movement of water that takes place below the Earth's surface'. It is an important source of water and is used all over the world for water supply (domestic and industrial), and irrigation purposes. When precipitation takes place a portion of it infiltrates into the ground and when a surface of impervious layer is met with, it is stored over it and forms a 'ground water'. It forms an important source of water supply in areas where dry summers (as seen in Maharashtra) cause the stream flow to stop. The location and movement of the ground water is governed by the geological formation and thus it is a specialised and complex branch of hydrology. If the ground water table is very high, the surface streams also receive most of the portion of their flow from ground water. Elsewhere, water flowing from the surface stream forms the source of recharge for the ground water. The ground water may be available naturally in the form of lakes, river etc. or can be extracted artificially from open or tube wells etc.

4.2 OCCURRENCE OF GROUND WATER AND ITS DISTRIBUTION

Fig. 4.1 shows a schematic diagram of occurrence of ground water. The entire portion is divided into two parts by a 'water table'. The portion that lies below the water table is called as '*zone of saturation*' and that above is known as '*Zone of aeration*'.

After precipitation the infiltrated water moves downward through zone of aeration. Some portion of this water is held by capillary forces in the pores of soil and is called as 'soil moisture'. Subsequently, the water moves down into the regions and all the pores of soil in this zone get completely filled with water and is known as 'zone of saturation'.

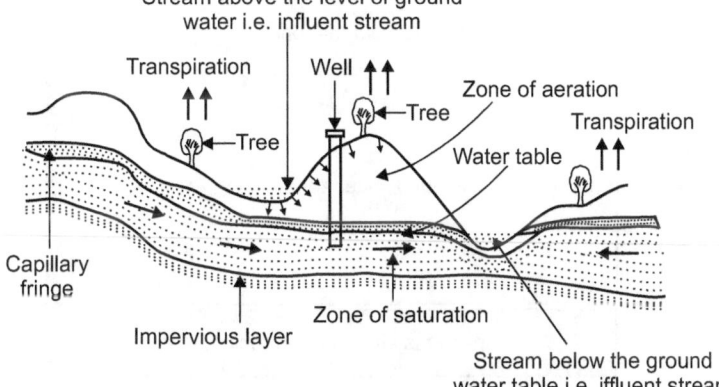

Fig. 4.1 : Occurrence of ground water

The water contained in the zone of saturation is called as 'ground water'. The replenishment of the 'ground water' by the water moving downwards is known as recharge of ground water.

Water Table : The portion of the earth enclosed between 'zone of aeration' and zone of saturation is known as the water table. It can be located from the level of water that rises in an open well that penetrates the top of zone of saturation. The water table is higher below the hills as compared to adjacent valleys.

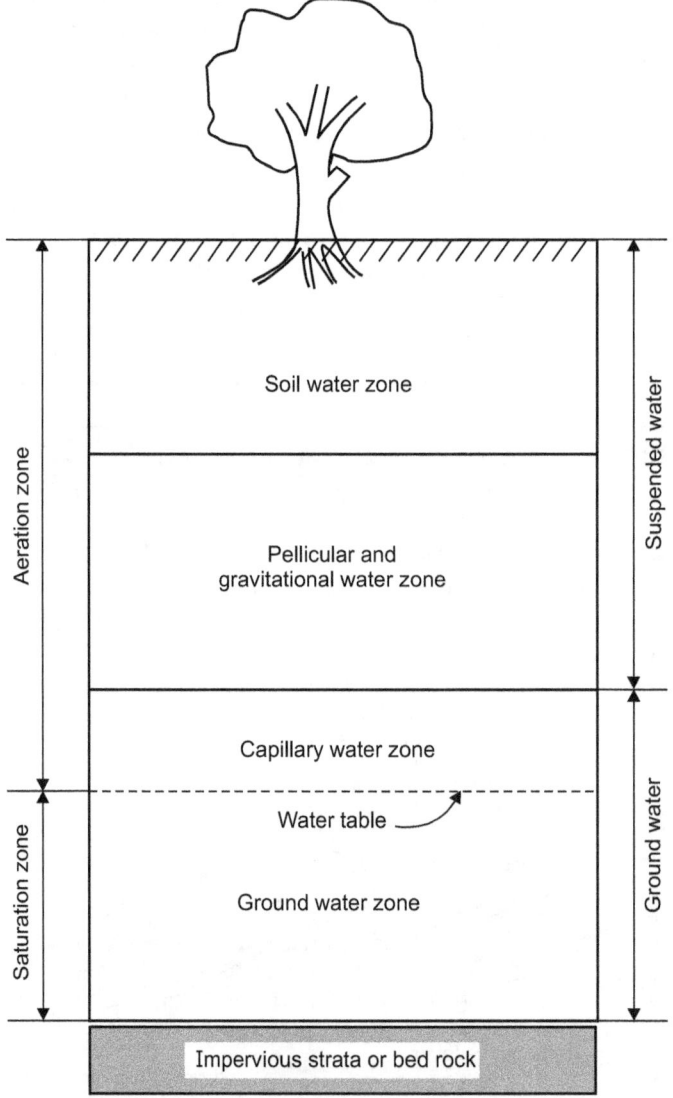

Fig. 4.2 : Divisions of sub-surface water in the earth

The portion lying immediately above the water table is called as 'capillary fringe' where the water pressure is always less than atmospheric pressure. The water table is the surface of water body that continuously adjusts itself towards an equilibrium condition. In the Fig. 4.1 there are two streams shown. The one which is situated above the level of water table, contributes to the ground water and is known as *'influent stream'* and other situated below the level of water table, draws water from the ground water and is called *'effluent stream'*.

4.3 DEFINITION OF TERMS

4.3.1 Aquifer
It is a geologic formation which contains and transmits ground water in sufficient quantity to support springs or wells. Aquifer may be either *confined* or *unconfined*.
A confined (also called as artesian) aquifer is surrounded above and below by impervious strata and an unconfined aquifer is surrounded from above by the water table only with a overlying zone of aeration.

4.3.2 Aquiclude
It is a geologic formation of somewhat impermeable material that contains large volumes of water but due to its less rate of movement is unable to transmit water in large quantities for its economical development.

4.3.3 Aquifuge
It is a geologic formation of impermeable material having no inter connected opening and thus can neither absorb or transmit water.

4.3.4 Aquitard
It is a geologic formation of very less permeable material that can store water but offers resistance to the movement of ground water.

4.3.5 Porosity (n)
It is defined as 'the ratio of volume of pores (i.e. openings) V_p in the material to its total volume V' and is expressed in percentage i.e.

$$n = \left(\frac{V_p}{V}\right) \times 100$$

Porosity indicates the capacity of the formation to hold water. The porosity of fine grained soils such as clay is about 65% and that of coarse grained sand is about 20%.

4.3.6 Specific Yield (of an aquifer) (S_y)
It is defined as 'the ratio of volume of water that after being saturated, can be drained by gravity action, to its own volume, always expressed as percentage'.

i.e. Specific yield (S_y) = $\dfrac{\text{Volume of water that can be drained by gravity}}{\text{Total volume}}$

$$S_y = \left(\frac{W_y}{V}\right) \times 100$$

It enables in determining the water yielding capacity of an (unconfined) aquifer.

4.3.7 Specific Retention (of a soil) (S_r)

It is 'the ratio of the volume of water that can be retained (after saturation) against the gravity force to its volume'.

i.e $$S_r = \left(\frac{W_r}{V}\right) \times 100$$

Obviously porosity = Specific yield + Specific retention

i.e. $n = S_y + S_r$

The specific yield is a function of size of grain, its shape, distribution pores and the compaction of stratum. The yield from coarse grained particles will obviously be more than from fine grained one and thus the former serves as an aquifer.

4.4 DIVISIONS OF SUB-SURFACE WATER (IN THE EARTH)

As shown in the Fig. 4.2 the divisions of the subsurface water will be as indicated below :

4.4.1 Zone of Aeration

This can further be classified as soil water zone, (intermediate) gravitational and pellicular zone and capillary zone.

4.4.2 Zone of Saturation

In this zone, all the interstices are filled with (ground) water and is under hydrostatic pressure.

4.5 TYPES OF AQUIFERS

As stated in Article 4.3.1 an aquifer may be a unconfined or confined as shown in the Fig. 4.3. The confined aquifer is also called as *artesian aquifer*.

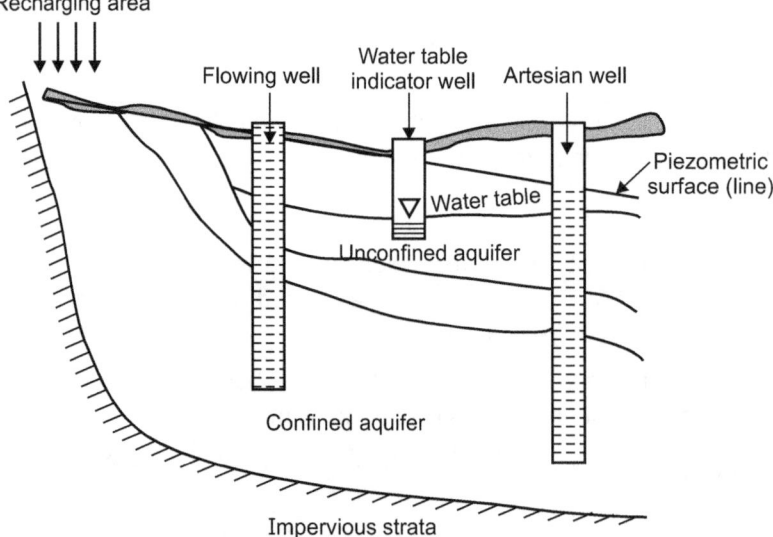

Fig. 4.3 : Aquifers-confined and unconfined

4.5.1 Unconfined Aquifer (or water Table Aquifer or Non-Artesian Aquifer)

It is defined as 'an aquifer in which the water surface forms the upper surface of the zone of saturation'. The level of water table increases or decreases depending upon to the recharge of water more or less.

4.5.2 Confined Aquifer (or Artesian Aquifer)

It is an aquifer in which ground water is confined (i.e. enclosed) under pressure which is greater than atmospheric pressure by overlying impermeable strata. This aquifer is analogous to a pipe line. The static pressure at any point within this aquifer is equivalent to the elevation of water table after subtracting the loss of head through the aquifer to the point which is under consideration

If a well is penetrated through such an aquifer the water will rise to the local static pressure level or artesian head.

4.5.3 Perched Aquifer

It is a type of special unconfined aquifer (as shown in the Fig. 4.4) that occurs when a ground water body gets separated from the main ground water by a relatively small areal extent by the zone of aeration above the main body of the ground water. The quantity of water obtained from well in such aquifer is somewhat less as these are not recharged.

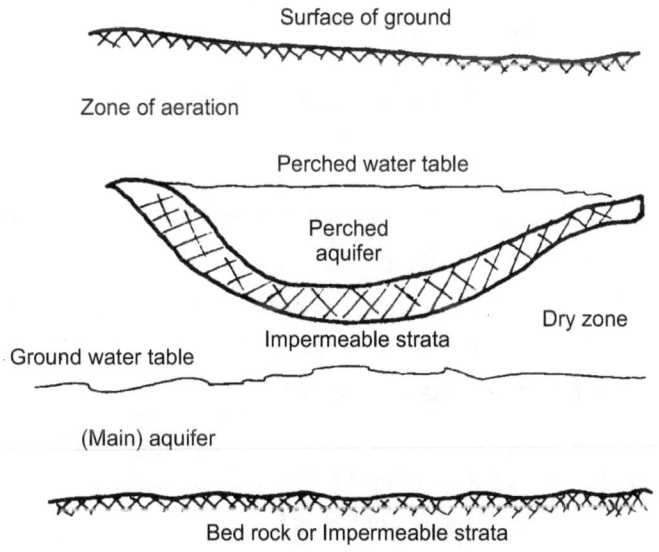

Fig. 4.4 : Perched water table or perched aquifer

4.6 MOVEMENT OF GROUND WATER

4.6.1 Introduction

Normally, the flow of the ground water is assumed to be laminar, as the velocities are low as the water traverses an irregular path through the interstices of the strata. The flow may be either under gravity following the water table slopes or it may be under pressure while flowing through the undulating confined stratum.

4.6.2 Darcy's Law and Coefficient of Permeability (K)

Darcy (1856) was the first to demonstrate the movement of ground water in filtered sand beds. As per Darcy's law for flow of water through porous media, the *rate of flow* is directly proportional to the hydraulic gradient.

i.e. $$v \propto \frac{h}{l}$$

or $$v = k\frac{h}{l} \text{ or } v = ki$$

where, v = rate of flow = $\frac{Q}{A}$

h = difference in pressure head measured in a distance l.

and k = constant depending upon the physical properties of the aquifer

and $i = \frac{h}{l}$ = hydraulic gradient

Further the rate of (specific) discharge (denoted by q) of an aquifer is expressed as:

$$q = \left(k \cdot a \frac{h}{l}\right)$$

where q = rate of discharge per unit cross-section per unit gradient

and a = cross-sectional area

k in the above equation is called as the coefficient of permeability and has the units of metres per day.

4.6.3 Coefficient of Transmissibility (T)

It is the rate of flow of water measured in m^3/day passing through the vertical strip of aquifer of unit width (i.e. metre) and under the unit hydraulic gradient, at 60°F.

The relation between k and T will be expressed as follows:

$$T = k \cdot b$$

where, b = thickness of the aquifer

4.6.4 Storage Coefficient

It is the water yielding capacity of a confined aquifer and is defined as 'volume of water that an aquifer can release from or take into storage per unit surface area of aquifer taken per unit change in component of the head measured normal to that surface.

i.e. Storage coefficient $= \dfrac{\text{Volume of water}}{\text{Volume of aquifer}} = \dfrac{m^3}{m^3}$

i.e. a non-dimensional number.

4.7 SAFE YIELD OF BASIN

Safe yield of groundwater may be defined as 'the amount of water which can be withdrawn from it annually without producing any undesirable effects'. Any withdrawn in excess of safe yield is called *overdraft*.

$$\text{Basin Self Yield} = \dfrac{\text{Basin yield + Well}}{\text{Reservoir storage credit} - \text{Environmental protection factor}}$$

In many cases the safe yield may simply be taken to the amount of water that enters the groundwater basin every year. When the withdrawals exceed long term mean annual recharge of the basin, the excess must come from the storage within the aquifer. Such permanent deflection is often referred to as mining of ground water.

In most basins the quantity of water in the storage is the many times annual recharge. Therefore, in any one year the draft can exceed the recharge without causing permanent deflection. But on long time basin, if the draft exceeds the average annual recharge it become overdrafts.

The safe yield may be less than the average annual recharge to the basin due to many factors that includes economics, water quality and water rights. Higher drafts may lower water table resulting in increasing pumping costs. Pumping in a coastal aquifer could include sea water intrusion into the basin.

Higher draft rates may causes interferences with prior water rights within a basin or in adjacent basins. If economic, quality or legal problems are created by plumpage from the ground water basin, its safe yield is then governed by the average annual recharge to the basin.

4.8 HYDRAULICS OF WELLS

4.8.1 Introduction

Fig. 4.5 shows a well penetrating an extensive homogenous aquifer having isotropic hydraulic conductivity where initially the water table is horizontal.

When the pumping commences water will be extracted from the aquifer and the water table takes the shape of a depression called as the 'cone of depression' or 'drawdown curve' and the lowering of the water level S is called as drawdown.

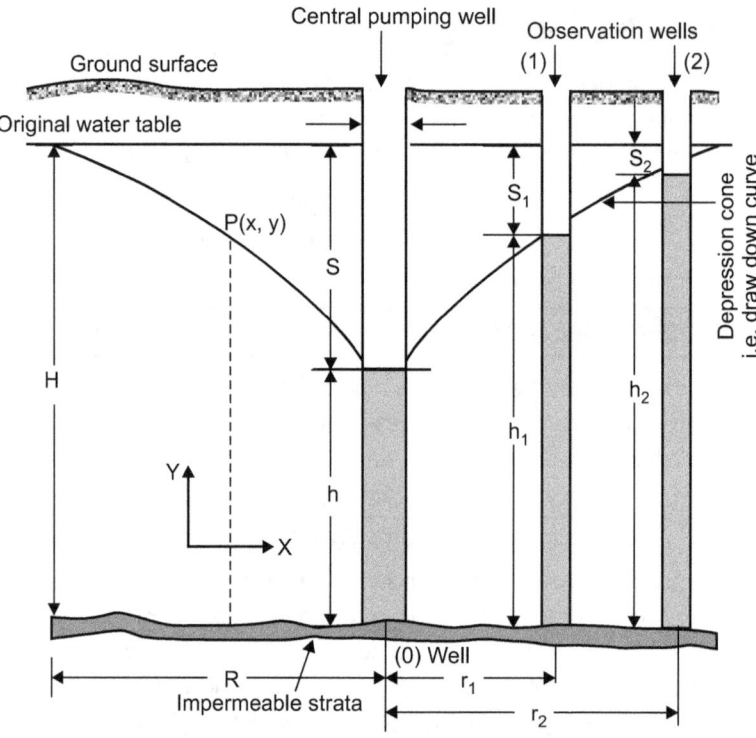

Fig. 4.5 : Well through an unconfined aquifer

4.8.2 Assumptions in the Analysis of Radial Flow

The analysis of radial flow towards a well was proposed originally by Dupit (1853) and subsequently modified by Thiem (1906). The assumptions made by them in derivation of formula are as follows :

- The ground water flow is horizontal and laminar and Darcy's law holds good.
- The aquifer is homogenous and isotropic.
- The coefficient of transmissibility is same every where.
- The well penetrates and receives water from the whole thickness of aquifer.
- For hydraulic gradient, tan θ (instead of sin θ) will be adopted, 0 being the angle between horizontal and hydraulic grade line.
- The pumping of water is to be continued till an equilibrium steady flow condition is reached.

4.8.3 Types of Aquifers

Now, we will consider two types of aquifers :
- Unconfined aquifer and
- Confined aquifer to establish radial flow equations i.e. relation between the discharge and drawdown for steady state conditions of flows.

Case (i) Unconfined Aquifers :

Referring to the Fig. 4.5, let the radius of the well be r and H the thickness of aquifer and S the draw down at the well portion and h the depth of water column in the well. Let the centre of the well (0) be the origin and the co-ordinates of any point P on the depression cone be (x, y).

∴ As per Darcy's law,

$$Q = KiA$$

where, A = Cross-section area of the saturated portion of aquifer at P
= Perimeter × Height
= $(2\pi x)(y)$

and i = hydraulic gradient at P = $\dfrac{dy}{dx}$ (as per assumption)

∴ $Q = K(2\pi xy) \cdot \dfrac{dy}{dx}$

∴ Rearranging the terms

$$Q \cdot \left(\dfrac{dx}{x}\right) = 2\pi K y \, dy \qquad \ldots (4.1)$$

On integrating the equation (4.1) between the limits $x = r$, $y = h$ and $x = R$ and $y = H$.
We may write

$$Q \int_r^R \dfrac{dx}{x} = 2\pi k \int_h^H y \, dy$$

or $\quad [\log_e x]_r^R = 2\pi K \left[\dfrac{y^2}{2}\right]_h^H$

or $\quad Q = \left[\dfrac{\pi K (H^2 - h^2)}{\log_e (R/r)}\right] \qquad \ldots (4.2)$

$\quad = \dfrac{\pi K (H^2 - h^2)}{2.3 \log_{10} (R/r)} = \dfrac{1.36 \, K (H^2 - h^2)}{\log_{10} (R/r)} \qquad \ldots (4.3)$

Now, from the Fig. 4.5

$$S = H - h$$

i.e. $\quad H = S + h$

or $\quad H + h = S + 2h$

Multiplying both sides by $(H - h)$

then $\quad (H + h)(H - h) = (S + 2h)(H - h)$

i.e. $\quad H^2 - h^2 = S(S + 2h)$ ... (4.4)

Substituting this value of $H^2 - h^2$ from (4.4) in equation (4.2) above we may write

$$Q = \frac{\pi K\, S(S + 2h)}{\log_e(R/r)}$$

$$= \frac{1.36\, K\, S(S - 2h)}{\log_{10}(R/r)}$$

For small value of draw down S.

then $\quad (H + h) \approx H + H \approx 2H$

$\therefore \quad (H^2 - h^2) = (H - h)(H + h)$

but $\quad H \approx h$

$\therefore \quad H^2 - h^2 = 2H(H - h)$

but $\quad (H - h) = S$

$\therefore \quad H^2 - h^2 = 2HS$

$\therefore \quad Q = \dfrac{2\pi K\, HS}{\log_e(R/r)}$

or $\quad Q = \dfrac{2.72\, KHS}{\log_{10}(R/r)}$

In case of an unconfined aquifer $T = kH$.

$\therefore$ Substituting T for kH in the above equation

$$Q = \frac{2.72\, T.S.}{\log_{10}(R/r)}$$

The above equation can be used if the radius of influence R is known.

An another expression for Q, which will be independent of radius of influence R can be derived by establishing two observation wells (1) and (2), as shown in the Fig. 4.5.

Let the radii of the two wells (1) and (2) be r_1 and r_2 respectively and the water depths as h_1 and h_2 respectively.

Then writing the same equation (4.1) above,

$$Q \frac{dx}{x} = 2\pi K y\, dy$$

$\therefore$ On integration, the limits of integration being

$\quad x = r_1$ and $y = h_1$, for well point (1)

and $\quad x = y_2$ and $y = h_2$, for well point (2)

We may write,
$$Q = \frac{\pi K \left(h_2^2 - h_1^2\right)}{\log_e \left(\frac{r_2}{r_1}\right)}$$

$$= \frac{3.142\, K \left(h_2^2 - h_1^2\right)}{2.303 \log_{10} \left(\frac{r_2}{r_1}\right)}$$

$$= \frac{1.36\, K \left(h_2^2 - h_1^2\right)}{\log_{10} \left(\frac{r_2}{r_1}\right)}$$

Where $h_2 = H - S_2$ and $h_1 = H - S_1$ or $H = h + S$

Where S_1 and S_2 are drawdowns of the well no. (1) and No. (2) respectively.

Now, substituting these values in the original equation

$$Q = \frac{1.36\, K\, (H^2 - h^2)}{\log_e (R - r)}$$

We get,
$$Q = \frac{\pi K\, (H + h)\, (H - h)}{\log_e (R/r)}$$

$$= \frac{\pi K s\, (S + 2h)}{\log_e (R/r)}$$

Notes :

- If the value of k in the above equation is written in term of m^3/day per m^2 of sub soil area, then the value of Q obtained will be in m^3/day.
- The selection of value of R (i.e. radius of influence) is arbitrary and approximately it may be assumed in the range of 150 to 300 m.
- The value of R can also be calculated by Sichardt formula.
  i.e. $R = 300 \sqrt{K}\, S$; where R and S are in metres and K is in m/sec.

Case (ii) Confined Aquifer :

Fig. 4.6 is a case of a well having radius r, that penetrates a confined aquifer, of thickness b.

Let P(x, y) refer to the co-ordinates of any point on the cone of depression (i.e. draw down curve), the centre of the well (0) being the origin.

Then as per Darcy's law

$$Q = KiA$$

where A = (perimeter of cylinder) × (height of thickness of confined aquifer)

$$= 2\pi \cdot x \cdot b$$

and i = hydraulic gradient at p = dy/dx (as per assumption)

$$\therefore \quad Q = K\left(\frac{dy}{dx}\right) 2\pi \cdot x \cdot b$$

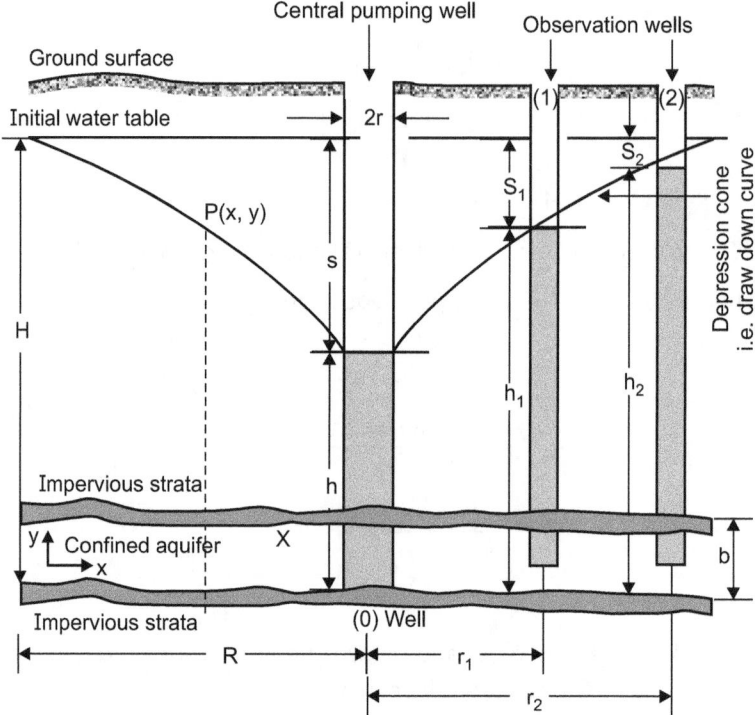

Fig. 4.6 : Well through a confined aquifer

∴ Rearranging the terms

$$Q \cdot \frac{dx}{x} = 2\pi K b \, dy$$

On integrating between the limits

$$x = r, \; y = h \text{ and } x = R, \; y = H$$

We get,

$$Q \int_r^R \frac{dx}{x} = 2\pi K b \int_h^H dy$$

or $\quad Q[\log_e(x)]_r^R = 2\pi Kb [y]_h^H$

i.e. $\quad Q = \dfrac{2\pi Kb (H-h)}{\log_e (R/r)} \rightarrow$ Thiem's equilibrium equation

$$= \dfrac{2\pi Kb (H-h)}{2.3 \log_{10} (R/r)}$$

$$= \dfrac{2.72\, kb\, (H-h)}{\log_{10} (R/r)}$$

but $\quad H - h = S =$ Draw down at the well

$\therefore \quad Q = \dfrac{2.72\, Kb \cdot S}{\log_{10}(R/r)}$

but $\quad kh = T =$ Coefficient of transmissibility

$\therefore \quad Q = \dfrac{2.72 \cdot T \cdot S}{\log_{10}(R/r)}$

As the exact value of R is not known, it can be avoided by observations from two (observation) wells situated at radial distances r_1 and r_2, the corresponding water depths being h_1 and h_2 respectively.

Now, $\quad \displaystyle\int_{r_1}^{r_2} Q \dfrac{dx}{x} = \int_{h_1}^{h_2} 2\pi kb\, dy$

$\therefore$ On integration, $\quad Q = \dfrac{2\pi Kb (h_2 - h_1)}{\log_e (r_2/r_1)}$

$$= \dfrac{2.72\, Kb\, (h_2 - h_1)}{\log_{10}(r_2/r_1)}$$

Now, for the depths of water h_x at any radial distance x, the discharge Q may be written by making use of the above equation as :

$$Q = \dfrac{2\pi Kb (h_x - h)}{\log_e (r_x/r)}$$

but $\quad Q = \dfrac{2\pi Kb (H - h)}{\log_e (R/r)}$

or $\quad (h_x - h) = (H - h) \dfrac{\log_e \left(\dfrac{r_x}{r}\right)}{\log_e (R/r)}$

Which indicates that the head $(h_x - h)$ linearly varies with the logarithm of distances and is independent of the discharge Q.

4.9 DETERMINATION OF COEFFICIENT OF TRANSMISSIBILITY (T)

The coefficient of transmissibility (T) for steady state flow condition is determined by carrying out pumping test and by the observation of draw down in the various observation wells.

Case (i) Unconfined Aquifer : Referring to Fig. 4.5, we may write

$$h_1 = H - S_1 \text{ and } h_2 = H - S_2$$

or

$$h_2^2 - h_1^2 = (H - S_2)^2 - (H - S_1)^2$$

$$= (H^2 - 2HS_2 + S_2^2) - (H^2 - 2HS_1 + S_1^2)$$

$$= 2H\left[\left(S_1 - \frac{S_1^2}{2H}\right) - \left(S_2 - \frac{S_2^2}{2H}\right)\right]$$

Putting

$$\left(S_1 - \frac{S_1^2}{2H}\right) = S_1' \text{ (i.e. modified draw down) and}$$

$$\left(S_2 - \frac{S_2^2}{2H}\right) = S_2' \text{ (i.e. modified draw down)}$$

We get,

$$\left(h_2^2 - h_1^2\right) = 2H\,[S_1' - S_2']$$

Now the earlier equation,

$$Q = \frac{1.36\,k\,(h_2^2 - h_1^2)}{\log_{10}(r_2/r_1)}$$

can be written in following form

$$Q = \frac{1.36k\,[2H\,(S_1' - S_2')]}{\log_{10}(r_2/r_1)}$$

$$= \frac{2.72\,kH\,(S_1' - S_2')}{\log_{10}(r_2/r_1)}$$

but $\quad kH = T = $ coefficient of transmissibility

$$\therefore \quad Q = \frac{2.72 \cdot T\,(S_1' - S_2')}{\log_{10}(r_2/r_1)}$$

or

$$T = \left[\frac{Q}{2.72\,(S_1' - S_2')}\right]\left[\log_{10}\frac{r_2}{r_1}\right]$$

Assuming $(r_2/r_1) = 10$ so that $\log_{10}(10) = 1.00$

$$\therefore \quad T = \left[\dfrac{Q}{2.72\,(S_1' - S_2')}\right] = \dfrac{Q}{2.72 \cdot \Delta s}$$

Where $\Delta s = (S_1' - S_2')$ i.e. difference between the two values of S taken over one long cycle of distance r.

Case (ii) Confined Aquifer :

Referring to the Fig. 4.6.

We have for the well (1); $S_1 = H - h_1 =$ drawn down and $\therefore h_1 = H - S_1$

for the well (2), $S_2 = H - h_2 =$ draw down and $\therefore h_2 = H - S_2$

$\therefore \quad (h_2 - h_1) = (H - S_2) - (H - S_1)$

$\therefore \quad h_2 - h_1 = S_1 - S_2$

Now, substituting this value of $(h_2 - h_1) = (S_1 - S_2)$ in the equation

$$Q = \dfrac{2.72\,T\,(h_2 - h_1)}{\log_{10}(r_2/r_1)}$$

We get, $\quad Q = \dfrac{2.72\,T\,(S_2 - S_1)}{\log_{10}(r_2/r_1)}$

or rearranging $\quad T = \left[\dfrac{Q}{2.72\,(S_1 - S_2)}\right] \times \log_{10}(r_2/r_1)$

Again assuming $r_2/r_1 = 10$ $\therefore \log_{10}(10) = 1$

$\therefore \quad T = \dfrac{Q}{2.72\,(S_1 - S_2)} = \dfrac{Q}{2.72\,\Delta s}$

Where $\Delta s = S_1 - S_2 =$ draw down difference of wells (1) and (2) selected so that $r_2/r_1 = 10$.

4.10 WELL LOSSES, SPECIFIC CAPACITY OF WELLS AND EFFICIENCY OF WELL

4.10.1 Well Losses

When the pumping of water from the well takes place the draw down is not only due to the logarithmic draw down curve but is also due to draw down caused by flow of water through well screen and axial flow within the well. This latter loss is termed as well loss. Due to the presence of turbulent flow at the well face, the well loss is assumed as proportional to the (discharge)^n, where n is a constant which is greater than unity i.e. well losses = CQ^n.

Rewritting the equation,

$$Q = \dfrac{2\pi TS}{\log_e(R/r)}$$

i.e.
$$S = \frac{Q}{2\pi T} \log_e (R/r)$$

∴ Adding the well loss to the above equation, we may write
$$S = \frac{Q}{2\pi T} \log_e (R/r) + CQ^n$$

The value of C depends upon the condition of the well and its radius substituting $\frac{1}{2\pi T} \log_e (R/r) = B$.

∴ $S = QB + CQ^n$ (i.e. Aquifer losses + Well losses)

4.10.2 Specific Capacity

It is defined as 'yield or the discharge of the well per unit of draw down' i.e. specific capacity
$$= \frac{\text{Discharge}}{\text{Draw down}} = \frac{Q}{S}.$$

Thus, the specific capacity is equal to the specific draw down of a well substituting $S = QB + CQ^n$ in the above equation,

$$\text{Specific capacity} = \frac{Q}{QB + CQ^n} = \frac{(Q/Q)}{\left(\frac{QB + CQ^n}{Q}\right)}$$

$$= \left[\frac{1}{B + CQ^{n-1}}\right]$$

i.e. specific capacity decreases as the discharge increases.

4.10.3 Efficiency of Well

'It is the ratio of the actual specific capacity of the well ascertained in the field to the theoretical specific capacity'.

∴ $\quad \text{Efficiency} = \left[\frac{(Q/S)}{Q/BQ}\right] \times 100 = \frac{QB}{S} \times 100$

But $\quad S = BQ + CQ^n$

∴ $\quad \text{Efficiency} = \left(\frac{BQ}{BQ + CQ^n}\right) \times 100$

4.11 WELL IRRIGATION

A water well is usually a vertical hole excavated in the earth, for bringing the ground water to the surface. Wells may be classified as follows :

- Dug or open wells
- Tube wells

4.11.1 Dug or Open Wells

4.11.1.1 Introduction

It is the most common simplest type of well consisting of a pit mostly circular in section excavated little below the water table. The diameter of this well varies from 2 to 8 m and depth from 5 to 20 m and is suitable for discharges upto 5 litres/sec. It may be constructed of bricks, stones or pre-cast concrete rings of thickness from 0.4 to 0.7 m.

Open well may be classified as :

- Shallow well
- Deep well

A shallow well is excavated upto the pervious strata and draws its supplies from surrounding area. A deep well on the other hand rests on an impervious 'mota layer' and draws water from the pervious layer lying underneath the 'mota layer' through a hole bored into it.

The mota layer consists of clay, sand, and kankar and hard material etc. The mota layer helps in giving structural support to the well. The water may be lifted from the well by bucket and hoist or by a pump.

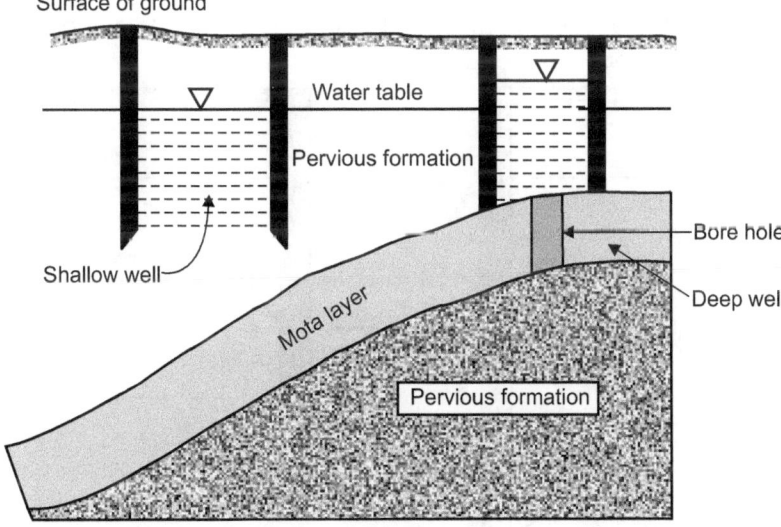

Fig. 4.7 : Schematic diagram of shallow and deep wells

Fig. 4.7 shows a schematic diagram of shallow and deep open wells. The open wells may be unlined, or provided with impervious or pervious lining. Temporary (also called as kachha) wells are constructed when the water table is near the ground surface. The life of such wells is very short.

Such wells are possible only in unconsolidated material. However, if more water is extracted, the water table may be lowered below the well bottom and well becomes useless. Wells provided with impervious lining are most common in use. The impervious lining of thickness 0.3 to 0.6 m given to such wells also provide stability to it.

The well curbs may be provided of wood, steel or R.C.C. The entry of water into such wells is from its bottom and the flow is not radial.

The wells with pervious lining are constructed in coarse grained formations. The dry bricks or stones without any binding material (i.e. mortar) serves as pervious lining. The flow in such cases is radial, if it is concreted at the bottom.

4.11.1.2 Yield of An Open Well

The yield of an open well, which differs from a tube well, is carried from following (two) tests :

(1) Constant level pumping test and

(2) Recuperation test

(1) Constant Level Pumping Test : As shown in Fig. 4.8, after the pumping, let the level of water be lowered by an amount h, called as *depression head*. The pumping is thereafter to be so adjusted that the constant level is maintained in the well after attaining the depression head (h). The quantity of water pumped out is actually measured by a notch or weir. The quantity of water pumped out under the steady state in one hour is called yield of the well per hour.

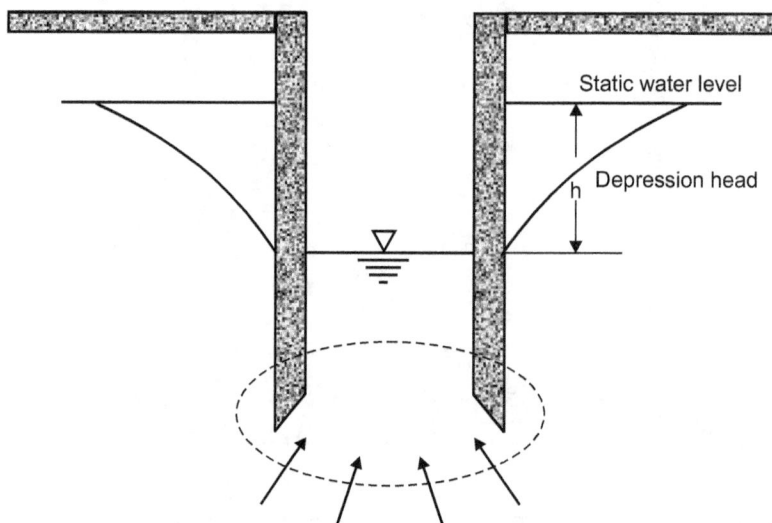

Fig. 4.8 : Pumping test (at constant level)

i.e. $Q = kAi$

$\qquad = k \cdot A \dfrac{h}{L}$

Putting,   k/L = C, percolation intensity coefficient

We may write,   Q = CAh

Due to the formation of cavity at the well bottom, the value of A is taken as $4/3^{rd}$ the area of cross-section at the bottom of the well. As the percolation head 'h' increases, the discharge also goes on increasing. The value of 'h' at which the velocity becomes critical is termed as *critical depression' head*. The working head is usually adjusted to $1/8^{th}$ of the critical head.

Maximum safe yield is the yield that corresponds to that under working head (h) and critical or maximum yield will be under the critical head.

(2) Recuperation Test : Even though the results obtained by constant pumping test are fairly accurate, it is however, sometimes difficult to adjust the pumping rate to maintain constant level of water in the well. In such cases, recuperation test is adopted.

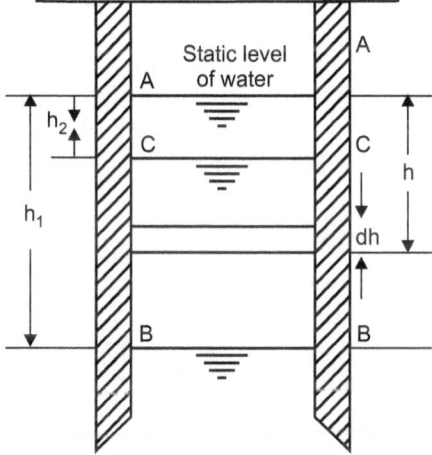

Fig. 4.9 : Recuperation test

In this test, the water level is depressed to a level below the normal water level and the pumping is stopped. There after the level of water will start rising. The total time required for the water to recover to its original normal level is recorded and the discharge or yield from the well is then computed as explained below. As shown in Fig. 4.9.

Let,   AA = Static water level before the starting of pump (in metres).

         BB = Water level in the pump after the pump was stopped (in metres).

         CC = Water level in the well after a time T after the stopping of the pump (in metres).

         h_1 = Depressed head in the well when the pumping was stopped (in metres).

         h_2 = Depression head after time T (in hours) after the pumping was stopped (in metres).

h = Depression head measured in the well at any time t in hours after pumping was stopped (in metres).

dh = Decrease in the depression head measured in time dt in hours.

As shown in the Fig., in the time t (in hours) after the pump was stopped, the level of water is recuperated (i.e. recovers) by vertical distance ($h_1 - h$) in metres. Further in time 'dt' is recuperated by dh metres.

Small volume of water dv that enters in the well in time dt is given as –

$$dv = A \cdot dh \qquad \ldots (4.5)$$

where, A = area of cross-section at the bottom of well

Now,

if Q = rate of discharge inside the well at the time t, under the depression head h, then volume of water entering the well in time dt will be –

$$dv = Q \cdot dt \qquad \ldots (4.6)$$

However as $Q \propto h$

i.e. $Q = kh$

where k is a constant that depends upon the nature of the soil at the bottom of the well through which water enters into the well then,

$$dv = kh \cdot dt \qquad \ldots (4.7)$$

∴ Equating the equation (4.5) and (4.7), we may write

$khdt = -Adh$, the negative sign indicates that as t increases, the value of h decreases

Rearranging $\quad dt = -\dfrac{A}{k} \cdot \dfrac{dh}{h} \quad$ or $\quad \dfrac{k}{A} dt = -\dfrac{dh}{h}$

Integrating the above expression between the limits –

at $\qquad t = 0, \; h = h_1$ and
at $\qquad t = T, \; h = h_2$

∴ $$\dfrac{k}{A} \int_0^T dt = \int_{h_1}^{h_2} -\dfrac{dh}{h}$$

or $$\left(\dfrac{k}{A}\right) \cdot T = (\log_e h)_{h_2}^{h_1}$$

i.e. $$\dfrac{k}{A} = \dfrac{1}{T} \log_e \left(\dfrac{h_1}{h_2}\right)$$

∴ $$\dfrac{k}{A} = \left(\dfrac{2.303}{T}\right) \log_{e} \left(\dfrac{h_1}{h_2}\right) \qquad \ldots (4.8)$$

The term $\dfrac{k}{A}$ on the left hand side of expression is called as specific capacity or specific yield of an open well and is defined as the volume of water which percolates into well measured in cubic metres per hour per square metre area of percolation under unit depression head. However, the following table which gives approximate values of $\frac{k}{A}$ as suggested by Marriot may be used when such a test cannot be carried out.

Sr. No.	Type of Soil	Value of $\frac{k}{A}$ (Measured in m³ per Hour per Square Metre Area Operating at 1 Metre Depression Head)
1.	Clay	0.25
2.	Sand (fine)	0.50
3.	Sand (coarse)	1.0

Thus, after the values of h_1, h_2 and T are known from recuperation test, the value of $\frac{k}{A}$ (i.e. specific yield) can be determined as explained below :

$$\therefore \quad Q = kH = \left(\frac{k}{A}\right) A.H.$$

Substituting, the value of $\frac{k}{A}$ from above expression

$$Q = \frac{2.303}{T} \log_{10}\left(\frac{h_1}{h_2}\right) \cdot A \cdot H \text{ (m}^3\text{/hour)}$$

Notes :
- It is to be remembered that if the value of T in the above equation is taken in hours, then Q will be in m³/hour and if it is taken in seconds, then Q will be in m³/sec.
- The discharge Q, corresponding to maximum depression head H_m is called as *maximum yield* of the well.
- For the mean or average depression head, H_a the discharge Q is known as *average yield*.

4.12 TUBE WELL

4.12.1 Introduction

It consists of a long pipe driven into the ground that passess through one or more water bearing layers or strata. It is provided with a strainer so that only water will pass trhough it and will prevent the entry of coarse material sand etc. into it. The diameter of tube well which is very small varies from 100 mm to 600 mm. As the flow of water towards the well is radial and more area of section will contribute to the flow, the discharge from tube well is much more as compared to an open well. A tube well may be shallow (depth upto 30 m) or deep (depth upto 600 m).

4.12.2 Types of Tube Wells

The tube wells may be of the following three types.

    (1) Strainer type   (2) Cavity type   (3) Slotted type

(1) Strainer Type Tube Well : This type of tube well is so common that the word 'tube well' generally used refers to the strainer type only. It is made up of strainers and blind pipes which are arranged (as shown in the Fig. 4.10) in such a way the former rests against water bearing strata (i.e. aquifer) and the latter passes through the impervious strata or layer (called as aquicludes). The strainer in general consists of a (special variety of) wire mesh, wrapped round the pipe provided with slots or perforations. In order to maintain constant velocity of flow, the total area of openings in the slotted pipe is kept same as the area of openings of strainers.

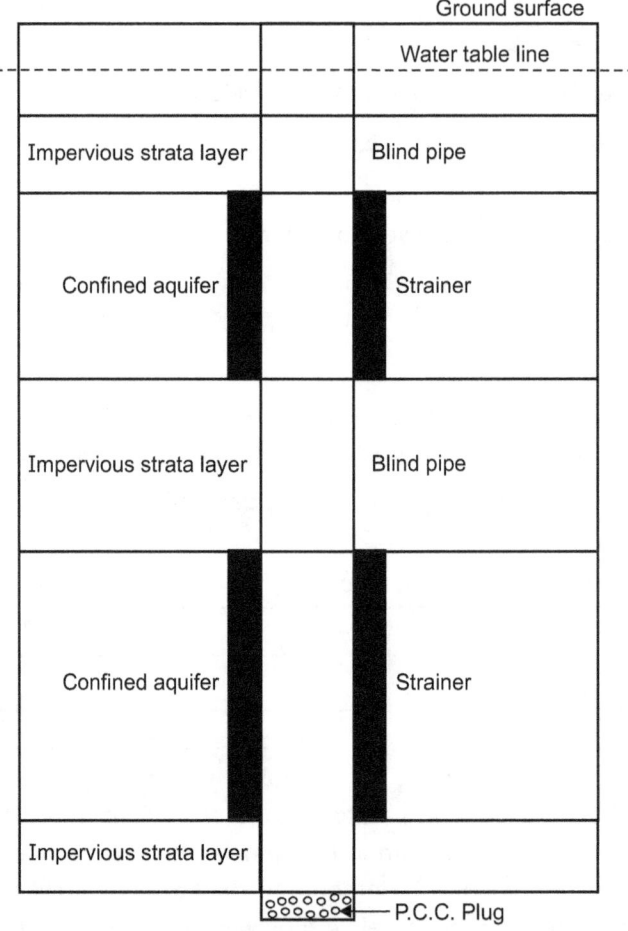

Fig. 4.10 : Strainer (Type) tube well

The strainers permits only the water to flow into it and thus prevents the entry of sand particles into the well. The mesh size of strainer is usually equal to D_{60} to D_{70} of the surrounding soil. The strainer type of tube well draws water from both unconfined aquifer of unlimited extent or from (one or more) confined aquifer strata. A short blind pipe provided at the bottom of the tube well collects the sand particles, that may enter the strainer. The well is plugged at the bottom by a layer of plain cement concrete. A special type of strainer tube well having a well pipe diameter of 1.5" (37.5 mm) and strainer of length 4 to 5 ft. (1.2 to 1.5 m) is known as *Abyssinian tube well*. The material used for strainers may be steel, brass, stainless steel, thermoplastics etc.

- **Types of Strainers (for strainer type tube wells) :** The strainers commonly used for tube wells may be as follows :
  (a) Cook strainer (USA made)
  (b) Tej strainer (Indian made)
  (c) Brownlie strainer
  (d) Ashford strainer
  (e) Legget strainer
  (f) Phoenix strainer (Chemical resistant)
  (g) Layne and Bowler strainer

A brief description of above types of strainers is given in a tabular form on the next page.

- **Brief Description of Various Types of Strainers**

Sr. No.	Cook Strainer	Tej Strainer	Brownile Strainer	Ashoford Strainer	Legget Strainer	Phoenix Strainer	Layne and Bowler Strainer
(1)	It is a soild drawn brass tube with wedge shaped horizontal slots.	It consists of a brass tube manufactured from brass sheet bent round to form the tube.	It is manufactured from a polygonal steel convoluted perforated plates surrounded by a copper wire mesh.	It is a perforated tube a wire that surrounds it.	In this type a cleaning device in provided.	It is made up of m.s. tube.	It is a wedge shapped steel wire wound to a suitable pitch round a perforated steel or W.I. pipe.

Contd...

(2)	Slots are wider towards inside and narrower at outside.	The vertical joints are brazed. The slots are made before bending.	The mesh consists of heavy parallel copper wires woven with copper ribbens.	A wire mesh is soldered above the tube that maintains the mesh away from the tube.	The cleaning device has the shape of a cutter.	The slots in this case are cut from inner side.	The joining of strainer pipes is done by screwed collars.
(3)	The gauge of the solts will depend upon coarseness of the surrounding material and varies from 0.15 to 0.4 mm.	Manufactured in our country from 7.5 cm diameter brass sheet of 2.5 m length.	The wire mesh is kept away from the main tube.	The wire mesh is protected and also strengthened by a wire net around it.	The cutters are operated from the ground surface.	The tube is plated with cadmium.	It is a robust type of strainer, mostly used for extracting oils.
(4)	It is USA patented and costly.	Widely used in our country	It is considered as the best available strainer.	As the strainer is declicate it required proper care during its handling.	By turning the cutters the slits in the strainers can be cleared off the clogged material.	Due to the cadmium plating the tube is kept free from choking and corrosion that may be caused by chemical action.	It is a USA patented strainer.

(2) Cavity Type Tube Well : As the name suggests, it draws water from the cavity formed at the bottom of the well and not from the sides of the strainer. Here when the tube well starts pumping initially fine clay mixed with water is extracted and strong cavity is formed at the bottom through which the water (from the pervious layer) enters the tube well. Formation of the large cavity at the bottom ultimately decreases the radial velocity of flow and stops the entry of sand particles into the tube well and then a clean water starts coming out of the tube well.

The drawback of this type of tube well is that since water is drawn from the bottom portion it can tap water from only one pervious layers (i.e. aquifer) at a time, i.e. cavity type of tube well is similar to deep open well. The aquifer from where the water is to be pumped should have sufficient good specific yield. The discharge through the strainer tube well can be increased by increasing the length of strainer pipe but in the cavity type tube well, the area of cavity at the bottom will have to be increased for pumping more water. (See Fig. 4.14)

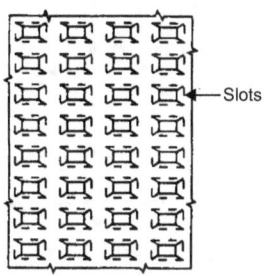

Fig. 4.11 : Cooks strainer

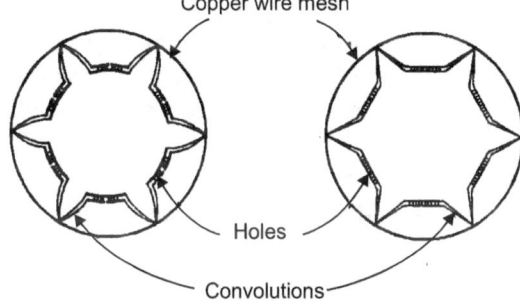

Fig. 4.12 : Brown-lie strainer

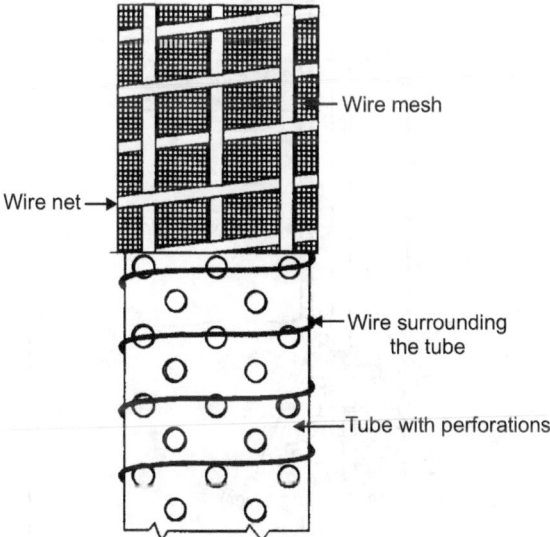

Fig. 4.13 : Ashford strainer

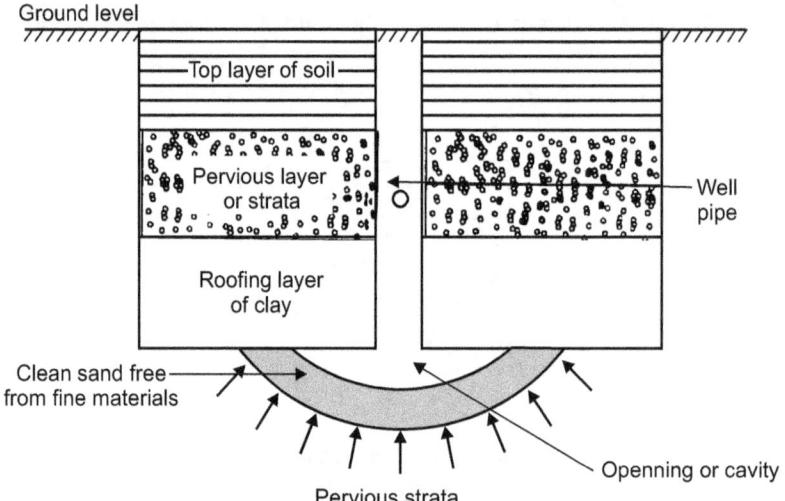
Fig. 4.14 : Cavity type tube well arrangement

(3) Slotted Type Tube Well (Fig. 4.15) : It consists of a slotted pipe penetrating the confined aquifer, the size of the slots being 25 mm × 3 mm and are spaced 10 to 12 mm apart.

The entry of fine sand particles into the pipe is prevented by 'Shrouding'. The shrouding consists of a mixture of gravel and coarsed sand that surround the slotted portion of the well pipe.

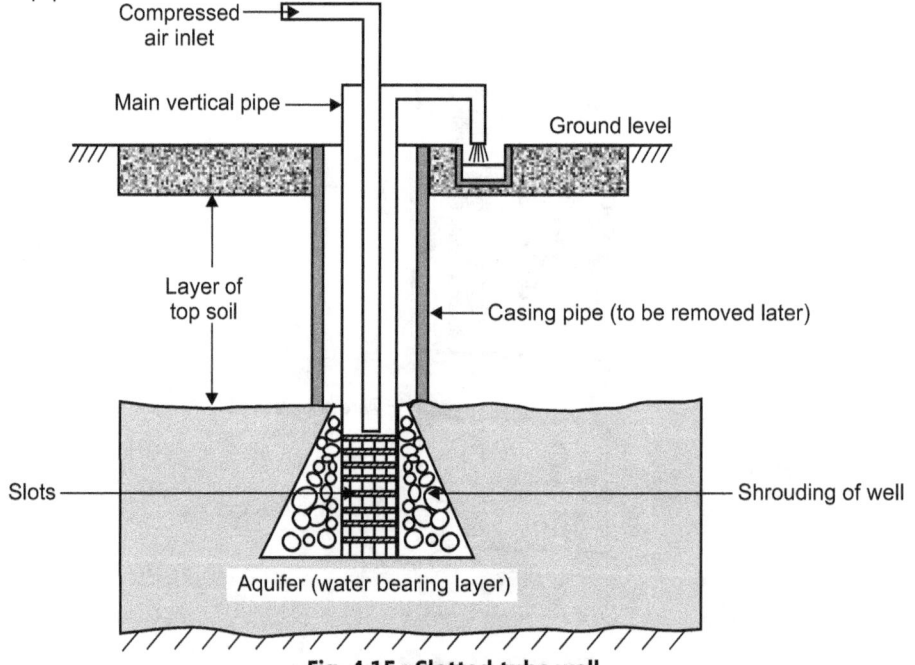
Fig. 4.15 : Slotted tube well

The main difference between the slotted type tube well and strainer type tube well is an follows :

Straomer Type Tube Well	Slotted Type Tube Well
(1) The wire mesh that surround the strainer pipes prevent the entry of sand particles into the tube.	(1) The gravel and coarse sand (i.e. shrouding) surrounding the well pipe prevents the entry of sand into the pipe.
(2) The strainer type tube well, at one time, can tap one or more confined aquifers.	(2) As the slotted length of the pipe is provided only at the bottom, it can tap water from only one aquifer at a time.

4.13 CONSTRUCTION (OR DRILLING) OF TUBE WELLS

In order to insert a tube well into the ground, for withdrawing water, it is necessary to bore a hole of slightly larger in size than the diameter of the tube well pipe.

The tube well may be either a shallow or deep and accordingly the methods of constructions differ.

4.13.1 Shallow Tube Wells

The shallow tube wells are constructed by :

   (1) Boring   (2) Driven wells,   (3) Wash boring method

4.13.1.1 Boring

The bored wells may be excavated in unconsolidated material where water table is found at shallow depths. The three common types of earth augers employed for boring are 'bucket augers', 'solid stein augers' and 'hollow stem augers'. They excavate the material by means of cutting blades provided at the end of a drilling rod or pipe. In case of 'bucket auger' the excavated material is collected in a cylindrical bucket provided with cutting blades. After the bucket becomes full, it is lifted from the hole and the excavated material is dumped out.

In case of 'solid stem' and hollow-stem augers, the excavated material from the bottom is lifted from the hole by the use of spiral flange known as *flighting*. Each section of the auger is called flight as shown in the Fig. 4.16. Holes of diameters 15 cm to 35 cm with a depth upto 45 m can be bored by such augers.

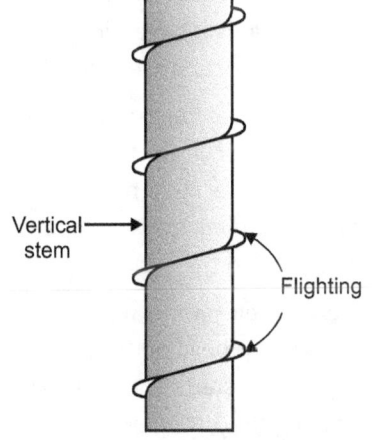

Fig. 4.16 : Auger fighting

4.13.1.2 By Driven Wells

A driven well of about 10 cm in diameter and 20 m deep can be constructed by the use of 'well point' in an unconsolidated material. A well point essentially consists of a perforated pipe having pointed end (i.e. driven point) at the bottom for driving it into the unconsolidated soil (Fig. 4.17).

It is driven into the ground by power driven drop hammers. As the well point is driven into the ground additional lengths of pipes can be connected to it by means of threaded couplings. This process is to be continued, till the required stratum of aquifer is reached by the well point. Due to its limitations of size i.e. (diameter) and depth, they are usually adopted for small domestic colonies, or for temporary supplies of water. A series of such well points may be used to increase the quantity of water to be lifted. The merits of this method are that it can be constructed in the shortest possible time with minimum cost.

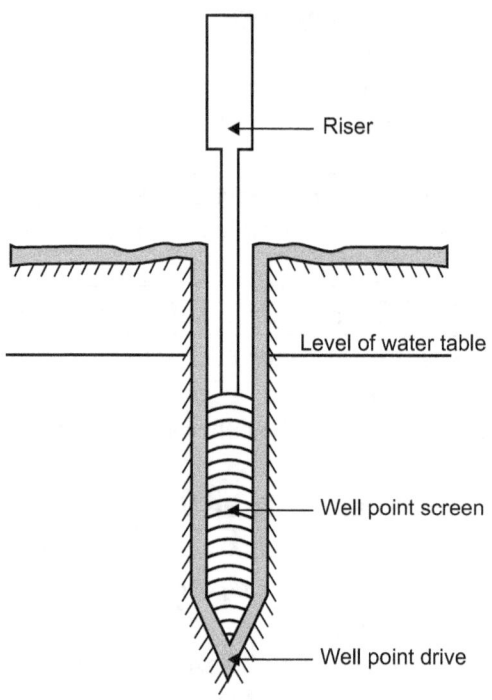

Fig. 4.17 : Well point system

4.13.1.3 Wash Boring Method or Jetted Method

In this method, a high velocity of jet of water is used for boring purposes. The method in short consists in first erecting the outer casing pipe in a suitably dug trench and then jet pipe with a nozzle is lowered into it. A jet of water with high velocity is then forced through the jetted pipe to loosen the soil in the hole.

These loose particles mixed with water (which is called as slurry) is then lifted up by the water that comes up from the annular space between casing and jetting pipes. The casing pipe with a shoe at the bottom is then lowered into the hole. After the casing pipe penetrates the aquifer the well pipe with a strainer is lowered into it and the outer casing is then pulled out and the annular space is filled with gravel.

Alternatively, a self jetting well point system may also be adopted (Fig. 4.18). In this case instead of casing pipe, a perforated brass tube ending into a nozzle is screwed at the end. As the jetting action starts the well pipe goes on sinking. When the well pipe sinks to the desired aquifer, the jetting action is discontinued, and the annular space is filled with gravel.

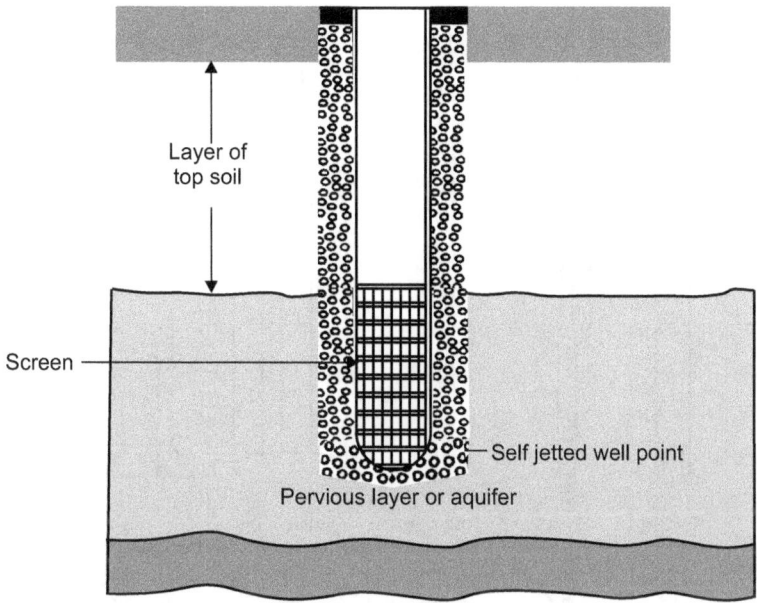

Fig. 4.18 : Well point self jetting type

4.13.2 Deep Tube Wells

The deep wells are constructed by drilling as stated below :

(1) Cable tool method (or percussion method) (2) Hydraulic rotary method (3) Reverse rotary method

A brief description of the above methods is as given below :

4.13.2.1 Cable Tool Method (or Percussion Method or Standard Method)

The common method adopted for drilling deep tube wells (of diameter 40 cm and upto a depth of 1500 m) through consolidated rock materials is by the use of cable tool rig. The well hole is drilled by hammering and cutting action at the bottom by means of heavy drill bit suspended from a cable which is raised and lowered alternatively in the hole. Sufficient quantity of water is introduced as required so that the crushed material can be lifted at intervals by a bailer made up of a hollow tube with a flap valve at the lower end.

A portable standard well drilling rig consists of a multi-line hoist, a walking beam and an engine properly assembled and mounted on the truck. The entire string of tools consists of a rope socket, a set of jars, a drill stem and the drilling bit. These drilling bits are available in lengths of 1 to 3 m, weighing upto 1500 Kgf.

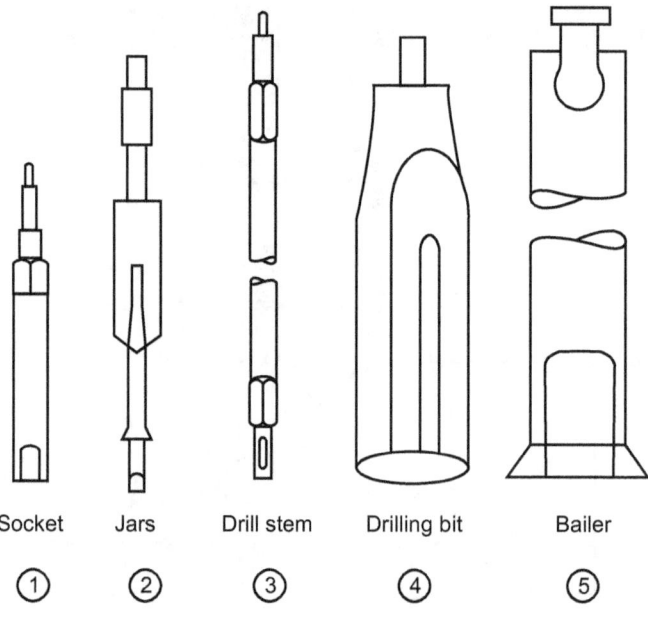

Fig. 4.19 (a) : (Percussion or) Cable tool equipments

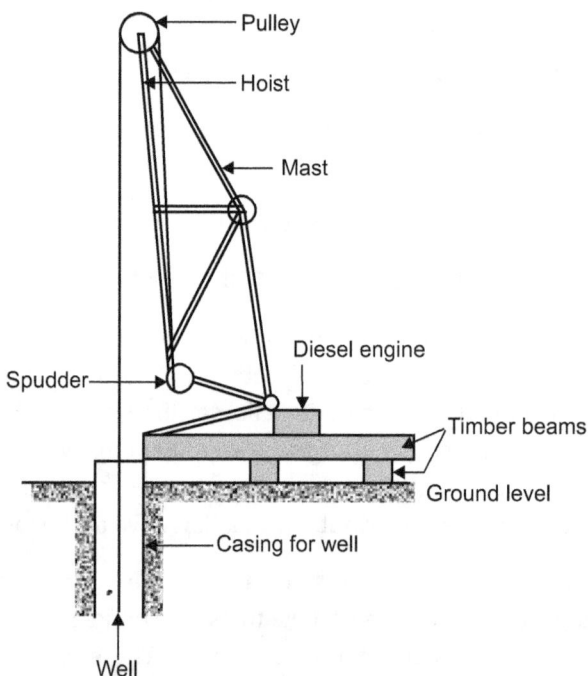

Fig. 4.19 (b) : Sketch showing various components of percussion drilling system

At first, a pit of about 2.5 m diameter and 6 metre deep is excavated at the site where the tube is to be constructed and a casing pipe with a cutter shoe at its bottom is inserted into the pit. The spring of tools is then introduced into the casing pipe and then the drilling is carried out mechanically by alternate lifting and dropping the (drilling) bit into the hole. In this process, the tools make about 40 strokes per minute, ranging from 0.4 to 1 m in length the drilling line being kept rotating to form a circular hole. After the bit has penetrated to about 1.5 m depth through the formation, the entire string of tools is taken out and a bailer (Fig. 4.20) which consists of a section of pipe with a flap valve, is inserted into the hole to the cutting materials. The valve at the bottom of the bailer gets automatically opened due to the upward thrust of the cutting material mixed with water and reaches the bailer. The valve also prevents the above mixture from moving downwards during lifting. When the bailer gets filled, it is lifted to the surface and emptied. The bailers may be upto 10 m in length having a capacity of about 0.2 m³. After removing the cuttings, the string of tools are reinstated into the hole and the process of drilling is repeated till the required depth is achieved.

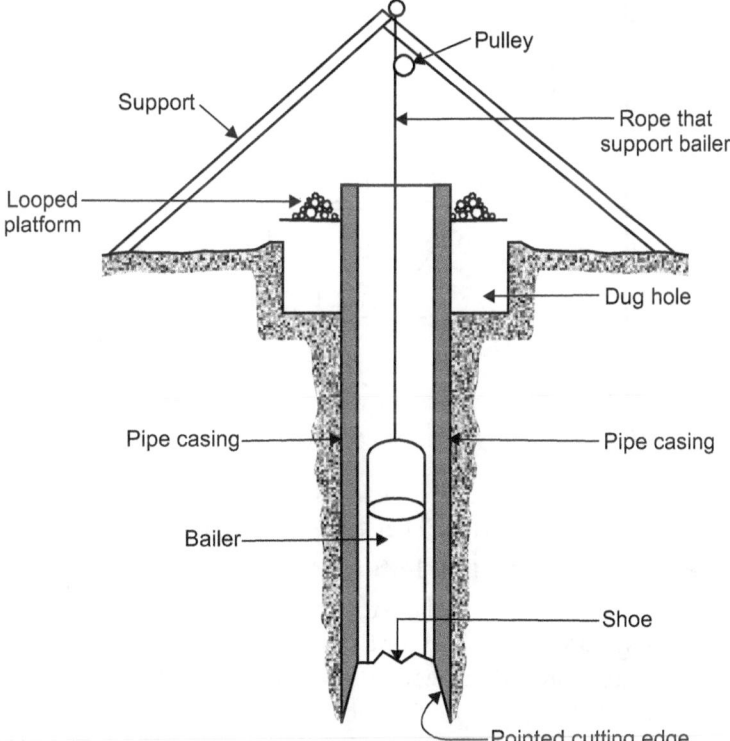

Fig. 4.20 : (Percussion) Boring by the use of bailer

In unconsolidated soil formation, casing is driven as the hole is drilled by attaching drive clamps fastened to the drill stem. The vertical (up and down) movement of the tools transferred to the top of casing, enables it to drive in downward direction.

4.13.2.2 Hydraulic Rotary Method

Large diameter, deep wells in unconsolidated formation are constructed by the fastest method of rotary drilling. In this method, a bit attached at the end of the string of hollow pipe is continuously rotated to drill the hole. At the time of drilling a mixture of clay and water i.e. drilling mud is continuously forced through the drilling pipe into the hole. The cuttings of the bit are carried up in the hole by the rising mud. Usually, no casing is required during drilling as the mud itself forms a clay lining on the walls of the hole to prevent casing. The arrangement of drilling rig for hydraulic rotary methods as shown in the Fig. 4.21 essentially consists of a mast (or derrick), a rotating table, a pump for inserting mud a hoist and the engine. The mud as it flows out of the hole is carried to a settling tank where the cutting settles at the bottom and the mud is reused for pumping into the hole. After the drilling is completed the casing is inserted into the hole, the clay deposits into the well are washed away by water. After the washing is completed, at this level, the bit is again raised and the process of drilling is repeated till the required depth is achieved.

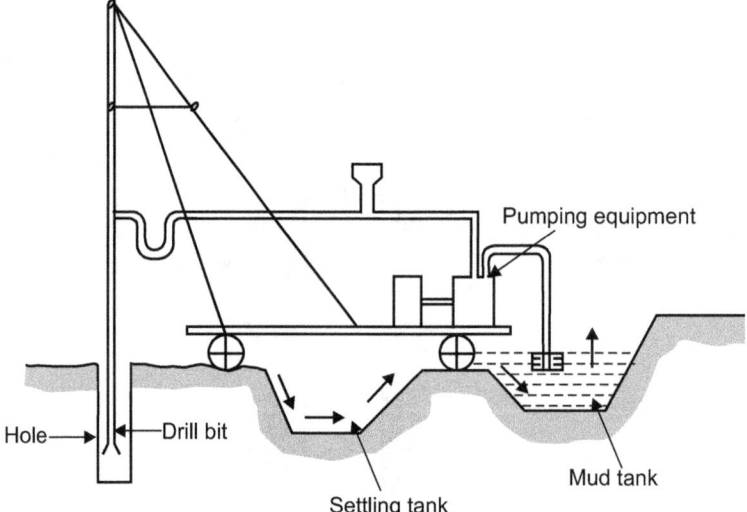

Fig. 4.21 : (Hydraulic) Rotary drilling method

4.13.2.3 Reverse Rotary Method (i.e. Jetting Method)

Reverse rotary method is quite similar to the hydraulic rotary method with little modifications. It is most popular method for drilling large wells upto 1.5 metres in diameter and over 1500 metres deep in unconsolidated soil formations. The drilling arrangement for this method is quite similar to the hydraulic drilling method. In this method, the water moves down to the bit through the annular space and the cuttings are extracted by water through the drilling pipe. These contents are further carried to a settling tank where the cuttings drops down and clear water on the top is repumped into the hole. The walls of the drilled hole are supported by hydrostatic pressure acting against the film of fine grained material resting on the walls by the drilling water.

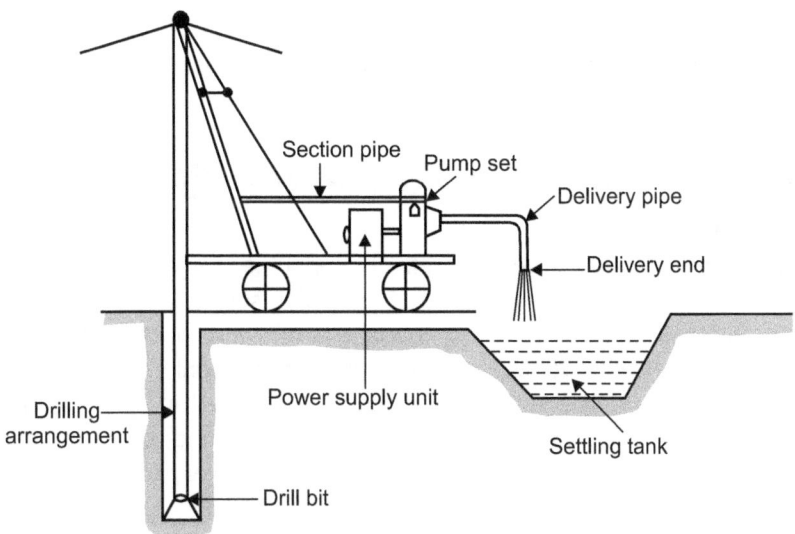

Fig. 4.22 : Reverse rotary type system

The casing and cleaning operations are similar to the hydraulic rotary method.

It may be noted that hydraulic rotary method is the faster method used to drill larger holes than the cable tool method. However for drilling shallow holes, the cable tool method is found to be economical. Moreover, the cable tool method (being mounted on the truck) is portable and requires less amount of water for its entire process (as compared to hydraulic rotary method).

4.14 WELL COMPLETION AND ITS MAINTENANCE

In the previous Article 4.12 the various methods of drilling shallow and deep tube wells have been discussed in details. However mere drilling of holes does not complete the job of construction of wells. Except in cases of wells drilled in sound hard consolidated rocks, it is necessary to protect it from collapsing by providing a suitable casing. Moreover to permit entry of water into the tube well, it should be covered with perforated or slotted casings. The casing commonly adopted may be of steel and thermoplastics.

There are two ways of providing the casings. In the first case the casing is introduced as the work of drilling is in progress as seen in case of cable-tool methods. In the second case, the casing is inserted into the position after the entire drilling work is over such as in case of rotary drilling method. The slotted or perforated casing may be made of steel, brass, fibreglass or thermoplastics etc. After this casing is inserted in position, the well is developed by pumping at very high rate. The agitated material surrounding the casing and the mud slurry still remaining move inside the well and is taken out by pumping. This operation enables the water to flow freely towards the well and the yield from the well increases.

In order to maintain the tube well in good working condition, it should never be pumped at excessive rate (i.e. more than its specified rate). Such an excessive pumping results in the movement of the fine particles in aquifer and choking of the casings and ultimate failure of the pumping equipment. As regards leakage arising due corrosion of casing, the entire casing may be replaced if possible. However, in case of tube wells drilled in unconsolidated materials, replacement of casing may not be possible and the well will have to be abandoned.

4.15 WELL SHROUDING AND WELL DEVELOPMENT

4.15.1 Well Shrouding

The operation of interposing a layer of coarse material (i.e. gravel and coarse sand) in the annular space between the well-pipe and the aquifer soil is called as *'shrouding'*. The purpose of shrouding is to prevent fine soil particles coming in contact with the strainer and ultimately choking it. The shrouding also assists in permitting only the water, without sand, to flow into the well pipe. The shrouding is specially required in case of unconsolidated sandy formations of aquifer and also for slotted type of tube wells not provided with screens. Such shrouded tube wells are sometimes called as gravel packed wells.

4.15.2 Well Development

It is defined as 'the process of removing the fine material from the formations that surround the strainer pipe'. The purpose of well development is to increase its specific capacity, prevent the fine sand from flowing into it and to attain its maximum economic life. Once the screen is inserted the well is to be developed by any one of the following processes.
- By pumping the well at very high rate or
- Surging the well with plunger, or
- Jetting the entire screen either with water or compressed air.

The above methods help in agitating the material surrounding the screen and also any drilled slurry material still remaining inside the well that forces the finer materials to enter the well and which is subsequently pumped out of the well, till free and clean water starts flowing out of the well. The development of the well as explained above results in increasing the yield from the given well without any losses. The various methods of well development commonly adopted are as follows :
- Pumping method
- Surging method
- Compressed air method
- Back washing method and
- Dry ice method

A brief description of various methods of development are given below in a tabular form.

4.16 RADIAL WELLS OR COLLECTORS

All the wells described above are drilled vertical. However sometimes the wells are driven horizontally or with a slight upward slope into the hilly portion till it encounters the water table. The advantage of such types of well is that water can be conveyed to a place situated at lower level without pumping and moreover such wells are easier to construct. The maintenance cost of such wells is also very less. However, the initial investment of construction of such wells is much more as compared to tube wells.

A typical horizontal radial well or collector is as shown in Fig. 4.23. It is constructed of R.C.C.

casing of about 5 to 6 m in diameter driven into the aquifer to the desired depth. Horizontal screened pipes of lengths 30 to 300 m as shown in the Fig., spread radially (at the bottom) depending upon local conditions of the strata. Such wells are installed in the vicinity of the natural rivers, where they induce and increase the rate of percolation from the stream and recharge ground water table. Such collector wells are adopted in case of highly permeable aquifer having small thickness. The arrangement of radial pipe lines increases the yield from the well considerably.

Methods of Development of Wells

Pumping Method (1)	Surging Method (2)	Compressed air Method (3)	Back washing Method (4)	Dry ice Method (5)
The method consists in using a variable speed pump that agitates the small particles that surround the well, so that it enters the well and is then pumped out. The pumping is carried out in steps so that after all the materials are removed, a clear water starts flowing out.	The method consists in creating surging action to the water in the well by up and down movement of the surge block. During the upward movement of the surge block the water is sucked and bailed out. The process is to be repeated till all the materials i.e. sand particles are practically removed and the clearer water starts flowing from the well.	The method consists in using a compressed air that enters the air pipe inserted into the discharge pipe which moves into the tube well. The sudden entry of compressed air into the well generates surges that help in loosening of particles that surround the strainer and helps in increasing the pressure. The water with loosened particles entres the well when the air pressure falls. The water with fine material is then pumped out till a clear water starts flowing.	The method consists in sealing the well at the top to make it air-tight and is provided with three way cock. The compressor, the air pipe and discharge pipe are inserted in the way as explained in the method (3), with a little change i.e. end of air pipe is slightly above the discharge pipe. Initially as the air enters the air pipe that results in air and water flowing out of the well through the discharge pipe. The valve is closed and clear water comes out. This increases the level of water in the well. The valve is then turned in such a way that air starts flowing through the air pipe and this back washes the water from the well and also agitation process starts and the water comes out. The process is repeated till a clear water starts coming out of well.	The method consists in using hydrochloric acid and dry ice for the devleopment process. At first, acid is poured into the well and the well is capped at the tope and the compressed air is allowed to enter into the well. This results in entering the acid into the adjoining well formation. The dry ice is then inserted into the well after removing the cap. This results in the release of CO_2 that generates high pressure. Thereafter, the water with sand comes out and finally clear water flows out.

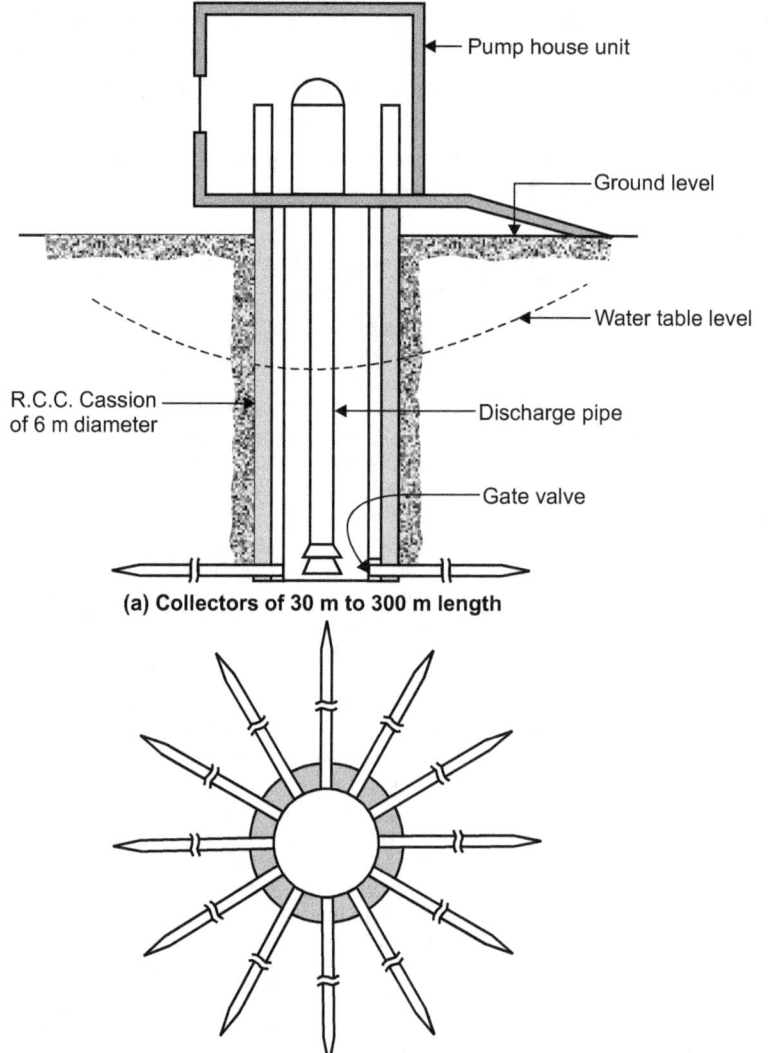

(a) Collectors of 30 m to 300 m length

(b) Plan showing collector radial pipes

Fig. 4.23 : Radial wells or collectors

4.17 COMPARISON BETWEEN (TUBE) WELL IRRIGATION AND CANAL IRRIGATION SYSTEMS

The two systems of irrigation i.e. well irrigation and canal irrigation have their own merits and demerits as stated below :

(A) Merits of Well Irrigation (over Canal Irrigation) :
- Well irrigation can be adopted for irrigating any isolated remote agricultural land.
- As wells belong to private owners, they can be driven constructed and efficiently managed by such owners.

- A fairly constant discharge can be maintained by well irrigation.
- The conveyance losses in well irrigation are considerably less as compared to canal irrigation.
- An area where water table has been considerably increased due to canal irrigation can advantageously be used for well irrigation which ultimately will lower the ground water table.
- The duty of water under well irrigation will be higher as compared to canal irrigation (because of reduction in transit losses).
- The well water being cool in hot weather and warm in cold weather is more suitable for the growth of the crops.
- The well irrigation system is less expensive as compared to the entire canal system.
- Well irrigation is not affected by ordinary drought conditions.

(B) Demerits of Well Irrigation :

- Failure of electric power and/or mechanical defects in the pumping system may result in the irregular supply of water to the crops.
- Maintenance and repair charges of machinery under well irrigation are high as compared to gravity canal system.
- Daily working expenses of lifting water from the well are considerably high.
- As the tube well becomes old, the strainers get choked and the yield from such wells gets reduced considerably.
- The well water being clean does not contain any manures and as such, it is inferior to canal irrigation water (that contains silt and manure).
- Well irrigation is not suitable for very large command areas as the yield from the wells is limited.

SOLVED PROBLEMS

Problem 4.1 : A 50 cm diameter well completely penetrates a confined aquifer of permeability 2 m/hr. The thickness of aquifer is 20 m. Under steady state of pumping, the draw down at the well was found to be 3.00 m and the radius of influence was 300 m. Calculate the discharge. What would be the percentage increase in the discharge, if the diameter of the well is increased to 75 cm ?

Solution : Using Dupits Equation

$$Q_{(initial)} = \frac{2.72 \, Kbs}{\log_{10}(R/r)}$$

Here $K = 2$ m/hour, $b = 20$ m, $s = 3$ m, $R = 300$ m, $r = \frac{0.50}{2} = 0.25$.

$$\therefore \quad Q_{(initial)} = \frac{2.72 \times 2 \times 20 \times 3}{\log_{10}\left(\frac{300}{0.25}\right)}$$

$$= 106 \text{ m}^3/\text{hour} = 0.0294 \text{ m}^3/\text{sec}$$

In the second case :

$$Q \text{ (fo 0.75 m diameter well)} = \frac{2.72 \times 2 \times 20 \times 3}{\log_{10}\left(\frac{300}{0.375}\right)} = 112.3 \text{ m}^3/\text{hour}$$

$$= 0.0312 \text{ m}^3/\text{sec}$$

$$\therefore \quad \frac{\text{Percentage increase}}{\text{in discharge}} = \frac{0.0312 - 0.0294}{0.0294} \times 100 = 6.10\%$$

Problem 4.2 : *A tube well fully penetrates in a confined aquifer of thickness 30 m and having a permeability coefficient of 38 m/day. Determine the radius of the tube well if the yield required is 40 lit/sec, under a draw down of 4 m. Use radius of influence circle as recommended by Sichardt.*

Solution : Using Sichardt equation for radius of influence R

$$R = 3000 \, S \sqrt{K}$$

Where,   K = coefficient of permeability in m/sec

            S = draw down in m

$$R = 3000 \times 4 \times \sqrt{\frac{38}{24 \times 60 \times 60}}$$

$$= 3000 \times 4 \times \sqrt{4.398 \times 10^{-4}}$$

$$= 251.66 \text{ m}$$

Now, using Dupits equation for the confined aquifer

$$Q = \frac{2.72 \, K \cdot b \cdot s}{\log_{10} R/r}$$

Where,   b = thickness of confined aquifer (m)

            R = radius of influence (m)

            r = radius of the tube well (m)

and   Q = 40 lit/sec = 40×10^{-3} m^3/sec

$$\therefore \quad 40 \times 30^{-3} = \frac{2.72 \times 4.398 \times 10^{-4} \times 30 \times 4}{\log_{10}\left[\frac{251.66}{r}\right]}$$

$$\therefore \quad r = 0.0645 \text{ m} = 6.46 \text{ cm}$$

Problem 4.3 : Calculate the diameter of the well that will have a discharge of 200 litre/sec with a draw down of 6 m excavated in a confined aquifer having thickness of 40 m. The radius of influence (R) is 300 m and the coefficient of permeability (K) 80 m/day.

Solution :

$$Q = \frac{2.72 \, K.b.s.}{\log_{10}(R/r)}$$

= Discharge through a well in confined aquifer

Here, $K = \frac{80}{24 \times 60 \times 60}$, b = 40 m, s = 6 m, R = 300 m, r = ?

$$\therefore \quad 200 \times 10^{-3} = \frac{\left[2.72 \times \left(\frac{80}{24 \times 60 \times 60}\right) \times 6\right]}{\log_{10}[300/r]}$$

∴ Solving for r, we get r = 0.29 m = 29 cm.
∴ Diameter of the well = D = 2r = 58 cm.

Problem 4.4 : During a recuperation test the water level in an open well was depressed by 3.5 m and is recuperated by 1.5 m in 60 minutes. Determine :

(i) The yield from a well 4.5 m diameter under a depression head of 4.5 m and
(ii) Diameter of well to yield 20 litres/second under a depression head of 3.00 m.

Solution : Data : S_1 = 3.5, S_2 = 1.5 m, Time = T = 60 min.

∴ Using the equation $\frac{C}{A} = \frac{2.3}{T} \log_{10}\left(\frac{S_1}{S_2}\right) = \left(\frac{2.3}{60}\right) \log\left(\frac{3.5}{1.5}\right)$

∴ C = 0.01411 A ... (i)

Now in the first case S = 4.5, diameter = d = 4.5 m.

$$\therefore \quad A = \frac{\pi}{4} \times d^2$$

$$= 0.7854 \times (4.5)^2 = 15.90 \, m^2$$

Now, Q = CS
Where C = 0.01411 A,

A = 0.01411 × 15.90
= 0.01411 × 15.90 × 4.50
= 0.0168 m³/sec = 16.8 litres/sec

In the second case, S = 3 m, Q = 20 lit/sec = 0.02 m³/sec

Q = CS
∴ Q = CS = 0.01411 × A × 3 = 0.02
∴ A = 28.35 m² = $\frac{\pi}{4} \times d^2$
∴ A = 6.0 m.

Problem 4.5 : *A well penetrate into an unconfined aquifer having a saturated depth of 30 m. The discharge is 100 litres per minute at 3 m draw down in the well. Assuming equilibrium flow condition and homogeneous aquifer, estimate the discharge at 5 m draw down in the well. Assume radius of influence as same in both the conditions.*

Solution : In the first case

$$Q_1 = \frac{\pi K (H^2 - h^2)}{2.3 \log_{10}(R/r)}$$

$$= \frac{\pi K [30^2 - 27^2]}{2.3 \log_{10}(R/r)}$$

$$\therefore \left[\frac{2.3 \log_{10}(R/r)}{\pi K}\right] = \left[\frac{(30^2 - 27^2)}{100 \times 10^{-3}}\right] = \frac{171}{100} \quad \ldots (i)$$

In the second case, $\quad Q_2 = \dfrac{\pi K (H^2 - h^2)}{2.3 \log (R/r)}$

$$\therefore \frac{2.3 \log(R/r)}{\pi K} = \frac{(30^2 - 25^2)}{Q_2} = \frac{275}{Q_2} \quad \ldots (ii)$$

Since the left hand side of both the equation (i) and (ii) are same, equating (i) and (ii).

$$\frac{171}{100} = \frac{275}{Q_2}$$

$$\therefore \quad Q_2 = 160.818 \text{ litre/sec}$$

Problem 4.6 : *During a recuperation test of an open well, the water level was depressed by pumping 4 metres and pumping was stopped. The recuperation was observed to be 1 m in 4 hour. Determine the yield from the well if the diameter of the well is 3.00 m and the draw down is 2.5 m.*

Solution : Using the formula,

$$\frac{C}{A} = \left(\frac{2.3}{T}\right) \log_{10} \frac{S_1}{S_2}$$

where $S_1 = 4$ m, $S_2 = 4 - 1 = 3$ m, $T = 4 \times 60 \times 60 = 14400$ sec.

$$\therefore \quad \frac{C}{A} = \frac{1}{14400} \times 2.3 \log_{10}\left(\frac{4}{3}\right) = 1.998 \times 10^{-5} \quad \ldots (i)$$

Now, $\quad Q = \left(\dfrac{C}{A}\right)$ (Area of C/s of well) $\times$ (S)

$$= 1.998 \times 10^{-5} \times \frac{\pi}{4}(3)^2 \times 2.5$$

$$= 3.530 \times 10^{-4} \text{ m}^3/\text{sec}$$

$$= 0.35 \text{ litres/sec}$$

Problem 4.7 : A pumping test was carried out for a well in 20 m deep aquifer. The normal ground water level was at surface. Observations holes were located at 4 m and 8 m distances from the well. At the steady stage discharge of 4 litres per second, the draw down observed at these holes was 1.5 m and 0.3 m respectively. Compute the coefficient of permeability of the soil.

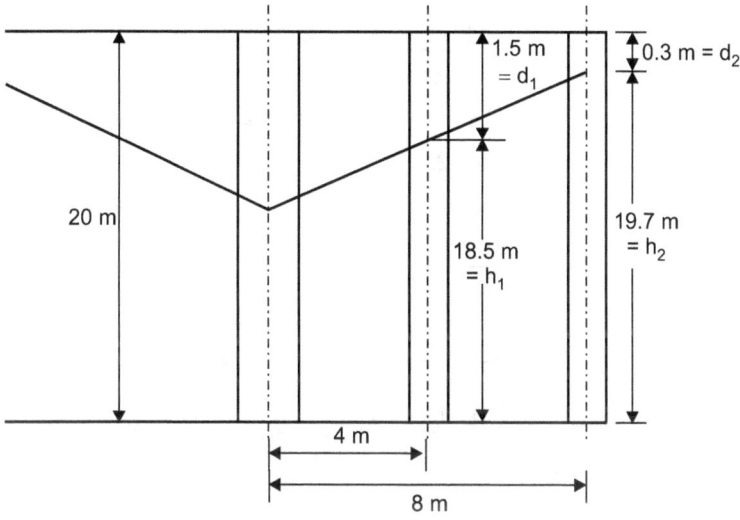

Fig. 4.24

Solution : Referring to Fig. 4.24, it will be seen that

$r_1 = 4$ m, $r_2 = 8$ m

$d_1 = 1.5$ m, $h_1 = 20 - d_1 = 18.5$ m

$d_2 = 0.3$ m, $h_2 = 20 - d_2 = 19.7$ m

$Q = 4$ litre/sec $= 4 \times 10^{-3}$ m³/sec

Using the formula for discharge, $Q = \dfrac{\pi K (h_2^2 - h_1^2)}{2.3 \log_{10} (r_2/r_1)}$

∴ Where K = coefficient of permeability of soil.

∴ Rearranging the terms,

$$K = \dfrac{(Q)(2.3 \log_{10} r_2/r_1)}{\pi (h_2^2 - h_1^2)}$$

$$= \dfrac{(4 \times 10^{-3})[2.3 \log_{10}(8/4)]}{\pi [19.7^2 - 18.5^2]}$$

$K = 1.921 \times 10^{-5}$ m³/s/m²

Problem 4.8 : A 30 cm diameter well fully penetrates a confined aquifer 30 metres deep. After a long time of pumping at a rate of 1200 litres/min, the draw downs in the wells at 20 m and 45 m from the pumping well were found to be 2.2 m and 1.8 m respectively. Determine the transmissibility coefficient of the aquifer and mention its units.

Solution : Using the formula for confined aquifer,

$$Q = \frac{2\pi Kb (h_2 - h_1)}{2.3 \log_{10} (r_2/r_1)}$$

$$h_2 = H - S_2 = 30 - 1.8 = 28.2$$
$$h_1 = 30 - 2.2 = 27.8$$
$$\therefore h_2 - h_1 = 0.4 \text{ m}$$

$$K = \frac{Q \times 2.3 \log_{10} (r_2/r_1)}{2\pi b (h_2 - h_1)}$$

$$Q = 1200 \text{ litres/min.} = \frac{1200 \times 10^{-3}}{60} \text{ m}^3/\text{sec}$$

$$\therefore K = \frac{\left[\left(\frac{1200 \times 10^{-3}}{60}\right) 2.3 \log_{10} (45 - 20)\right]}{2 \times 3.142 \times 30 \times (0.4)}$$

$$= 8.59 \times 10^{-5} \text{ m}^3/\text{s}/\text{m}^2$$

$$\therefore T = \text{Coefficient of transmissibility}$$
$$= K \times \text{depth of aquifer}$$
$$= 8.59 \times 10^{-5} \times 30$$
$$= 2.578 \times 10^{-3} \text{ m}^3/\text{s}/\text{m}$$

Problem 4.9 : A well penetrates into an unconfined aquifer having a saturated depth of 100 m. The discharge is 250 litres per minute at 12 m draw down. Assuming equilibrium flow conditions and a homogeneous aquifer estimate the discharge at 18 m draw down. The distance from the well where the draw down influences are not applicable may be taken to be equal for both the cases.

Solution : Using the equation for an unconfined aquifer.

$$Q = \frac{\pi K (H^2 - h^2)}{2.3 \log_{10} (R/r)} \quad \text{General form of equation}$$

∴ In the first case, $$Q_1 = \frac{\pi K (H_1^2 - h_1^2)}{2.3 \log_{10} (R_1/r_1)} \quad \text{... (i)}$$

and in the second cases,

$$Q_2 = \frac{\pi K (H_2^2 - h_2^2)}{2.3 \log_{10} (R_2/r_2)} \quad \text{... (ii)}$$

∴ Dividing equation (i) by (ii), we get

$$\frac{Q_1}{Q_2} = \frac{(H_1^2 - h_1^2)}{(H_2^2 - h_2^2)} \times \frac{\log_{10}(R_2/r_2)}{\log_{10}(R_1/r_1)}$$

But $R_2/r_2 = R_1/r_1 = R/r$ in this case

∴ $$\frac{Q_1}{Q_2} = \left[\frac{(H_1^2 - h_1^2)}{(H_2^2 - h_2^2)}\right]$$

Here, $H_1 = 100\ m = H_2$

and $h_1 = 100 - 12 = 88\ m$

$h_2 = 100 - 18 = 82\ m$

∴ $$Q_2 = \frac{Q_1(H_2^2 - h_2^2)}{(H_1^2 - h_1^2)}$$

$$= \frac{250 \times (100^2 - 82^2)}{(100^2 - 88^2)}$$

$$= 363.03\ \text{litre/min}$$

Problem 4.10 : *A population of 50,000 has to be supplied water at the rate of 300 litres per day per capita. Calculate the length of the drainage gallery that will have to be provided in a unconfined aquifer 6 m in depth. The water level in the gallery would be 2 m above the impervious stratum. Assume radius of influence as 200 m, and coefficient of permeability of 1.2 m/hour.*

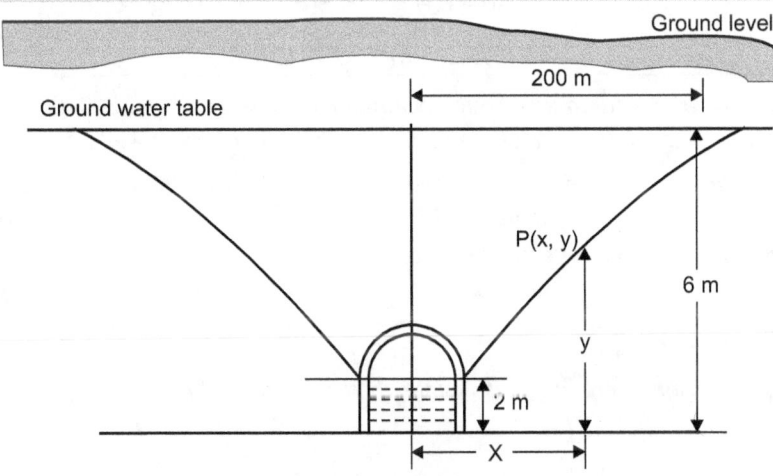

Fig. 4.25 : Drainage gallery

Solution : Using the Darcy's law for flow of water through porous media.

$$Q = KiA = K\left(\frac{dy}{dx}\right)(y \times L) \text{ from one side of the gallery}$$

∴ Q from both sides of gallery $= K\left(\frac{dy}{dx}\right)(y \times L) \times 2$

or $Qdx = 2KL\, y\, dy$

∴ Integrating both the sides

$$Q\int_0^R dx = 2KL \int_h^H y\, dy$$

$$QR = \frac{2KL}{2}(H^2 - h^2)$$

$$Q = \frac{KL}{R}(H_2 - h_2)$$

$$L = \frac{QR}{K(H^2 - h^2)}$$

Now, $Q = \dfrac{(300 \times 50000) \times 10^{-3}}{24 \times 60 \times 60} = 0.1735 \text{ m}^3/\text{sec}$

$R = 200$ m (given), $H = 6$ m, $h = 2$ m, $K = \left(\dfrac{1.2}{60 \times 60}\right)$

∴ $L = \dfrac{0.1732 \times 200}{\left(\dfrac{1.2}{60 \times 60}\right)(6^2 - 2^2)} = \dfrac{0.1738 \times 200 \times 3600}{(1.2)(32)}$

$= 3253.125$ m $= 3.2513$ km.

Problem 4.11 : *A 40 cm diameter well is pumped at the rate of 1200 litres per minute. Measurement of water levels made at the same time in a near by test well were as follows :*

Distance of the first test well and second test well from the well being pumped are 6 m and 18 m respectively, and the draw down in them are 5 m and 1.8 m respectively. The bottom of the well being pumped is 80 m below the water table.

Determine

(i) Coefficient of permeability.

(ii) If all the observations were in Dupit's curve, the draw down in the well during the pumping.

(iii) Specific capacity of the well.

(iv) The maximum rate at which the water can be drawn from the well.

Solution : **(i)** Data given : H = depth of aquifer = 80 m.

$$\text{Radius of well} = \frac{40}{2} = 20 \text{ cm} = 0.2 \text{ m}$$

$$Q = 1200 \text{ lit/min}$$

$$= \frac{1200 \times 10^{-3}}{60} = 0.02 \text{ m}^3/\text{sec}$$

For the first well : $r_1 = 6$ m, $S_1 = 5$ m.
For the second well : $r_2 = 18$ m, $S_2 = 1.8$ m.
Using the formula for the unconfined aquifer.

$$Q = \frac{1.36 \, K \, [h_2^2 - h_1^2]}{\log_{10}(r_2/r_1)}$$

$$h_2 = H - S_2 = 80 - 1.8 = 78.2 \text{ m}$$
$$h_1 = H - S_1 = 89 - 5 = 75 \text{ m}$$

$$\therefore \quad 0.02 = \frac{1.36 \times K \times [78.2^2 - 75^2]}{\log_{10}(18/6)}$$

$$\therefore \quad K = 14.2 \times 10^{-4} \text{ m/sec}$$

(ii) In the case r = 0.2 m i.e. at the well
and $r_2 = 18$ m i.e. at the well
$h_2 = 80 - 1.2 = 78.2$ m

and h is to be determined i.e. the draw down at the well is to be found out.

∴ Using the formula

$$Q = \frac{1.36 \, K \, (h_2^2 - h^2)}{\log_{10}(r_2/r)}$$

$$\therefore \quad 0.02 = \left[\frac{1.36 \, [14.2 \times 10^{-4}] \, [78.2^2 - h^2]}{\log_{10}\left[\frac{18}{0.2}\right]} \right]$$

on solving for h, we get,

$$h = 64 \text{ m}$$

∴ Draw down in pumping well = (80 − 64) = 16 m.

(iii) Specific, capacity : It is defined as 'the discharge per unit (i.e. 1 m) draw down in the pumped well'. In order to find the specific capacity of well it is necessary to calculate the value of R first using Dupits equation.

$$\therefore \quad Q = \frac{1.36 \, K \, (H^2 - h^2)}{\log_{10}(R/r)}$$

$$0.02 = \frac{1.36 \, K \, [80^2 - 16^2]}{\log_{10}(R/0.2)}$$

∴ Solving for R, we get,

$$R = 34.28 \text{ m}$$

∴ Specific capacity = Discharge per unit metre draw down

$$= \frac{1.36 \text{ K} [80^2 - 79^2]}{\log_{10}(34.28/0.2)} = 0.00138 \text{ m}^3/\text{sec} = 1.380 \text{ lit/sec}$$

$$= 1.380 \times 60 \text{ lit/min} = 82.8 \text{ lit/m}$$

(iv) To calculate the maximum discharge Q_{max}

$$Q = \frac{1.36 \text{ K} [H^2 - h^2]}{\log_{10}(R/r)}$$

For Q_{max}, $h = 0$

∴ $$Q_{max} = \frac{1.36 \times 14.2 \times 10^{-4} \times [90^2 - 0^2]}{\log_{10}\left(\frac{34.28}{0.2}\right)}$$

THEORETICAL QUESTIONS

1. Define the following terms :
   (i) Coefficient of transmissibility.
   (ii) Critical draw down head.
   (iii) Specific capacity of the well.
2. Explain the following terms
   (i) Aquifer.
   (ii) Aquiclude.
   (iii) Draw down curve.
   (iv) Perched aquifer.
3. Explain recuperation test for an open well.
4. Based on the Thiem's theory derive an equation for discharge from a tube well located in unconfined aquifer.
5. Derive an expression for the steady flow from a well penetrating in an unconfined aquifer.
6. Derive the Thiem's equilibrium formula for a discharge in a well in a homogeneous confined aquifer. State clearly the various assumptions made.
7. Discuss the assumptions and limitations of Dupits theory.
8. State clearly the assumptions made and derive the formula for the discharge of a well in an homogeneous unconfined aquifer.
9. Explain strainer type tube well.
10. Explain the pumping test of an open well.
11. Explain the construction of tube well.

12. Describe the cable tool method of drilling a hole for a tube well.
13. Derive the Dupits formula for a discharge of a well in a confined aquifer assuming equilibrium flow conditions. State all the assumptions made.
14. Derive an expression for yield from a tube well in an unconfined aquifer. State assumptions made and discuss their limitations.
15. Describe any one method of construction of tube well.
16. Derive an expression for determining the yield from a deep well located in a confined aquifer.
17. Derive an expression for yield from an open well based on recuperation test. Why is it preferred over pumping test ?
18. Write an explanatory note on well completion and its maintenance.
19. Explain the following :
    (i) Well shrouding
    (ii) Well development

NUMERICAL PROBLEMS

1. A 250 mm well penetrates 30 m in an unconfined aquifer. Radius of influence of the well is 200 m. The discharge from the well is 100 l.p.s., when depression is 8 m. Calculate the coefficient of permeability and coefficient of transmissibility.

   Find the maximum yield and percentage increase of maximum yield when the draw down increases to 10 m.

2. A 60 cm diameter well is being pumped at a rate of 1800 litres/minute. Observations made at nearby test well were as follows :
   (i) At a distance of 8 in from the well being pumped, the draw down was 6 m and at 20 m, the draw down was 2.0 m.
   (ii) The depth of unconfined aquifer below the undisturbed ground water table is 100 m.

   Determine :
   (i) Coefficient of permeability.
   (ii) Draw down in the well.
   (iii) Specific capacity of the well.
   (iv) Maximum rate at which water can be drawn from this well.

   Assume that the water surface in all the wells lies along Dupits surface.

3. A well 0.5 m in diameter is being pumped at the rate of 1500 litres per minute. The draw downs in the adjacent two wells at distances 6 m and 18 m respectively are 8 m and 2 m respectively. The depth of impervious strata is 100 m below the ground water level.

Determine :

(i) Coefficient of permeability (K)

(ii) Draw down in the well if the observed points lie on the same draw down curve.

(iii) Specific capacity of the well, and

(iv) Rate of maximum discharge from the well.

(**Ans.** : k = 0.46×10^{-3} m/min, Draw down = 28.1 m, R = 26.5 m = Radius of influence, Sp. capacity = 0.142 m³/sec, Max. discharge = 7.14 m³/min).

4. During a recuperation of an open well, the water level was depressed by pumping by 3 m and it recuperated by an amount of 1.4 m in 60 minute. Determine the yield from the well of 4 m diameter under a depression head of 3 m. Also determine the diameter of well to yield 15 litres per second for a depression head of 2.5 m.

(**Ans.** : 6.58×10^{-3} m³/sec, diameter = 6.61 m)

5. A 250 mm well penetrates 30 m in an unconfined aquifer. Radius of influence of the well is 200 m. The discharge from the well is 100 l.p.s. when the depression is 8 m. Calculate the coefficient of permeability and coefficient of transmissibility. Find the maximum yield and percentage of maximum yield when the draw down increases to 10 m.

6. A well penetrates into an unconfined aquifer with a saturated depth of 80 m. While pumping 200 litres per minute the draw down was found to be 10 m. Estimate the discharge at 15 m draw down. Assume equilibrium flow conditions and the extent of influence due to draw down to be same in both cases. (**Ans.** : 290 litres/min)

7. An infiltration gallery is used to tap the ground water from an unconfined aquifer 7.0 m deep. Determine its length for supplying water to a city with an ultimate population of 1,00,000 at 180 litres per capita per day. The depth of water in the gallery is 2.0 m and the zone of influence extends to 200 m both ways.

Take the coefficient of permeability to the aquifer as 0.002 cm/sec.

8. During a recuperation test of an open well the water level was depressed by pumping by 3.00 m and it recuperated by an amount of 1.8 m in 60 minutes. Determine the yield from a well of 3.5 m diameter under a depression head of 2.5 m.

Also determine the diameter of a well to yield 15 litres per second under a depression head of 30 m.

9. During a recuperation test of an open well, the water level was depressed by pumping by 3 m and it recuperated by an amount of 1.8 m in 60 minutes. Determine the yield from the well of 3.5 m diameter under a depression head of 2.5 m. Also determine the diameter of a well to yield 15 litres per second under a depression of 3.00 m.

IRRIGATION AND CROP WATER REQUIREMENT

5.1 INTRODUCTION

A crop requires certain amount of water at different intervals throughout its growth period. If it rains as and when required by the crop, it is not necessary to supply water to it, artificially. However, as it happens in our country, it may not rain when required by the crops and sometimes it may rain in excess of its requirements thus damaging the crops. Thus, instead of depending entirely on the mercy of nature, man thought of storing the water during the excessive rainfall and utilizing it during the scanty or less rainfall period. Thus, irrigation may be defined as 'the scientific artificial application of water to the agricultural land to supply necessary moisture to the crop as and when required for its healthy growth'.

5.2 FUNCTIONS AND NECESSITY OF IRRIGATION

If it rains as and when required by the agricultural crop, throughout its growth period, it is not at all necessary to store water and then apply it artificially to the agricultural crop. However, the India monsoon is erratic and not evenly distributed due to diversified climatic and topographic conditions. The growth of the crop depends upon the soil fertility, sun shine and the assured supply of water. In topical country like India whose more than 70% of population depends upon agriculture, there is plenty of fertile soil and sufficient sunshine for the growth of crop. However, the rainfall is uncertain, untimely and unevenly distributed resulting in the necessity of artificial application of water by efficient irrigation system.

The following are the factors which governs the necessity of irrigation :

- Insufficient rainfall
- Uneven distribution of rainfall
- Improvement of perennial crops
- Development of agriculture in desert area

- **Insufficient Rainfall :** When the seasonal rainfall is less than the minimum requirement for the satisfactory growth of crops, the irrigation system is essential.
- **Uneven Distribution of Rainfall :** When the rainfall is not evenly distributed during the crop period or throughout the culture able area the irrigation is extremely necessary.
- **Improvement of Perennial Crops :** Some crops like sugarcane, cotton, etc require water throughout the major part of year. but the rainfall may fulfill the water requirement in rainy season only. so for the remaining part of the year, irrigation becomes necessary.
- **Development of Agriculture in Desert Area :** In desert area where the rainfall is very scanty, irrigation is required for the development of agriculture.

5.3 ADVANTAGES OF IRRIGATION

It hardly needs to emphasize the importance and benefits of irrigation when our country has to increase the overall food production to meet the food requirements of growing population. Even then, some of the direct and indirect benefits of irrigation are as follows :

5.3.1 Direct Benefits

(1) Increased Food Production : As there is assured supply of water to the agricultural crop, there is bound to be increase in food production. This is the most important benefit for our country in view of tremendous growth in population and sizeable quantities of food grains that are to be imported every year.

(2) Protection from Famine : With the artificial application of water, there will be assured growth of crop resulting in protection from famine thus reducing the amount to be spent by the Government on famine relief works.

(3) No Necessity of Mixed Cropping : In areas where irrigation facilities are not available, farmers generally adopt 'mixed cropping' system i.e. sowing together of two or more crops in the same agricultural land. If the weather conditions are not favourable to one of the crops, they may be beneficial for the other and thus the cultivator gets at least some yield from the land. When irrigation facilities are made available, farmers need not adopt the mixed cropping system.

(4) Cultivation of Cash Crops : With the assured supply of irrigation water, the farmers may cultivate more remunerative crops such as tobacco, sugarcane etc. in place of conventional crops such as Bajara, Jowar etc.

(5) Plantation : Plantation of trees along the canal banks leads to the increase in the timber wealth of the country and also prevent the erosion of soil in such areas.

(6) Navigation : The large irrigation canals may serve as the cheapest means of transport and thus serve the useful purpose of inland navigation.

(7) Appreciation of Value of Agricultural Land : Due to assured supply of irrigation water, the value of agricultural land in the command area gets appreciated.

(8) Generation of Hydro-Electric Power : Water stored in the reservoirs and also from the canal falls can be used for the generation of hydro-electric power.

(9) Drinking Water Supply : Irrigation water stored in the reservoirs can also be used as supply of drinking water to the towns and cities.

5.3.2 Indirect Benefits

(1) Increase in Revenue : Large irrigation projects serve as a permanent sources of additional income to the government.

(2) Overall Development of the Area : Due to the availability of irrigation facilities, there will be overall development and prosperity and the general standard of living in the area increases.

(3) Employment Opportunities : The constructions of large irrigation projects, creates employment to the people in that area.

(4) Increase in the Ground Water Table : Irrigation facility in an area increases the general level of ground water table due to seepage of water through the reservoir and canal and thus the cost of lifting water from the adjoining open wells and tube wells gets reduced.

5.4 DISADVANTAGES OF IRRIGATION

Irrigation is beneficial only when it is properly managed and controlled. Faulty and careless irrigation does harm to crop and damage lands, besides causing waste of valuable water. Wide knowledge and experience are required for effective water management. When plenty of water is available, farmers are tempted to over irrigate their lands without being conscious of the harmful effects.

Some of the ill-effects of irrigation are as follows :

- **Water Logging :** Due to over irrigation and seepage from canals the ground water table rises and in the absence of proper drainage of the soil, leads to water logging. Water logging renders the soil infertile and useless for cultivation.
- **Bad Climate :** Due to intense irrigation of an area, the climate becomes and cold and damp resulting in unhealthy climate causing outbreak of malaria disease.
- **Increase in Humidity :** Excess and intense irrigation may result in increasing the humidity of the area.
- **Marshy Land :** Excess irrigation of the land with poor drainage may convert it into a marshy land.
- **Impaired Soil Aeration :** Excess irrigation fills all soil pores expelling soil air completely. This leads to deficiency of oxygen in the soil and disturbs seriously the root respiration and root growth.
- **Loss of Soil Fertility :** Uneven and excess irrigation leads to leaching of nutrients beyond plant root zone. Often, careless and heavy irrigation causes erosion of fertile surface soil and runoff that washes out plant nutrients into drains.
- **Restricted Root System :** Excess water and lack of adequate oxygen in soil restrict the root development and feeding zone of plants. Roots do not grow in wet soils and

usually shallow particularly where water table rises and encroaches the normal rrot zones of crops.

- **Activities of Micro-Organisms :** Excess soil water due to excess irrigation causes deficiency of oxygen in soil. Useful aerobic bacteria such as ammonifying, nitrifying and nitrogen fixing bacteria cannot function well or at all under oxygen deficiency.

5.5 INTRODUCTION TO IRRIGATION METHODS

The water flowing through the irrigation canals may be applied to the agricultural crops either by 'surface irrigation' or 'sub-surface irrigation' methods. The 'surface irrigation method' may further be classified as, '(gravity) flow irrigation' or 'lift irrigation', depending upon whether the available water is at higher or lower level than the level of the agricultural land to be irrigated.

In the former case, the water flows by gravity to the land to be irrigated whereas in the latter case it is to be lifted from the source by mechanical means such as pumps etc. before applying it to the agricultural crop. The latter method is found to be expensive as compared to the former one. Fig. 5.1 shows component parts in details of a surface flow irrigation system from a storage reservoir.

5.6 BASIC FUNCTIONS OF IRRIGATION WATER

When water is made available to the agricultural land, the yield of the crop increases considerably. The basic functions of water are as follows :

- The crop can not extract the mutrients present in the soil directly. The water acts as a solvent for the nutrients which can be readily absorbed by the roots of the plants or crops.
- Bacterias that produce food for the growth of the plants, need water for their growth.
- Water controls the temperature of the soil in which plants are grown.
- The unwanted salts present in the soil can be removed by the application of irrigation water i.e. by leaching.
- Application of irrigation water helps in maintaining optimum moisture in the root zones of the soil.

5.7 METHODS OF APPLYING IRRIGATION WATER

Application of irrigation water to be agricultural soil to maintain optimum moisture in the root zone of the crops depends upon various factors such as type of the crop to be grown and its water requirements, type of the soil to be irrigated, the quantity of irrigation water available etc. For applying irrigation water either 'surface' or 'sub-surface' irrigation methods may be utilized.

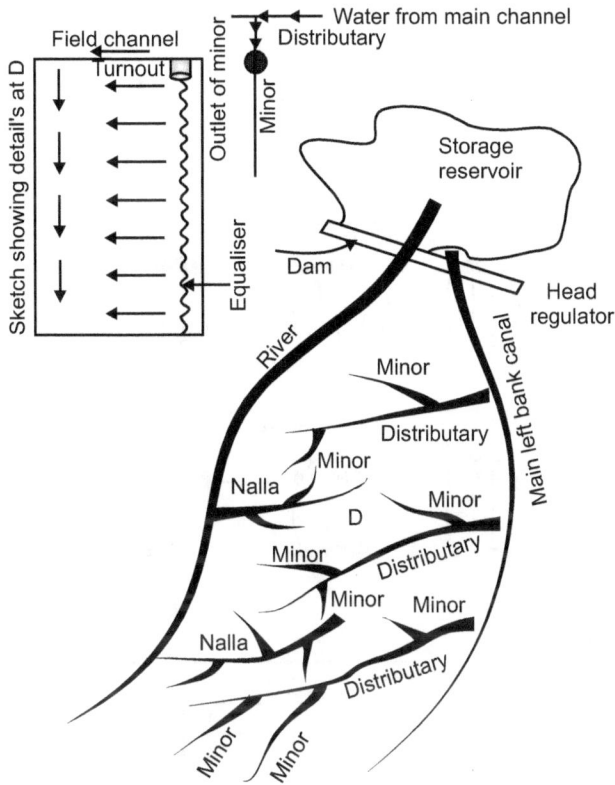

Fig. 5.1 : Component parts of surface (flow) irrigation system

5.7.1 Surface Irrigation System

The most commonly adopted method of irrigation is by surface irrigation. The entire agricultural land is flooded with the irrigation water standing on it to a few millimetres. After the water is applied, some portion of it will be retained by the root zone and the remaining will flow by gravity to join the ground water. The water retained by the root zone of the crops is extracted by the roots and is utilised for building the plant tissues and subsequently it is released to the atmosphere through transpiration.

The surface irrigation system is further classified as follows :

- Free flooding (or uncontrolled) system
- Controlled flooding system which may further be sub-classified as :
    (a) Border flooding (or Border strip method)
    (b) Check flooding
    (c) Basin flooding

- Furrow system which may be either :
   (a) Deep furrows
   (b) Shallow furrows (or corrugated method)

5.7.1.1 Free Flooding (or Uncontrolled) System

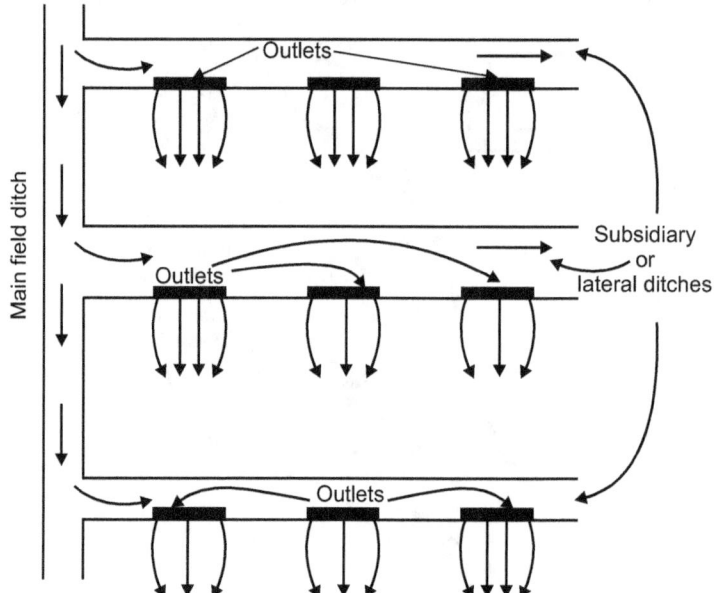

Fig. 5.2 : Free flooding or uncontrolled system

This is the method commonly adopted in our country for irrigating the crops. The method consists in applying water from the field ditches having no embankments or levees to guide its flow or otherwise restrict its movement. Water from such ditches, flows across the field without any restriction and hence it is also known as *'wild flooding'* (Fig. 5.2).

The method is generally adopted for smooth and flat land surfaces, especially in *'inundation irrigation'* in which the water overflows the banks of the stream or river during its floods. However, there is wastage of water as all water cannot be utilised for irrigating the land. The method may be economical in places where water is inexpensive and available in plenty. The initial investment in the preparation of agricultural land is low. However due to loss of water, the efficiency of water appliation is low as compared to other methods. The method is generally adopted where the topography of the land is very irregular and where other methods cannot be economically adopted.

5.7.1.2 Controlled Flooding System

(1) Border Flooding (or Border Strip Method) Fig. 5.3 : The popular system adopted in our country is border flooding or border strip method (Fig. 5.3). The method consists in dividing the agricultural land into number of strips of about 10 to 18 metres in width and 100 to 400 m long separated by low levees known as borders, to prevent overtopping of water from one strip to the other. Irrigation water from the supply ditch is diverted into such strips through the higher end and flows towards the lower end with non-scouring velocity, thus irrigating the land over which it advances. When the water reaches the lower end of the strip, the supply of water to that strip is discontinued. Generally a longitudinal slope for such strips of 2 to 5 m per 1000 m is considered to be sufficient for the water to flow by gravity.

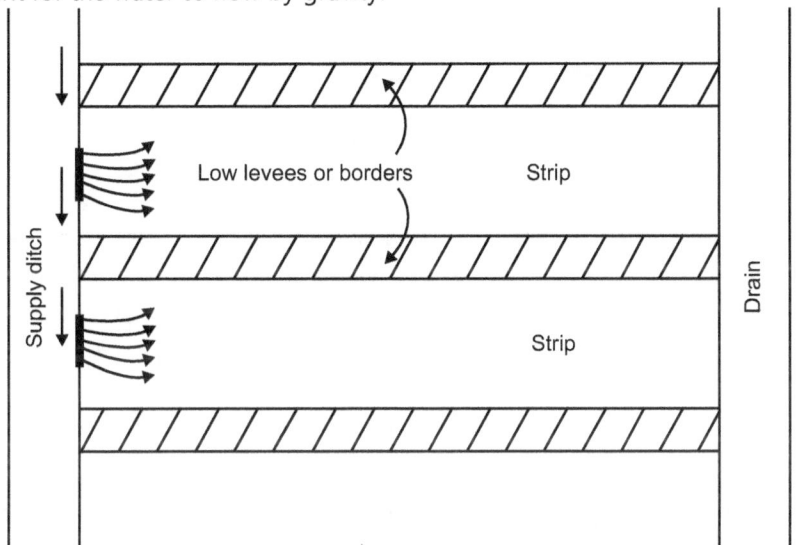

Fig. 5.3 : Border flooding or Border strip method

The time (T) required to cover a given area of a strip is given by the equation :

$$T = 2.303 \frac{y_a}{f} \log_{10}\left(\frac{Q}{Q - f_A}\right),$$

where,
- y_a = Average depth of water in the strip in m.
- f = Rate of infiltration capacity of soil in m/hr.
- A = Area of strip to be irrigated in hectares in time t.
- Q = Discharge from the supply ditch in hectare-metre per hour

and
- T = Time required to irrigate the given area A in hectares.

The method is convenient for close grown crops on soils having moderate infiltration capacity. Moreover, the efficiency of application of water is good and cost of labour involved is also less. However if the topography of the land is undulating, the cost of levelling the ground will be too high.

(2) Check Flooding (Fig. 5.4) : In this method comparatively large streams discharge water to a relatively level plots surrounded by checks in the form of levees, 2 to 3 m base width and about 30 cms in heights. Construction of such low levees will not obstruct the farming work carried out by farm machinery. The plots may be rectangular in case of level grounds enclosed by levees or levees may follow contours.

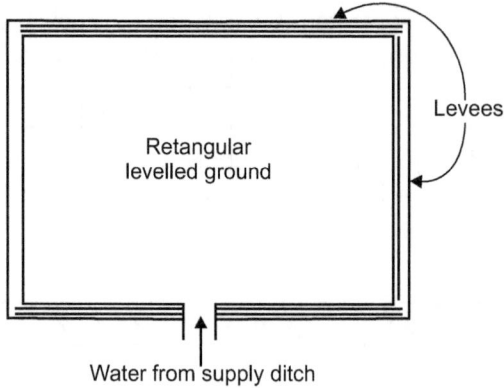

Fig. 5.4 : Checking flooding

The method is preferred in case of permeable soils having excessive percolation losses. In this method, the entire area is filled with water at very high rate which is in excess of its infiltration capacity, thus preventing excessive percolation losses. The water remains on the area till it infiltrates into the soil to the required depth. Some of the merits of this method are even distribution of water over the entire area, ease of operation and adoption of unskilled labour. However, it has low irrigation efficiency, moreover it needs large streams of irrigation water and its labour cost is high.

(3) Basin Flooding (Fig. 5.5) : It is a special form of check flooding adopted for orchards. In this method, water is applied to a level area encircled by low embankment called as basin till it is absorbed into the soil. In some cases two or more trees are covered by the same basin. The basin surface is flooded by water from the ditch.

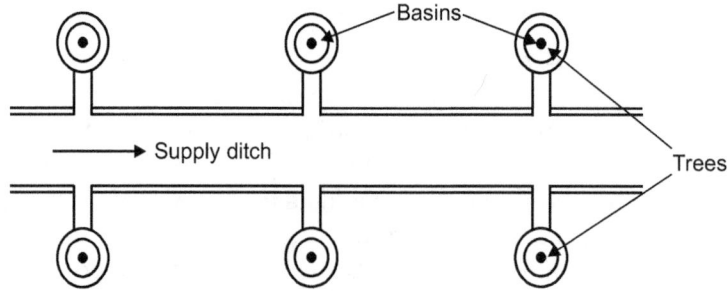

Fig. 5.5 : Basin method

Portable pipes or hoses can also be used instead of ditches. Some of the advantages of this method are that different types of crops can be sown in sequence and there is very title loss of water due to surface flow. However, the irrigated land is to be levelled perfectly.

5.7.1.3 Furrow System (Fig. 5.6)

(1) Deep Furrow Method : In this system a part of the land suface 20 to 50 % in wetted by the irrigation water as compared to flooding methods which covers the entire irrigated land. This results in reducing the evaporation losses, and also helps in reducing the pudding of heavy soil. This helps in easy cultivation immediately after the irrigation water is applied. The method is used for row crops such as jowar, sugarcane etc. Furrows, which are narrow field ditches, excavated between the plant rows, convey water through them. The size of furrows may be 10 to 30 cm in depth and about 300 to 400 m long and have longitudinal slope of about 1 to 5 %.

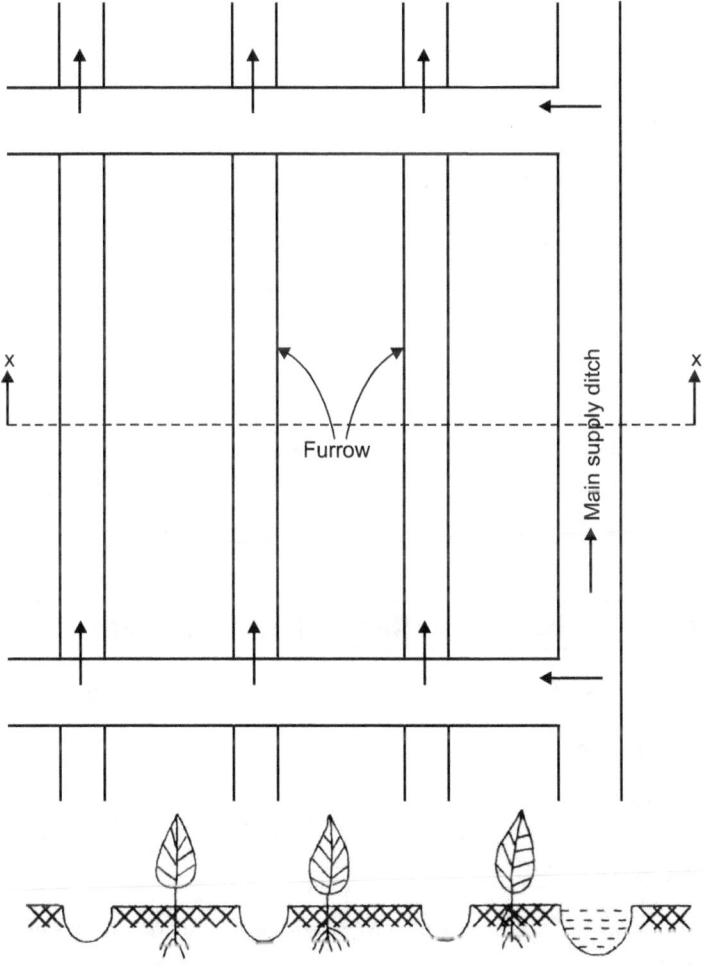

Fig. 5.6 : Furrow method (section along x-x)

(2) Shallow Furrows or Corrugation Method : In is a slightly modified form of furrow method usually adopted for undulating, ground surface. It is used for crops which are grown very close to each other. e.g. small grains and meadows, alfaalfa etc. These are usually small channels flowing with the uniform slope in the direction of irrigation. In this case the eater does not flow directly into the corrugations from the main supply ditch but is first collected into another distribution basin along the lower side of the ditch. Water flowing through the corrugations seeps into the soil and spreads laterally and thus irrigates the space between the corrugations, which are usually U or V shaped, about 10 to 12 cm in depth placed 50 to 80 cm centre to centre.

The method is mostly suitable for smooth level ground surface having gentle slope of 1 to 10 % for closely grown crops in an area having less rainfall. The efficiency of irrigation is also high. However, the method needs proper maintenance of the corrugations for which more labour is required.

5.7.2 Surface Irrigation System

As the name suggests, the irrigation water is applied to the root zone of the crops directly. The water does not wet the soil but the plants extract water from the under water through the roots by capillary action. The sub-surface irrigation system may be either *natural* or *artificial*.

In the former, the water while seeping through the channels through the sub-soil joins ground water and while doing so irrigates the crops grown on the lower side by capillary action, whereas in the latter case a system of open jointed drains is to be laid below the surface of the soil that supplies water to the plants by capillary action. The artificial sub-surface irrigation is however costly.

5.8 MODERN METHODS OF IRRIGATION SYSTEM

The two modern methods of applying the water to the land to be irrigated are as follows :

- Sprinkler irrigation and
- Drip or trickle irrigation

5.8.1 Sprinkler Irrigation

In this method, the water is applied in the form of spray, through a sprinkler nozzle. which falls on the land to be irrigated. The water is applied uniformly at a rate less than the infiltration capacity of the soil. This system of irrigation is used in the United States of America, Israel and to certain extent in our country.

The system is very useful for the land where surface irrigation is not economical due to undulating nature of the excessive sloping ground, where the preparation of the land surface is costly and the soil is erodable.

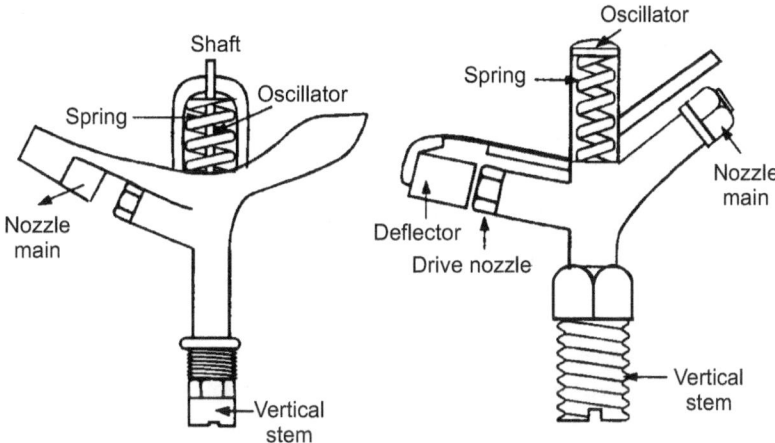

Fig. 5.7 : Rotating types of sprinklers

Sprinkler irrigation system is similar to creating artificial rains which can be distributed uniformly and thus yield good results. Moreover, it can be adopted for all types of soil having undulating topography.

The method is more suitable for the crops having small root zone, that need frequent irrigation. However, the method is very costly as the initial investment is very high.

Classification of Sprinkler System :

The sprinkler system is classified as follows :

- Permanent system
- Semi-permanent
- Portable system

Earlier, stationary over-head perforated pipe installations were generally used but with the introduction of light weight steel pipes and quick couplers, portable sprinkler system have been developed now-a-days. In the permanent sprinkler system, as the name suggests, the pipes are buried permanently in such a manner that they do not interfere with the normal farming activities of the cultivators. In the semi-permanent system main (pipe) lines are buried underground and the laterals are portable. In the portable sprinkler system, both the mains and laterals are portable and thus can be moved from one farm to the another.

The sprinkler system in general consists of main and sub-mains through which water flows under pressure. A pump first lifts water from the source and then flows through the distribution system and then flows out through the sprinkler nozzles mounted on the top of rising pipes connected to the laterals.

The sprinkler arrangement may be either in the form of revolving head sprinklers or the perforated pipe itself. The perforated pipe system works under low pressure whereas the revolving head system operates under low as well as high pressure, depending on the type of rotary head used.

Merits of Sprinkler System :
- Uniform distribution and application of water.
- No prior preparation of land is required as in the other conventional methods.
- Seepage losses are entirely eliminated.
- No fertile land is lost in preparing ditches as in conventional methods.
- The rate of application of sprinkler water being less than the infiltration capacity of the soil, there is no surface run-off that may lead to wastage of water and soil erosion.
- As fertilisers are mixed with water before sprinkling, it can be applied uniformly.
- The method does not lead to water logging of the area.
- High efficiency call be achieved.

Demerits of the Sprinkler System :
- High wind blowing in the area may distort the sprinkling pattern.
- Water if not clean and free from sand may clog, the impeller of the pump and also the nozzles of the sprinklers.
- The method is not suitable for plants which need larger depth of water and frequent irrigation.
- The initial and operating cost of the system is very high.
- A constant supply of water is required for commercial use of equipment.
- Constant expert supervision of the system is required.
- System is not suitable for heavy soil with poor intake capacity.

    The efficiency of application of water (η) for the sprinkler system may be worked out by the following expression.

$$\eta = \frac{V_s}{V_p} \times 100, \text{ where}$$

V_s = Volume of water stored in the root zone of crop.

V_p = Volume of water entering the pump.

The value of η may be about 75 to 80%.

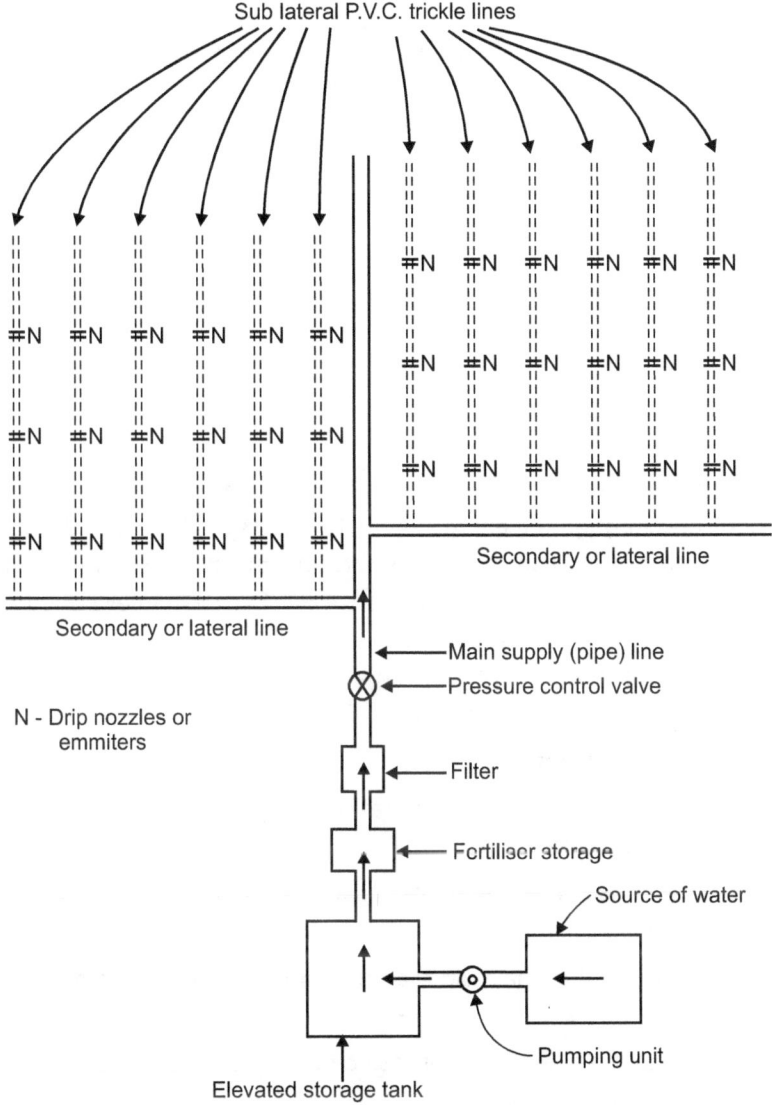

Fig. 5.8 : Layout of a drip or trickle irrigation system

5.8.2 Drip or Trickle Irrigation System

This latest system aims at applying the water directly to the root zone of the crops, in the form of drops. The system consists in conveying water through a flexible pipe line arrangement, operating under low pressure and applying water to the root zones of plant through drip nozzles. The system thus reduces the loss of valuable water by evaporation and percolation.

The system enables to maintain just desired amount of moisture in the root zone of the soil required for consumptive use of the plant growth. The system was first adopted in Israel which was facing acute shortage of irrigation water. It is a sub-irrigation or sub-surface irrigation systems in which water is applied below the ground surface direct to the root zone of the crops.

The drip irrigation system consists of the following :

- Head
- Mains
- Sub-mains
- Laterals and
- Drip nozzles

The pump lifts water and stores in the tank which maintains desired pressure for ensuring required flow of water through the entire system. Fertilisers are then mixed with the water in the tank and the mixture is allowed to pass through the filter to remove the impurities present in the water. The mains and sub-mains are P.V.C. pipes either buried underground or laid on the surface. The laterals are very small P.V.C. pipes about 10 to 15 mm in diameters fitted with drip nozzles (also known as emitters) at an interval of about approx. 1 m and carry discharge at the rate of about 4 to 10 litres/hours.

Merits of Drip Irrigation System :

- Saving of water due to reduction of evaporation and percolation losses and achievement of irrigation efficiency to the extent of 90%.
- There is no possibility of water logging of the area as the system avoids deep percolation of water.
- The water can be applied to maintain the optimum moisture required for the growth of the crop.
- The system results in the higher yield of cash crops e.g. orchards, tobacco etc.
- The method avoids the possibility of over irrigation of the area.
- The cost of labour as compared to other conventional methods is less.
- Due to saving of water more area can be brought under cultivation.
- The erosion of soil is eliminated by this method.

Recently all automatic drip irrigation system comprising of micro-process based controller provided with a soil moisture sensor has been developed by the Vasantadada Sugar Institute at Manjari in the Pune District (Maharashtra). It is claimed that this new system will result in 50 per cent saving of irrigation water and will increase the crop yield by 30 per cent.

Demerits of Drip Irrigation System :
- **High Cost :** The initial cost of installation is very high as compared to the other systems e.g. sprinkler system.
- **Blockage of Nozzles :** There is every possibility of nozzles whose diameter is very small (0.5 to 1.5 mm) being blocked due to presence of soil or salts which could not be removed by filtration.
- **Shallow Depth of Root Zone :** The system develops shallow depth of root zone for the fruit trees and are thus likely to be toppled by the blowing in of high wind.
- **Insoluble Fertiliser :** The fertilisers (e.g. super phosphate) which are insoluble in water cannot be applied by this system.

5.9 WATER REQUIREMENT FOR CROP

As Irrigation Engineering is related to the *'agricultural soil', 'soil moisture'* and *'the crops to be cultivated over it'*, it is necessary to have thorough knowledge of the soil classification, soil moisture and crop water relationship. Knowing such a relationship it may be possible to arrive at certain decisions regarding the type of crop to be grown in the soil, its water requirements, frequency of irrigation etc. After identifying the type of soil, its optimum moisture capacity and the type of crop to be grown and the crop period, it is possible to determine the total water requirements of crops (to be grown in the area).

The *'water requirement'* of a crop is the total amount of water required for a crop during its *'crop period'* to come to maturity before it is harvested.

5.10 SOIL CLASSIFICATION

Soil may be defined as 'loose material formed of non-coherent particles derived mostly from rocks'. For agriculturist and irrigation engineer, the soil is that part of the loose material at the surface of the earth that provides support, nutrients, air (i.e. oxygen) and water required for the growth of plant life. The general classification of soil based on the grain size will be *'coarse-grained'* and *'fine grained'*. It can also be classified as cohesive and non-cohesive depending upon its binding properties or as organic and inorganic based upon its composition. The important characteristics of the soil that affect the growth of the plant or crop are its 'texture' and 'structure'.

Depending on the grain size distribution the textural classification of soil is as follows :

Sr. No.	Name of the Soil Group	Grain Size Diameter in mm
1.	Gravelly soil	60 to 2
2.	Sandy soil	2 to 0.5
3.	Silty soil	0.5 to 0.002
4.	Clayey soil	< 0.002

However, as the soil found in nature rarely belongs to any one group, the common classification of the soil based on its clay content is as follows :

- Light soils,
- Medium soils and
- Heavy soils

The structure (i.e. arrangement of particles) of the soil also plays important role as regards its fertility, permeability and growth of the roots of crop.

5.11 SOIL MOISTURE AND WATER REQUIREMENTS OF CROPS

5.11.1 Water Requirements of Crops

The main functions of water in the plant growth are as follows :

- It acts as a solvent for the nutrients to rise from the soil to the crop or plant.
- Bacteria, present in the soil prepare food for the growth of the plant and they in turn need water in the form of moisture for their growth.
- Water is also essential for the chemical action that takes place during growth of the plant.
- The presence of water also controls the temperature of the soil.

5.11.2 Classification Water Stored in Soil

The water stored in the soil pores is generally divided into the following categories :

(1) Free or Gravity water, (2) Capillary water and (3) Hygroscopic water.

(1) Free or Gravity Water : When water is applied to the soil surface, part of it is absorbed by the root zone (i.e. depth of overburden to which the roots of plants can extend to extract the water present in the soil) and the remaining flows out under the influence of gravity and is known as *'free or gravity water'*.

(2) Capillary Water : Even after all gravity water has drained down, a certain amount of it is still held by the surface tension against gravitational forces and plants can extract it by capillary action and is called *'capillary water'*.

(3) Hygroscopic Water : The part of the water that is attached to the soil particles by loose chemical bonds and as such cannot be extracted by capillary action is known as *'hygroscopic water'*.

5.11.3 Field Capacity

It is the moisture contents of the soil after free drainage under the influence of gravity has taken place for 2 to 5 days and consists of two parts i.e. *'capillary water'* and *'hygroscopic water'*.

Mathematically, field capacity

$$\text{F.C.} = \frac{\text{Weight of water contained in a soil volume}}{\text{Weight of the same volume of soil}} \times 100$$

If
- ρ_s = Mass density of soil in kg/m³
- γ_s = Weight density of soil in N/m³
- d = Depth of root zone in m

Considering 1 sq. m of soil area,

Volume of soil = 1 (sq. m) × d (m)
= d m³

∴ Weight of soil = $\gamma_s \cdot d$ newtons

∴ $\text{F.C.} = \left\{\dfrac{\text{Weight of water contained in unit area of depth of d metres}}{\text{Weight of same volume of soil}}\right\} \times 100$

where, weight of same volume of soil = $\gamma_s \cdot d$

∴ (Weight of water in unit area of soil of depth d metres) = F.C. $\gamma_s \cdot d$ (N/m²)

If γ_w = Weight density of water in N/m³

Then, depth of water storage capacity of soil in m = $\dfrac{\text{F.C.} \cdot g_s \cdot d}{g_w} \left(\dfrac{N/m^2}{N/m^3}\right)$

$= \text{F.C.} \left(\dfrac{g_s}{g_w}\right) \cdot d$ (m)

But $\dfrac{g_s}{g_w}$ = Relative density or specific gravity of the soil

∴ Depth of water storage capacity of the soil in m = (F.C.) × (Relative density) × d (m)

The field capacity (F.C.) depends on :
- Soil texture,
- Soil structure,
- Surface area of the soil grain particles and
- Voids present in the soil.

5.11.4 Permanent Wilting Point

It is defined as 'the moisture contents of the soil at which plants cannot extract water from the root zone of soil for its growth and starts wilting up'.

5.11.5 Available Water or Moisture

It is the water or moisture which is available for the plant growth and is equal to the difference between the water contained at the field capacity (F.C.) and the permanent wilting point. This is also known as maximum possible storage capacity of the soil.

5.11.6 Readily Available Moisture

Out of the available water or moisture, certain portion about 75 to 80% of it can be readily extracted by the plant and is termed as *'readily available moisture'*.

5.11.7 Soil Moisture or Field Moisture Deficiency

It is the water required to bring the moisture content of the soil to its field capacity (F.C.).

From the above, it is obvious that irrigation water is to be supplied when the moisture contents of the soil reaches wilting point and the amount of water to be supplied should be just sufficient to bring the moisture content of the soil from the wilting point to the field capacity. The above criteria helps in determining the frequency of irrigation and the amount of water to be applied during its watering, after allowing for application or transit losses.

5.12 WATER REQUIREMENTS OF A CROP

As already mentioned, the water requirement of a crop is the total quantity of water required for the crop to come to maturity before harvesting. Thus, water requirement will vary from place to place depending upon the type of soil and also from crop to crop depending upon its requirement to come to maturity. Definitions of some of the common terms used in the above context are as follows :

Definitions of Terms :

(1) **Base Period of the Crop (B) :** It is defined as 'the interval of time in days between the first watering of the crop at the instant of its sowing to last watering before it is harvested'.

Base Period of Crops in Maharashtra :

(a) Rabi	15th October to 28th February	0.0283 cumes for 137 days.
(b) Hot Weather	1st March to 30 June	0.0283 cumes for 122 days.
(c) Monsoon	1st July to 14th October	0.0283 cumes for 106 days.

(2) **Crop Period) :** 'It is the time interval in days between the sowing of the crop to its harvesting'. Thus, it can be seen that base period of crop will be slightly less than the crop period.

However, in practice both the above terms are taken as synonyms and expressed as B number of days.

(3) **Delta (Δ) :** A crop needs certain quantity of water at fixed interval of time throughout its growth period. Usually 4 to 5 waterings (each watering varying from 5 to 12 cm) are to be given during its base period. Thus, the total depth of water required by a crop to come to maturity is known as a delta (Δ) of a crop which may be expressed in metres or centimetres.

(4) Duty of Crop (D): It expresses the relationship between the volume of water supplied and the area of the crop it irrigates.

If one cubic metre of water per second is applied to the crop throughout its base period i.e. B number of days, it may irrigate say 100 hectares of crop, then its duty is said to be 100 hectares per cumec for the base period of B days.

(5) Relation between Duty and Delta of a Crop: From the above definitions of base period, duty and delta of crop, a relationship between them may be established as follows:

Let B = Base period in days for which one cubic metre of water per second is applied to the crop.

Then,

$$\begin{bmatrix} \text{Total volume of water applied} \\ \text{in B number of days} \end{bmatrix} = B \times 24 \times 60 \times 60 \times 1 \text{ m}^3$$

$$= B \times 86400 \text{ m}^3 \qquad \ldots (5.1)$$

As one cumec to water supplied for B number of days irrigate D hectares of land, the depth of water applied being Δ.

Volume of water supplied = D (hectare) × Δ (metres)

= D · Δ hectare.metres

∴ Volume of water supplied = D × Δ × 10^4 m³ (∵ 1 hectare = 10^4 m²) ... (5.2)

Equating (5.1) and (5.2) we get

$$B \times 86400 = D \times \Delta \times 10^4$$

or

$$\Delta = \frac{B}{D} \times \frac{86400}{10^4} = 8.64 \frac{B}{D} \text{ metres}$$

or (Δ i.e. total depth of water required = $864 \times \frac{B}{D}$ cm

where B = Base period expressed in number of days and

D = Duty of crop expressed in hectares/cumec

(6) Points to be Remembered Regarding Duty: The following points may be remembered regarding duty of water for a crop.

- A crop requiring more water will have less duty as the area irrigated will be less.
- A crop which needs less water, will have more duty as the water in this case can irrigate more area.
- Duty at the entry of water at the head of main canal will be different from the duty at the outlet of minor (Fig. 5.9) because as the water flows from the main canal to

the branch canal and then through distributary to the outlet of the minor and then to the field channel, certain amount of water is lost due to evaporation and seepage. Such losses are termed as conveyance or transit or transmission losses in the canals.

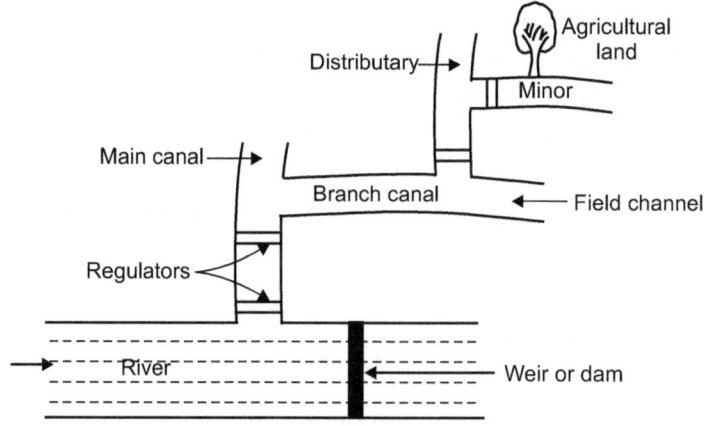

Fig. 5.9 : Typical canal system

Thus, the duty of water at the outlet of the minor will always be less than the duty at the head of the main canal because as the water flows from head of the main canal to the outlet of the channel, some amount of water is lost during its passage as transit losses. Thus, duty of water varies along the whole length of the canal i.e. from head of the main canal to the outlet of the minor and it goes on increasing towards the downstream end. The water from the outlet of minor passes through the field channel (i.e. water course) to the cultivators field. The responsibility of the Irrigation Department ends at the outlet of the minor, the field channel (i.e. water course) being maintained by the individual cultivators. The duty at the outlet of the minor (i.e. water course), is known as *outlet discharge factor*.

Duty may further be expressed as *'flow duty'* or *'quantity duty'* depending upon whether it is expressed in terms of hectares/cumec in case of direct irrigation or as hectares/million cubic metre of water stored in the reservoir.

5.13 FACTORS AFFECTING DUTY OF WATER

Duty of water used for irrigation depends upon the following main factors :

- **Type of Crop Grown :** A crop requiring more water will have less duty and the one requiring less water will have more duty.
- **Climatic Conditions and Season :** Depending upon the temperature and humidity, the evaporation losses along the canal vary, thus affecting duty.

  Similarly the seepage losses through the canal will be more in summer than in rainy season, thus affecting the duty.

- **Base or Crop Period :** The duty of water varies in direct proportion to the length of the base or crop period. Longer the base period for a particular crop, lower will be its duty. In case of different crops, longer the base period of one crop than another, more quantity of water will be required for that crop and its duty will be less and vice-versa.
- **Type of Agricultural Soil :** The soil having less permeability will have more duty whereas the soil having more permeability will have less duty.
- **Rainfall :** If the rainfall in the irrigated area is useful for the growth of the crop, less irrigation water will be required by the crop, thus increasing its duty.
- **Method of Cultivation :** The method of cultivation should be efficient so as to reduce the wastage of water during its application, thereby increasing the duty.
- **Condition of Canal :** For an unlined canal, the transit losses will be more and the duty will be less. For a lined and properly maintained canal, the transit losses will be less and its duty will increase.
- **Soil Characteristics :** The duty of water directly depends on the soil characteristics. if the soil of canal is porous and course grained, there will be more water seepage, resulting in the reduction of duty.
- **Skill of Cultivator :** skilled cultivator will use water properly whereas unskilled cultivator will waste more quantity of water.
- **Method of Irrigation :** Duty of water is more in case of perennial irrigation, as compared with non perennial irrigation.
- **Use of Irrigation Water :** When the irrigation charges are on the basis of volume of water, the farmers will use water economically, thus increasing the duty of water.

Note : The duty of the water is very useful in designing the capacity of the canal. Thus, knowing the various types of crops to be irrigated and their water requirements i.e. duties, the total water requirements can be worked out. After determining the total water requirements, the transit losses are added to it to arrive at the quantity of the discharge that should be passed through the canal system.

Average duties of the common types of crops grown in our country.

Sr. No.	Name of the Crop	Duty (Hectares/Cumec)
1.	Rice	775 to 800
2.	Sugar cane	730 to 750
3.	Kharif crops	1500 to 1600
4.	Rabi crops	1800 to 1850
5.	Hot weather	2000 to 2100

5.13.1 Method of Improving Duty

The duty of water can be increased by the following methods :

- By adopting such methods of applying water, which would reduce or minimize the conveyance losses of water.
- By properly ploughing and leveling the fields, so that the water can be evenly applied in thin layer to the field.
- By frequent ploughing the field, when the ground water is within the capillary reach of the ground surface, become it will reduce loss of moisture.
- By active farmers participation in irrigation management and by training framers to use water economically.
- By lining the of main canal and network of canals, because it will minimize the percolation losses.
- By using application of law and punishing the persons who use water unlawfully or cut canal.
- By increasing the irrigation charges, and using volume of water by volumetric basis duty is increase.
- By using pipe network for distribution of water.
- By avoiding the canal route through sandy or porous reaches and reducing the length of canal network.
- Duty of water can be improved by improved modern cultivation methods (Drip irrigation / sprinkle cal irrigation / ploy house) preferably be adopted.
- Rotation of crops should be preferred, as this will ensure increasing crop yields with minimum use of water.

5.13.2 Factor Affecting Water Requirements of Crops

Following factors are affecting water requirement of crops :
  - Water table
  - Climate
  - Type of soil
  - Method of ploughing
  - Intensity of irrigation
- Ground slope
- Method of application of water
  - Type of crop grown
  - Base period of crop
  - Condition of canal
  - Method of cultivation :

Water Table : Depending upon position of water table nearest to ground surface or much below, water requirement may be less or more respectively.

Climate : The evaporation loss is more in hot climate, hence water requirement will be more and cold climate water requirement of crop will be less comparatively.

Method of Ploughing : In deep ploughing, soil can retain water for a longer period and water requirement is less.

Intensity of Irrigation : More the intensity of irrigation more requirement of water required.

Ground Slope : In steep ground water flows down quickly, find little time to absorb require amount of water, hence water requirement is more as compare to flat slope.

Method of Application of Water : water requirement is more in surface irrigation as compared to sub-surface irrigation due to evaporation loss in minimum in sub-surface irrigation.

5.14 CROP SEASONS IN INDIA

The two main crop seasons in our country are called as *Kharif* and *Rabi* crops, as shown below in a tabular form.

Sr. No.	Crop Season	Name of Crop	Approximate Base or Crop Period
1.	Kharif	Bajara, Jowar, Cotton, Rice, Groundnut, Tobacco, Maize	Beginning of April to the end of September.
2.	Rabi	Gram, Wheat, Barley, Linseed, Potatoes	Beginning of October to end of March.

Note : Sugarcane which is a cash crop falls in both the seasons i.e. it requires water in both the crop seasons and is said to be an overlap crop and additional provision of water is to be made in the next season also and is termed as overlap allowance or provision.

5.15 CROP SEASONS IN MAHARASHTRA

In Maharashtra there are three crop seasons i.e. Kharif, Rabi and Hot weather crops as shown below.

Sr. No.	Crop Season	Name of the Crop	Crop or Base Period
1.	Kharif	Bajara, Maize	15th June to 14th October
2.	Rabi	Wheat, Jowar, Gram	15th October to 14th February
3.	Hot weather	Fodder crop	15th February to 14th June

Note : There are certain crops such as sugarcane, garden fruits that need water throughout the year and are known as 'perennial crops'. Some crops have base period of two seasons and are known as eight monthly crops. e.g. onions, turmeric, garlic, etc.

5.16 CLASSIFICATION OF CROPS INDIA

These seasons are based on the general trends of sowing and maturity of the respective crops.

Following are the classification of the crops generally grown on the irrigation tank :

(a) Perennials :
- Sugarcane / Banana'
- Pan Gardens,
- Fruit Tress (Graps, Oranges) and,
- Lucern and Elephant Grass Etc.

(b) Two Seasonals :
- Turmeric,
- Chilly,
- Vegetables,
- Cotton and,
- Tobacco
- Kharif Seasonal
- Jawar,
- Bajara,
- Paddy,
- Kara,
- Mung,
- Udid and
- Kharif Groundnut

(c) Rabi Seasonal :
- Wheat
- Gram
- Rabi Jawar

(d) Hot Weather Seasonal :
- Hot Weather Groundnut
- Kadawal (Green Fodder)

5.17 WATER REQUIREMENTS OF CROP

The water requirement of a crop is the quantity of water required for that crop for its normal growth and to come to maturity. This requirement is inclusive of consumptive use, transit or conveyance losses and other unavoidable losses. This is usually expressed as depth of water required per unit area in a given time.

In the equation form, it may be written as follows:

$$\begin{bmatrix} \text{Water requirement} \\ \text{of a crop} \end{bmatrix} = \begin{bmatrix} \text{Consumptive} \\ \text{use} \end{bmatrix} + \begin{bmatrix} \text{Transit or} \\ \text{conveyance} \\ \text{losses} \end{bmatrix} + \begin{bmatrix} \text{Water required for} \\ \text{preparation of land} \\ \text{transplanting and} \\ \text{leaching etc.} \end{bmatrix}$$

Net Irrigation Requirement (N.I.R.) of a Crop:

The net irrigation requirement of a crop is 'the amount of water required to be supplied to the crop for its normal healthy growth and come to maturity'. This excludes the effective rainfall and contribution from the ground water.

i.e. $\quad$ N.I.R. $= \begin{bmatrix} \text{Water requirement} \\ \text{of the crop} \end{bmatrix} + \begin{bmatrix} \text{Effective or} \\ \text{useful rainfall} \end{bmatrix} + \begin{bmatrix} \text{Contribution from} \\ \text{ground water} \end{bmatrix}$

Consumptive Use of Water (C.U.) by a Crop:

It is defined as 'the depth of water required (i.e. consumed) by the plant for its normal growth plus the losses due to evaporation and transpiration during its growth, including water absorbed by accompanying weed growth'. This is usually expressed as depth of water required in cm or mm.

The consumptive use (C.U.) is for all practical purposes taken as equal to the evapo-transpiration (i.e. evaporation from the surface and transpiration from plants). However, the term consumptive use also includes the quantity of water required for building up plant tissues in addition to evapo-transpiration.

Mathematically,

$$\text{Consumptive use (C.U.)} = \text{N.I.R.} + \begin{bmatrix} \text{Useful or} \\ \text{effective rainfall} \end{bmatrix} + \begin{bmatrix} \text{Change in the} \\ \text{soil moisture storage} \end{bmatrix}$$

where N.I.R. is taken as equal to amount of irrigation water that should be stored in the root zone to satisfy the consumptive use required by that crop.

The consumptive use of water depends upon the rate of evaporation, mean monthly temperature, velocity of wind, day light hours, humidity, type of soil, rainfall in the area and the depth of (irrigation) water applied.

5.18 DEFINITION OF SOME TERMS

(1) Kor Watering: After sowing of the crop and application of first watering, it grows a few centimeters above the ground. At his stage it needs large quantity of water for its healthy growth and is known as *'Kor Watering'* i.e. it is the maximum amount of watering given to a crop after it has grown a few centimetres high and the depth of this watering is known as *'Kor depth'* and the period during which this watering is applied is known as *'Kor period'*.

(2) Crop Ratio : 'It is the ratio of area of crop irrigated during Kharif season to that irrigated in Rabi season. The usual crop ratio is taken as 1 : 2.

i.e. $\dfrac{\text{Area of crop irrigated in Kharif}}{\text{Area of crop irrigated in Rabi}} = \dfrac{1}{2}$

(3) Rotation of Crop : If the same crop is grown in agricultural land every year, then, the fertility of the land decrease because the soil becomes deficient in certain nutrients required for that particular crop and the yield from land gets reduced. In order to maintain fertility of the soil, it is advisable to grow another crop that does not require the same nutrients as required by the earlier crop or to keep the land fallow without any cultivation. Such a systematic arrangement of growing different crops in rotation in the same land is termed as *'crop rotation'*.

Advantages of Crop Rotation
- Prevents soil depletion
- Maintains soil fertility
- Reduces soil erosion
- Controls insect/mite pests. Crop rotation as a means to control to insect pests is most effective when the pests are present before the crop is planted have no wide range of host crops; attack only annual/biennial crops; and do not have the ability to fly from one field to another.
- Reduces reliance on synthetic chemicals
- Reduces the pests' build-up
- Prevents diseases
- Helps control weeds

(4) Cash Crops : Crops, other than food grains, which cannot be consumed directly by the cultivators and are to be sent to the market for further processing for encashment are called cash crops : Sugarcane, tobacco, tea, jute etc. are some of the examples of cash crops.

Paleo or Paleo Irrigation : It is the application of irrigation water to the land before the sowing of crop. This is required when the land is initially dry at the time of sowing.

5.19 OPTIMUM CROP REQUIREMENTS

If the conditions such as fertility of the soil, temperature, humidity, etc. are identical, there will be a certain optimum consumptive use of water for a particular crop. Now, if only the depth of water (Δ) is varied under absolutely identical conditions, the yield from such a land varies and will have the shape as shown in the Fig. 5.10.

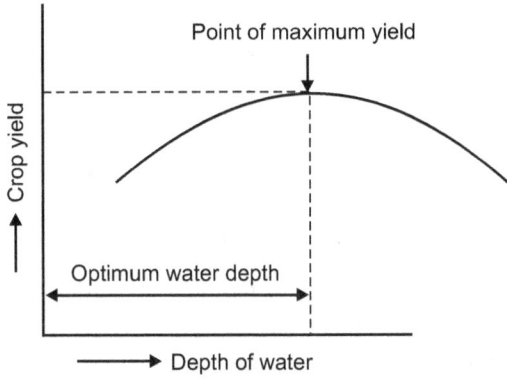

Fig. 5.10

It will be observed that the crop yield increases with water initially, and thereafter attains a certain maximum value and then decreases gradually. The depth of water that results in maximum yield is known as *'optimum depth'* for optimum crop requirement.

5.20 COMMAND AREAS

(1) Gross Command Area (G.C.A.) : It is the total area that is enclosed inbetween two drainage boundaries which can be brought under the command of irrigation canal system without considering the availability of water. The G.C.A. includes all cultivable (i.e. which can be irrigated) and uncultivable (which cannot be irrigated) areas such as villages, ponds, roads, hilly portion etc.)

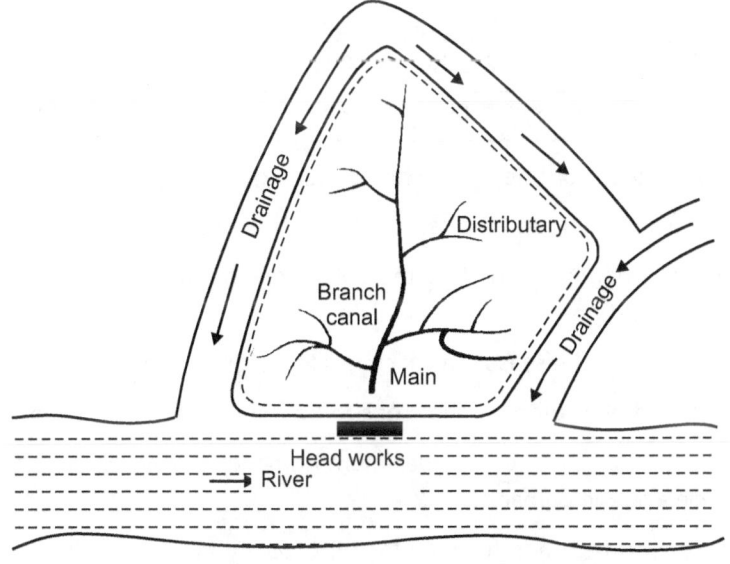

Fig. 5.11 : Gross Command Area (G. C. A.) shown dotted

(2) Culturable Command Area (C.C.A.) : It is the area that can be cultivated and will be equal to C.C.A. minus the areas of uncultivable (i.e. unculturable) land such as forests, roads, ponds, fallow lands, etc.

(3) Intensity of Irrigation (I.I.) : Due to limitations of available water, it may not be possible to irrigate the entire culturable area. Thus a certain percentage of C.C.A. is irrigated. Thus, intensity of irrigation (I.I.) is defined as 'the ratio of actual area brought under cultivation to the total culturable (irrigable) commanded area'.

Once the intensity of irrigation is determined, the actual area to be brought under irrigation can be worked out. Further knowing the type of crop to be grown in such areas, its total water requirement can be found out for different seasons and the capacity of the canal can be decided.

(4) Time Factor : Time factor is defined as 'the ratio of number of days the canal has actually supplied water to a crop at one time to the number of days between two successive water intervals'. Usually the interval between two waterings is 10 to 15 days. Thus, if irrigation water is supplied for say only 4 days, the period of intervals being say 10 days. Then,

$$\text{Time factor} = \frac{4}{10} = 0.4$$

(5) Capacity Factor : It is defined as 'the ratio of mean capacity of the canal (Q_m) to its full capacity (Q_{max})'.

$$\therefore \quad \text{Capacity factor} = \frac{Q_{mean} \text{ for the canal}}{Q_{max} \text{ for the canal}}$$

5.21 COMPUTATION OF THE CAPACITY OF THE CANAL

The following points need consideration while designing the capacity of the canal.

- The various types of crops and the season in which they are to be grown.
- The intensity of irrigation and thus the total area of the land (out of C.C.A.) to be brought under irrigation.
- The area of each crop, the season in which it is to be grown and its water requirements.
- Maximum demand of water of all the crops to be irrigated in different seasons.
- The canal is to be designed for the maximum demand of water in any particular season and not for the average demand.
- Due allowance is to be made for time factor, capacity factor, transit losses in the canal etc. while calculating the capacity of the canal.

5.22 IRRIGATION EFFICIENCIES

In view of the maximum economisation of irrigation water all the available water should be used efficiently with minimum loss. The ratio of water utilized i.e. output to the water supplied i.e. input is called as irrigation efficiently and is expressed as percentage. irrigation efficiency may be considered in stages from the point of diversion of water from a source to its actual use of crops. the components are : (i) Water conveyance efficiency and (ii) Water application efficiency.

$$\eta_p = 100 \, (\eta_{c/100} \times \eta_{a/100})$$

Where,
- η_p = Project irrigation efficiency in %
- η_c = Water conveyance efficiency in %
- η_a = Water application efficiency in %

The various types of irrigation efficiencies are expressed on follows :

(1) Efficiency of Water Conveyance (η_c) is the ratio of water delivered to the field to the water supplied to it. Thus, it considers all conveyance or transit losses that take place.

$$\eta_c = 100 \, (W_f / W_d)$$

Where,
- η_c = Water conveyance efficiency in %
- W_f = Amount of water delivered to fields or farm.
- W_d = Amount of water diverted from sources.

(2) Efficiency of Water Application (η_a) is the ratio of actual quantity of water stored in the root zone of the plants i.e. crops to the actual quantity of water supplied to the field.

$$\eta_a = 100 \, (W_s / W_f)$$

Where,
- η_a = Water application efficiency in %
- W_f = Amount of water delivered to fields or farm.
- W_s = Amount of water stored in the crop root zone soil

(3) Farm Irrigation Efficiency is defined as the ratio of irrigation water consumed (i.e. consumptive use - effective precipitation) to the amount of water expressed as depth that should be delivered to the farm and it may be upto 60% to 80%.

(4) Efficiency of Water Used (η_u) is defined as the ratio of irrigation water beneficially used (inclusive of leaching water) to the total quantity of water delivered.

$$(\eta_u) = 100 \, (Y / W_r)$$

Where
- η_a = Water application efficiency in %
- Y = Economic crop yield in kilogram per hectare
- W_r = Water requirement of the crop in hectare- cm

(5) Water Storage Efficiency ($\eta_{w.s.}$) is defined as the ratio of water stored in the root zone of the crops at the time of irrigation to the water needed in the root zone prior to irrigation (i.e. field capacity minus the existing available moisture).

$$(\eta_{w.s.}) = 100\,(W_s/W_e)$$

Where η_a = Water application efficiency in %

W_e = Amount of water needed to meet the soil water depleted in the crop root zone soil prior to irrigation

W_s = Amount of water stored in the crop root zone soil

(6) Water Distribution Efficiency : It indicates the degree to which the water has entered uniformly throughout the root zone of the crops. It is given by the expression,

$$\eta_{dist} = \left(1 - \frac{d}{D}\right) \times 100$$

Where η_{dist} = Water distribution efficiency

d = Average of deviation (absolute value) in depth of water stored from the mean depth.

D = Mean or average depth of water stored during irrigation. Obviously if d is zero, the water distribution efficiency will be 100%.

Thus it can be said that efficiency of irrigation serves as a yardstick to compare the various methods that are adopted for application of water.

5.23 CROPPING PATTERN

The term cropping pattern refers to the yearly sequence of crops grown and the special arrangement of them and follows in a given area. it is formulated with a view to obtain maximum crop production under given situation.

Factors Governing Cropping Patterns :

There are many factors governing the cropping patterns in an irrigated area. The most important ones are as follows :

- Climate
- Soil characteristics
- Hydrology
- Hydrology water allowance and full supply days
- Water and irrigation requirement of crops.
- Intensity of irrigation
- Intensity o0f cropping and kharif, rabi and summer cropping ratio.
- Farmer's requirement.
- Size of holding and family

- Marketing and other facility
- Credit facilities
- Subsidy given by government etc.

Cropping patterns that exist in most of the tracts in India have been developed through years by way of farmers' experiences. The patterns are dynamic and changes occur with changes in factors of production and in physiological and social environments. Modifications made in the cropping pattern are always to derive the maximum benefit from changed crop growing conditions.

5.24 WATER QUALITY FOR IRRIGATION

Irrigation waters are grouped into six classes on the basis of soluble salt content and odium percentage. Interpretation of these classes in relation to their use follows :

Class 1 : Excellent :

The total soluble salt content and sodium percentage of this water are low enough that no problems should result from its use.

Class 2 : Good :

This water is suitable for use on most crops under most conditions. Extensive use of Class 2 water on clay soils where little or no leaching occurs may eventually cause a saline or sonic soil problem. Normal rainfall will usually dilute the soluble salts and eliminate the risk of salt accumulation. If the water's sodium percentage is high (above 30 per cent), gypsum can be used periodically to remedy the problem.

Class 3 : Fair :

This water can be used successfully for most crops if care is taken to regent accumulation of soluble salts including sodium, in the soil. Good soil management and irrigation practices must be followed. Class 3 water can be used with little danger on permeable, well-drained soils. The water table should be at least 10 feet below the surface to allow accumulated salts to be leached below the root zone by excessive irrigation when rainfall is limited.

Class 4 : Poor :

Use of this water is restricted to well drained permeable soils for production of salt tolerant crops. Irrigation practices must receive careful attention to avoid salt accumulation. Excess water must be applied when rainfall is not adequate to cause periodic salt leaching. Good soil management practices must be used to maintain good physical condition of the soil. Soil fertility levels must be maintained at adequate levels. Use of this water on medium textured soils may cause soil salinity problems if good practices are not followed. This water is not recommended for use on fine textured soils.

Class 5 : Very Poor :

Use of this water is restricted to irrigation of sandy, well-drained soils in areas of the state which receive at least 30 inches of rainfall. This water should not be used without advice from a person trained in irrigation water use.

SOLVED PROBLEMS

Problem 5.1 : Calculate the delta (Δ) for a crop from the following data :
(i) Base period = 120 days,
(ii) Duty = 1000 hectare/cumecs.

Solution :

Using the relation, $\Delta = \dfrac{8.64\, B}{D} = \dfrac{8.64 \times 120}{1000}$

$\therefore$ Delta (Δ) = 1.0368 m

Problem 5.2 : Calculate the duty of water for a crop from the following data :
(i) Delta for the crop = 80 cm,
(ii) Base period of crop = 140 days.

Solution :

Using the relation, Duty (D) = $\dfrac{8.64\, B}{D}$

$= \dfrac{8.64 \times 140}{0.80}$

= 1512 hectare/cumecs

Problem 5.3 : Calculate the discharge required at the head of the distributary from the following :
(i) Gross command area of distributary = 12000 hectares
(ii) Culturable irrigable area = 80% of gross area
(iii) Intensity of irrigation = 50% for Rabi
(iv) Intensity of irrigation = 25% for Kharif
(v) Average duty at the head of distributary = 2000 hect/cumecs for Rabi
(vi) Average duty at the head of distributary = 900 hect/cumecs for Kharif

Solution :

Given : Gross command area = 12000 hect.

$\therefore$ Culturable command area = $\dfrac{80}{100} \times 12000$ = 9600 hect.

Now, Area to be irrigated in Rabi = $\dfrac{50}{100} \times 9600$ = 4800 hect.

and Area to be irrigated in Kharif = $\dfrac{25}{100} \times 9600$ = 2400 hect.

Quantity of water required at the head of distributary to irrigate Rabi crop

$$= \frac{4800}{2000} = 2.4 \text{ cumecs} \qquad \ldots \text{(i)}$$

and quantity of water required at the head of distribution to irrigate Kharif crop

$$= \frac{2400}{900} = 2.67 \text{ cumecs} \qquad \ldots \text{(ii)}$$

∴ The discharge required at the head of the distributary will be greater of the (i) and (ii) i.e. 267 cumecs.

Problem 5.4 : *If in the above problem, the maximum requirements at the head of distributary of the crop are as follows :*

(i) Kharif crop (a) Kor period = 2.5 weeks
  (b) Kor depth = 190 mm
(ii) Rabi crop (a) Kor period = 4 weeks
  (b) Kor depth = 135 mm

Calculate the discharge needed at the head of the distributary to satisfy the above requirements.

Solution :

For Rabi : Outlet factor $= \frac{864 \, B}{D}$ where Δ is in cm

∴ Outlet factor for Rabi $= \frac{864 \times (7 \times 4)}{13.5} = 1792$ hect/cumecs

and Outlet factor for Kharif $= \frac{864 \times (7 \times 2.5)}{19.00} = 796$ hect/cumecs

∴ Water required for Rabi $= \frac{4800}{1792} = 2.685$ cumecs ... (i)

and Water required for Kharif $= \frac{2400}{796} = 3.025$ cumecs ... (ii)

∴ Taking the maximum of the (i) and (ii), the maximum requirement = 3.025 cumecs.

Problem 5.5 : *Calculate the design discharge at the outlet from the following data :*
(i) Gross command area = 3000 hectares
(ii) Culturable command area = 80% of gross command area
(iii) Intensity of sugarcane = 20%
(iv) Intensity of wheat = 40%
(v) Duly of crop for sugarcane at the water course = 730 hect/cumecs
(vi) Duty of crop for Rabi at the water course = 1800 hect/cumecs
(vii) Time factor = 0.80

Solution :

(i) G.C.A. = 3000 hectares

(ii) C.C.A. = $\frac{80}{100} \times 3000$ = 2400 hectares

∴ Area to be irrigated for Sugarcane = $2400 \times \frac{20}{100}$ = 480 hectares

and Area to be irrigated for Rabi = $2400 \times \frac{40}{100}$ = 960 hectares

∴ Discharge required for Sugarcane = $\frac{480}{730}$ = 0.658 hectares/cumecs ... (i)

and Discharge required for Rabi = $\frac{960}{1800}$ = 0.533 hectares/cumecs ... (ii)

It may be noted that Sugarcane is a crop that requires water for the entire year (i.e. for all the 12 months) whereas the wheat which is a Rabi crop needs water only during Rabi season.

∴ Water required at the head of water course = (i) + (ii)

= 0.658 + 0.533 = 1.1913 cumecs

As the time factor is given as 0.80 (i.e. channel flows for a period lesser than the crop period). Therefore, actual discharge required = $\frac{1.1913}{0.80}$ = 1.4891 cumecs.

Problem 5.6 : The following table shows the details of various crops grown in culturable area of 2000 hectares served by a field channel.

Sr. No.	Crop Grain	Intensity of Irrigation	Kor Period in Days	Kor Depth
1.	Wheat	40%	16	15 cm
2.	Jowar (Rabi)	50%	10	12 cm

Work out the discharge of field channel.

Solution :

The duty at the head of watercourse (i.e. outlet point of minor) is called as outlet discharge error.

∴ $\begin{bmatrix} \text{Outlet discharge factor} \\ \text{for Wheat i.e. (Rabi)} \end{bmatrix}$ = $\frac{864 \, B}{D}$ = $\frac{864 \times 16}{15}$ = 921.6 ha./cumecs

and $\begin{bmatrix} \text{Outlet discharge factor} \\ \text{for Jowar i.e. (Rabi)} \end{bmatrix}$ = $\frac{864 \times 10}{12}$ = 720 ha./cumecs

Now, Area under Wheat (Rabi) = $\frac{40}{100} \times 2000$ = 800 hect

Area under Jowar (Rabi) = $\frac{50}{100} \times 2000$ = 1000 hect

∴ Discharge requried for Wheat (Rabi) = $\frac{800}{921.6}$ = 0.868 cumecs ... (i)

and Discharge required for Jowar (Rabi) = $\frac{1000}{720}$ = 1.389 cumecs ... (ii)

∴ Total discharge required = (i) + (ii) = 2.257 cumecs

Problem 5.7 : *For an irrigated area, the data pertaining to the cropping pattern, with three seasons in a year, is as follows :*

Sr. No.	Name of Crop	Crop Period in Days	Area to be Irrigated in Hectares	Duty at the Head of Main Canal in hect./cumecs
1 (a)	Sugarcane	280	420	630
(b)	Overlap for sugarcane in hot weather	100	90	630
2.	Wheat (Rabi)	120	6750	1500
3.	Rice (Kharif)	120	2600	650
4.	Vegetables (Hot weather)	120	420	700

Find (i) Discharge required at the head of main canal.

(ii) The storage required.

Take time factor as 0.70 and capacity factor as 0.80.

Assume other suitable factors.

Solution :

(1) Amount of water required for

(a) Sugarcane = $\frac{420}{630}$ = 0.67 cumecs

(b) Sugarcane (H.W.) = $\frac{90}{630}$ = 0.14 cumecs

(2) Amount of water required for Wheat (Rabi) = $\frac{6750}{1500}$ = 4.5 cumecs

(3) Amount of water required for Rice = $\frac{2600}{650}$ = 4 cumecs

(4) Amount of water required for vegetables = $\frac{420}{700}$ = 0.6 cumecs

∴ Requirement of water for various crops in different seasons :

Sr. No.	Crop	Discharge Required in Cumecs		
		Kharif	Rabi	Hot Weather
1 (a)	Sugarcane	0.67	0.67	0.67
(b)	Sugarcane (H.W.)	–	–	0.14
2.	Wheat (Rabi)	–	4.5	–
3.	Rice (Kharif)	4	–	–
4.	Vegetables (H.W.)	–	–	0.60
	Sum	4.67	5.17	1.41

∴ Design for maximum i.e. 5.17 cumecs

Discharge required to satisfy the above requirements = 5.17 cumecs

∴ As time factor = 0.70

Actual design discharge = $\frac{\text{Design maximum discharge}}{\text{Time factor}}$

∴ Actual design discharge = $\frac{5.17}{0.70}$

and Capacity factor = $\frac{\text{Mean discharge required}}{\text{Maximum discharge required}}$ = 0.80

∴ Actual maximum design discharge considering capacity factor 0.80,

$$= \frac{5.17}{0.70} \times \frac{1}{0.80}$$

= 9.232 cumecs

Problem 5.8 : *(1)It is proposed to irrigate 40,000 hectares in western area of Pune district where the crop pattern is as follows :*

(1)	Sugarcane	10%
(2)	Other perennial crop	5%
(3)	Paddy	15%
(4)	Cotton	15%
(5)	Jowar	40%
(6)	Wheat	10%
(7)	Hot weather crop	5%

Assume suitable duty and time factor.
Find discharge of the canal and capacity of reservoir.

Solution :

The duties of various crops are assumed at the head of main canal as follows :

Sr. No.	Crop	Duty (hect/cumecs)	Area (hect)	Requirement of Water (cumecs)		
				Kharif	Rabi	Hot Weather
1.	Sugarcane	730	4000	5.48	5.48	5.48
2.	O.P. Crop	1000	2000	2.00	2.00	2.00
3.	Paddy	750	6000	8.00	–	–
4.	Cotton	900	6000	6.67	–	–
5.	Jowar	1500	16000	–	10.67	–
6.	Wheat	1800	4000	–	2.22	–
7.	Hot weather	2000	2000	–	–	1.00
	Sum		40000	22.15	20.37	8.48

The water requirement in Kharif is maximum i.e. 22.15 cumecs.

Assume time factor = 0.7 and capacity factor = 0.8

Capacity of canal at the head works $= \dfrac{22.15}{0.7 \times 0.8}$

$= 39.55$ cumecs ≈ 40 cumecs

∴ Capacity of canal is 40 cumecs.

To calculate total volume water stored in reservoir to meet the water requirements of crop, assume appropriate losses.

(1) First Method :

$$\Delta = \dfrac{8.64\, B}{D} \text{ (metres)}$$

Sr. No.	Crop	Base Period (days)	Duty (hect/cumec)	Delta in (m)	Area (hect)	Capacity (Mm³)
1.	Sugarcane	365	730	4.320	4000	172.80
2.	O.P. Crop	365	1000	3.154	2000	63.08
3.	Paddy	120	750	1.382	6000	82.92
4.	Cotton	120	900	1.152	6000	69.12
5.	Jowar	120	1500	0.691	16000	110.56
6.	Wheat	120	1800	0.576	4000	23.04
7.	H.W. crop	120	2000	0.518	2000	10.36
					Total	531.88 Mm³

Total capacity of the reservoir required (assume 15% losses)

$$= \frac{531.88}{0.85} = 625.74 \text{ Mm}^3 = \text{Live storage}$$

Gross storage required $= \frac{10}{9} \times \text{Live storage}$

$$= \frac{10}{9} \times 625.74 = 695.27 \text{ Mm}^3$$

(2) Second Method :

Sr. No.	Crop	Base period (days)	Discharge (Cumec)	Capacity (Mm³)
1.	Sugarcane	365	5.48	172.82
2.	O.P. Crop	365	2.00	63.07
3.	Paddy	120	8.00	81.94
4.	Cotton	120	6.67	69.15
5.	Jowar	120	10.67	110.59
6.	Wheat	120	2.22	23.02
7.	H.W. crop	120	1.00	10.34
			Total	531.95 Mm³

Assume 15% losses.

$$\text{Live storage required} = \frac{531.95}{0.85}$$

$$= 625.82 \text{ Mm}^3$$

$$\text{Gross storage required} = 625.82 \times \frac{10}{9}$$

$$= 695.36 \text{ Mm}^3$$

So the gross storage required by both the methods practically remains same.

Problem 5.9 : Estimation of gross storage capacity of reservoir.
Data given :

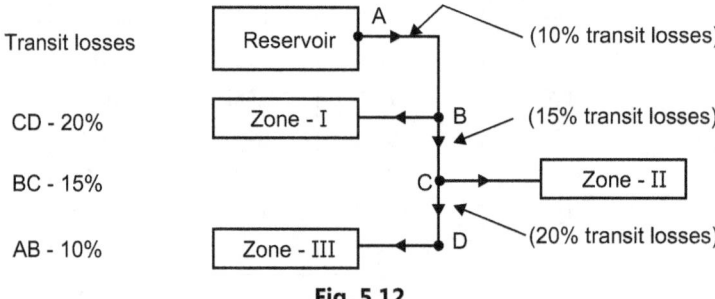

Fig. 5.12

Sr. No.	Crop	Season	Base Period (Days)	Duty (hect/m³)	Area (Hect-m)		
					Zone-I	Zone-II	Zone-III
1.	Sugarcane	Perennial	365	600	300	400	500
2.	Sugarcane overlap	Hot weather	100	600	100	125	150
3.	Rice	Kharif	122	700	700	500	600
4.	Jowar	Kharif	122	2000	1500	1500	1200
5.	Wheat	Rabi	121	1600	1600	2000	2400
6.	Vegetables	Hot weather	121	700	300	250	250

Time factor = 0.7

Capacity factor = 0.8

Tank losses = 10% of live storage

Dead storage = 10% of gross storage

Live storage = Effective live storage + Tank losses

Gross storage = Live storage + Dead storage

Important Terms :

Time Factor : It is the ratio of number of days the canal has actually run to the number of days of irrigation period.

Capacity Factor : It is the ratio of mean supply discharge to the full capacity discharge.

Duty of crop is generally the average duty. Hence, the average depth of water supplied is less than Kor-depth. The discharge required during Kor period is more than the average discharge. To account for this, the average discharge calculated is increased by capacity factor.

Live Storage : The volume of water stored in the reservoir between the minimum pool and normal pool levels is known as useful or live storage.

Dead Storage : The water stored in the reservoir below minimum pool level is known as dead storage. It is of no use in the operation of reservoir.

Procedure : From the given data, by using relationship discharge = Area/Duty. We will be finding discharge required for different crop seasons and for different zones tabulated as follows : (Sample calculation for Zone-I - Sugarcane).

∴ Discharge = Area / Duty

= 300 (hect) / 600 (hect/cumec)

= 0.5 cumecs

Discharge required for Zone-I :

Sr. No.	Name of Crop	Kharif (cumecs)	Rabi (cumecs)	Hot Weather (cumecs)
1.	Sugarcane	0.50	0.5	0.5
2.	Sugarcane (overlap)	–	–	0.167
3.	Rice	1.0	–	–
4.	Jowar	0.75	–	–
5.	Wheat	–	1.0	–
6.	Vegetables	–	–	0.43
	Total	2.25	1.5	1.097

Discharge required for Zone-II :

Sr. No.	Name of Crop	Kharif (cumecs)	Rabi (cumecs)	Hot Weather (cumecs)
1.	Sugarcane	0.667	0.667	0.667
2.	Sugarcane (overlap)	–	–	0.2083
3.	Rice	0.7143	–	–
4.	Jowar	0.75	–	–
5.	Wheat	–	1.25	–
6.	Vegetables	–	–	0.3571
	Total	2.1313	1.917	1.2315

Discharge required for Zone-III :

Sr. No.	Name of Crop	Kharif (cumecs)	Rabi (cumecs)	Hot Weather (cumecs)
1.	Sugarcane	0.833	0.833	0.833
2.	Sugarcane (overlap)	–	–	0.25
3.	Rice	0.8571	–	–
4.	Jowar	0.600	–	–
5.	Wheat	–	1.5	–
6.	Vegetables	–	–	0.3571
	Total	2.29	2.333	1.44

Design Discharge for Length CD :

From the table No. 3 for Zone-III :

$$\begin{bmatrix} \text{Maximum discharge} \\ \text{required at the field} \end{bmatrix} = [\text{Total discharge required in Rabi season}]$$

$$= 2.333 \text{ cumecs}$$

Time factor = 0.7

$$\text{Actual discharge} = \frac{\text{Average discharge}}{\text{Time factor}} = \frac{0.233}{0.7}$$

$$= 3.33 \text{ cumecs}$$

Capacity factor = 0.8

∴ Full supply discharge for peak demand,

$$= \frac{3.33}{0.8}$$

$$= 4.16 \text{ cumecs}$$

Considering canal transit losses given as 20%,

∴ Discharge required at field i.e. design discharge for C.D.,

$$= \frac{4.167}{0.8}$$

$$= 5.207 \text{ cumecs}$$

Design Discharge for Length BC :

From the table No. 2 for Zone-II :

$$\begin{bmatrix} \text{Maximum discharge} \\ \text{required at the field} \end{bmatrix} = \begin{bmatrix} \text{Total discharge required} \\ \text{in Kharif season} \end{bmatrix}$$

$$= 2.133 \text{ cumecs}$$

Time factor = 0.7

$$\text{Actual discharge} = \frac{\text{Average discharge}}{\text{Time factor}}$$

$$= \frac{2.133}{0.7}$$

$$= 3.326 \text{ cumecs}$$

Capacity factor = 0.8

∴ Full supply discharge for peak demand

$$= \frac{3.328}{0.8}$$

$$= 3.805 \text{ cumecs}$$

∴ Total discharge required = Design discharge for CD
+ Design discharge for BC
= 5.207 + 3.805
= 9.012 cumecs

Considering canal transit losses as 15%,

∴ Design discharge through canal BC

$$= \frac{9.012}{0.85}$$

$$= 10.6 \text{ cumecs}$$

Design Discharge for Length AB :

From table No. 1 : For zone-I,

$\begin{bmatrix} \text{Maximum discharge} \\ \text{required at the field} \end{bmatrix}$ = Total discharge requirement in Kharif season

= 2.25 cumecs

Time factor = 0.7

Actual discharge = $\frac{2.25}{0.7}$ = 3.214 cumecs

Capacity factor = 0.8

$\begin{bmatrix} \text{Full supply discharge} \\ \text{for peak demand} \end{bmatrix}$ = $\frac{3.214}{0.8}$ = 4.02 cumecs

Total discharge required = Design discharge through canal length BC
+ Design discharge through canal length AB
= 10.6 + 4.02
= 14.62 cumecs

Considering canal transit losses as 10%,

∴ Design discharge for length AB

$$= \frac{14.62}{0.9} = 16.244 \text{ cumecs}$$

Estimation of Gross Storage Capacity of Reservoir :

Using the relationship,

Volume required = Discharge × Base period (in sec)

(Sample calculation for Zone-I)

For sugarcane, $V = \frac{0.5 \times 365 \times 24 \times 3600}{10^6} = 15.8 \text{ Mm}^3$

Tabulating the Same for Different Zone, We Get,

Sr. No.	Name of crop	Zone-I Mm^3	Zone-II Mm^3	Zone-III Mm^3
1.	Sugarcane	15.80	21.00	26.30
2.	Sugarcane (overlap)	1.44	1.80	2.16
3.	Rice	10.50	7.53	9.03
4.	Jowar	7.90	7.90	6.32
5.	Wheat	10.50	13.10	15.70
6.	Vegetables	4.44	3.70	3.70
	Total	50.58	55.03	63.21

Volume of water required in Zone-III
$$= 63.21 \text{ Mm}^3$$

Considering 20% as transit losses,

$\therefore$ Volume of water required $= \dfrac{63.21}{0.8} = 79.01 \text{ Mm}^3$

$\therefore$ Volume of water required at C = Volume of water required in Zone-III
+ Volume of water required in Zone-II
= 79.01 + 55.03
= 134.04 Mm^3

Considering transit losses as 15%,

$\therefore$ Volume of water required at C $= \dfrac{134.04}{0.85}$

$= 157.70 \text{ Mm}^3$

$\therefore$ Volume of water required at B = Volume of water required at C
+ Volume of water required in Zone-I
= 157.70 + 50.58
= 208.28 mm^3

Effective storage (live) of tank = 231.4 Mm^3

Gross storage = Live storage + Dead storage

G = L + 0.1 G

$\therefore$ G $= \dfrac{L}{0.9}$

$\therefore$ Gross storage $= \dfrac{257.11}{0.9} = 285.67 \text{ Mm}^3$

Results : For reservoir,

(1) Gross storage capacity = 285.67 Mm³
(2) Live storage = 257.11 Mm³
(3) Dead storage = 28.56 Mm³

Problem 5.10 : Calculate the depth and frequency of irrigation required for a crop pattern having the following data :

(i) Root zone of crop = 1 m
(ii) Field capacity = 22%
(iii) Wilting point = 12%
(iv) Specific weight of soil = 1.50 gm/cc
(v) Consumptive use = 25 mm per day
(vi) Irrigation efficiency = 50%

Assume 50% depletion of available moisture before application of irrigation water at field capacity.

Solution : Available moisture = Field capacity − Permanent wilting point
= 22 − 12 = 10%

Now, readily available moisture at 50% depletion = $10 \times \dfrac{50}{100}$ = 5%

∴ Optimum moisture = Field capacity − Readily available moisture
= 22% − 5% = 17%

Using the formula for depth of water stored in root zone

$$= \dfrac{g_s \cdot d}{g_w} \text{ (F.C. − Optimum moisture)}$$

$$= \dfrac{1.5}{1.00} \times 1.00 \,(0.22 - 0.17) = 0.075 \text{ m} = 7.5 \text{ cm}$$

∴ Irrigation water required at 50% efficiency

$$= \dfrac{0.075}{0.50} = 0.15 \text{ m} = 15 \text{ cm} = \text{Depth of water}$$

Now, given consumptive use of water = 25 mm/day = 2.5 cm/day

∴ $\begin{pmatrix}\text{Water is to be applied}\\ \text{at the frequency}\end{pmatrix} = \dfrac{\text{Depth of water}}{\text{Daily consumptive use}} = \dfrac{1.5}{2.5}$

∴ Frequency of irrigation = 6 days

Problem 5.11 : Determine the frequency of irrigation to be given to the soil to maintain the required quantity of irrigation water for a crop from the following data :
(i) Field capacity (F.C.) of soil = 30%
(ii) Permanent wilting point = 14%
(iii) Depth of effective root zone = 0.75 cm
(iv) Mass density of soil = 1.2 grams/cc
(v) Daily consumptive use of water for the above crop = 12.5 mm
Assume suitable data wherever necessary.

Solution :

Available moisture in the soil = (Field capacity) − (Permanent wilting point)
= 30% − 14% = 16%

Assuming (readily available moisture) = 75% of available moisture
= 0.75 × 16% = 12%

∴ Optimum level of moisture = F.C. − 12%
i.e. O.M.C. = 28% − 12% = 16%

Referring to the equation derived in Art 7.3.3 of this chapter, (the depth of water storage capacity of the soil)

$$= \frac{g_s}{g_w} \times d \times (F.C. - O.M.C.)$$

$$= \frac{1.2}{1.00} \times 0.75 \times (0.30 - 0.16)$$

$$= 1.2 \times 0.75 \times 0.14$$

$$= 0.126 \text{ m}$$

$$= 126 \text{ mm}$$

i.e. Total available water for consumptive use of crop = 126 mm
But (Daily consumptive use of water for the crop) = 12.5 mm

∴ 126 mm of water will be consumed in $\frac{126}{12.5} \approx 10$ days

i.e. frequency of irrigation i.e. interval between two irrigations i.e. waterings = 10 days.

THEORETICAL QUESTIONS

1. Explain the meaning of water requirements of crops.
2. What is soil ? State how it is classified.
3. State the important characters of soil that affect the growth of plant.
4. Explain the following terms :
   (i) Free or Gravity water,
   (ii) Capillary water,

(iii) Hygroscopic water,

(iv) Field capacity (F.C.),

(v) Permanent wilting point or wilting coefficient,

(vi) Available moisture,

(vii) Readily available moisture.

5. State the various factors in which the field capacity depends.

6. Explain the following terms :

   (i) Base period,

   (ii) Crop period,

   (iii) Delta (Δ) of a crop,

   (iv) Duty of water (D).

7. Derive a relationship between Base period (B), Duty (D) and Delta (Δ) of a crop.

8. State the various factors on which the duty of water for a crop depends. State the various methods of improving the duty.

9. Distinguish between 'flow duty' and 'quantity duty'.

10. Why duty at the outlet of the minor is more than the duty at the head of main canal ?

11. What is outlet discharge factor ?

12. State the various crop seasons commonly adopted in our country and also mention the crops that are grown in those seasons.

13. Explain the following :

    (i) Overlapped crop,

    (ii) Perennial crops,

    (iii) Eight monthly crops,

    (iv) Fodder crop.

14. Explain the meaning of consumptive use of water and state the factors on which the consumptive use depends.

15. What is net irrigation requirement (N.I.R.) of a crop ?

16. Explain the following terms :

    (i) Kor watering and Kor depth,

    (ii) Crop ratio,

    (iii) Crop rotation,

(iv) Cash crops,

(v) Optimum crop requirement,

(vi) Paleo irrigation.

17. State the meaning of the following terms :
    (i) Gross Command Area (G.C.A.),
    (ii) Culturable Command Area (C.C.A.),
    (iii) Intensity of Irrigation (I.I.).

18. Distinguish between 'time factor' and 'capacity factor'.

19. Explain clearly the entire procedure of determining the capacity of the irrigation canal.

20. Explain how the reservoir storage required is estimated based on the crop planning.

21. Define duty and delta and derivative relationship between them.

22. State factors affecting duty.

23. For a given cropping pattern explain how the required 'canal capacity' and 'storage' are determined.

24. State the duties for :
    (i) Sugarcane,
    (ii) Wheat,
    (iii) Rice and
    (iv) Cotton.

NUMERICAL PROBLEMS

1. Duty of crop in field is 1000 hectares. Calculate total volume to be supplied to bring the crop to maturity per 10,000 hectares of area under crop, if total losses are 20%. Base period of crop is 122 days. What is delta ?

   (**Ans.** : 140.544 Mm^3 and 1.054 m)

2. Water at the rate of 6 cumecs is available at the head sluice. If the duty at the field for a certain crop is 800 hectare/cumecs and the transit losses are 15%, determine the area to be irrigated.

3. Water requirements of crops during Kharif, Rabi and Hot weather seasons in an irrigation scheme are 15, 16 and 10 cumecs respectively. The other data is as given below :

   (i) Canal transit losses = 15%
   (ii) Capacity factor = 0.80

(iii) Time factor = 0.70

(iv) Tank losses = 20%

Estimate (i) Design discharge of canal and (ii) Live storage of reservoir.

(**Ans.** : (i) $\left(\dfrac{16}{0.85 \times 0.70 \times 0.80}\right)$ = 32.86 m³/sec.)

4. Compute the depth and frequency of irrigation required for a certain crop with the data given below.

   (i) Root zone depth = 80 cm

   (ii) Field capacity = 27%

   (iii) Wilting point = 12%

   (iv) Density of soil = 1.5 gm/cc

   (v) Readily available moisture = 80% of available moisture

   (vi) Daily consumptive use of water for a given crop = 15 mm/day.

   (**Ans.** : 9.6 i.e. say 10 days.)

5. The following table shows the details of various crops grown in a culturable area of 2000 hectares served by a field channel.

Sr. No.	Crop Grown	Intensity of Irrigation	Kor Period in Days	Kor Depth
1.	Wheat	40%	16	15 cm
2.	Jowar (Rabi)	50%	10	12 cm

Work out the discharge of field channel.

(**Ans.** : (0.868 + 1.388) = 2.257)

6. Estimate the discharge at the head of the canal irrigating the following crops.

Sr. No.	Name of the Crop	Base Period in Days	Duty in hect/cumec	Area to be Irrigated in Hectares
1.	Sugarcane	365	730	500
2.	Rice (Kharif)	123	775	300
3.	Jowar (Kharif)	123	15000	1000
4.	Wheat (Rabi)	122	1800	600
5.	Vegetables (H.W.)	120	800	400

Assume canal losses equal to 30%.

(**Ans.** : Assuming time factor = 0.7 $Q_{\text{at the head of main canal}}$ = 2.45 m³/sec.)

7. For an irrigation district, the data pertaining to cropping pattern with three seasons in the year, is as follows :

Sr. No.	Name of the Crop	Crop Period in days	Area to be Irrigated in Hectares	Duty at the Head of the Main Canal in hect/cumec
1 (a)	Sugarcane	280	420	630
1 (b)	Overlap for sugarcane in hot weather	100	90	630
2.	Wheat (Rabi)	120	6750	1500
3.	Rice (Kharif)	120	2600	650
4.	Vegetables (H.W.)	120	420	700

Find the discharge required at the head of the main canal and storage required. Take time factor for main canal as 0.7 and capacity factor as 0.8.

(**Ans.** : $Q_{max} = \dfrac{5.17}{0.8 \times 0.7} = 9.66 \text{ m}^3/\text{sec.}$)

8. In an irrigation project, the main canal is to be designed to irrigate the following crops.

Sr. No.	Name of the Crop	Crop Period in Days	Area to be Irrigated in Hectares	Duty at the Head of the Main Canal in hect/cumec
1 (a)	Sugarcane	280	325	650
1 (b)	Overlap for sugarcane in hot weather	100	130	650
2.	Wheat (Kharif)	120	500	2500
3.	Rice (Rabi)	120	850	1700
4.	Vegetables (H.W.)	120	200	800
5.	Rice (Kharif)	120	400	800

Determine the design discharge at the head of main canal taking time factor = 0.7 and capacity factor = 0.8. Determine the gross storage capacity of the reservoir taking dead storage = 10% of gross storage and tank losses equal to 10% water requirements of crops.

9. An area of 1950 hectares is to be irrigated under Kharif with a duty of 650 hectares/cumecs at the head of main canal. The canal is also to irrigate 1260 hectares of sugarcane with a duty of 630 hect./cumecs. If the time factor is 0.7 and capacity factor is 0.8, determine the design discharge of the canal.

10. The following crops and their areas are proposed to be irrigated from a reservoir.

Sr. No.	Crop	Area (ha)	Duty (ha/m³/s)	Base Period (days)
1.	Jowar	4000	1750	120
2.	Rice	2500	750	120
3.	Sugarcane	1000	600	365
4.	Wheat	3500	1500	120
5.	Gram	2000	1800	120

Canal losses are 10%, time factor 0.75, capacity factor 0.70, evaporation losses 10%. Calculate canal design discharge and live storage of the reservoir.

11. In an irrigation project, the main canal takes off from a storage reservoir. The cropping pattern is as follows :

Sr. No.	Crop	Base Period (days)	Duty at the Field ha/cumec	Area Under the Crop (Hectares)
1.	Wheat	120	1800	3000
2.	Sugarcane	360	800	2000
3.	Cotton	200	1400	4000
4.	Rice	120	900	4000
5.	Vegetables	120	700	1000

Find the reservoir capacity, if the canal losses are 30% and reservoir losses are 15%.

12. After how many days you will apply irrigation water to ensure healthy growth of the crop if :
    (i) Field capacity of soil = 29%
    (ii) Permanent wilting percentage = 11%
    (iii) Soil density = 1300 kg/m³
    (iv) Root zone of crop = 700 mm
    (v) Daily consumptive use of water by crop = 12 mm
    Assume that 75% of the available moisture is readily available for plant use.

13. Compute the depth and frequency of irrigation required for a certain crop with the following data given below.
    (i) Root zone depth = 80 cm
    (ii) Field capacity = 27%
    (iii) Wilting point = 12%
    (iv) Density of soil = 1.5 gm/cc
    (v) Readily available moisture = 80% of available moisture
    (vi) Daily consumptive use of water for a given crop = 15 mm/days.

✠ ✠ ✠

UNIT – VI

MINOR IRRIGATION WORKS AND WATERSHED MANAGEMENT

6.1 PERCOLATION TANKS

- Percolation tanks are needed to raise the ground water table in the command area. This increase in water table leads to raising of water levels in wells which helps in increasing lift irrigation. For reducing evaporation loss of water and reducing cost of irrigation, percolation tanks are necessary.

- **Construction :** It consists of earthen bund consisting of sandy casing and clayee hearting for retaining water on u/s side. Riprap is provided to protect the u/s slope of bund. Cut-off trench is provided at the centre of hearting in foundation of tank. Percolation tanks are constructed on previous soils so that percolation of water takes place through foundation soil and will be available on d/s in wells for lift irrigation when required. The typical c/s with dimensions is shown as below. [Fig. 6.1].

- Percolation tanks are constructed at suitable sites by providing earthen bunds. The water from percolation tank percolates through the tank bed and joins the ground water table. It raises the water level of the surrounding existing wells. The water is then pumped for irrigating crops. Thus, it is an indirect system of irrigation.

Construction of Percolation Tank is as Follows :

- The only component of these scheme is earthen bund may be in single or straight alignment with cut-off trench. A cut-off trench of 30 to 90 cm depth and 60 to 120 cm bottom with which is constructed with locally available material like moorum, soft rock, black cotton soil and stones for clipping. The earthen bund consisting of sandy casing and clayee hearting for retaining water on u/s side. The central core portion of bund is compacted, properly by adding proper moisture and then sandy type of soil is placed on the core as a cover with compaction and upstream. Side is packed with boulders or stones. Riprap is provided to protect the u/s slope of bund. Cut-off trench is provided at the centre of hearting in foundation of tank.

- Percolation tanks are constructed on previous soils so that percolation of water takes place through foundation soil and will be available on d/s in wells for lift irrigation when required. If height if bund will not generally exceed the limit of 10 m. The drainage arrangement should be provided in the bund seat to avoid slips by saturation.

6.1.1 Selection of Site for Percolation Tank

The following are the requirements of a site for percolation tank :

- The tank bed should be pervious so that water will percolate and join the ground water table.
- The nalla or stream should have sufficient discharge in monsoon.
- There should be sufficient number of wells on the downstream side of the tank. Otherwise wells will have to be dug.
- A good agricultural land should be available near each well for irrigating the crops.
- The flanks on both sides of the nalla should be rising with steep slopes.
- The availability of materials of construction, labour, machinery, approach road are other requirements.

6.1.2 Necessity and Importance

- Percolation tanks are necessary to raise the water table of the wells in command area to develop lift irrigation.
- In Maharashtra in most of the areas, the top soil is clayee and below this there is a permeable sandy soil or murum and soft rock. It represents an ideal condition for percolation tanks. It has been a proved fact that percolation tanks are effective in Maharashtra.
- Hence, the isolated patches of tank which cannot be served by minor irrigation tanks or bandhara schemes may be brought under cultivation by constructing percolation tanks.
- Moreover as there is no real water table existing in Deccan area, well irrigation also suffers and there becomes acute shortage of drinking water supply.
- In order to have assured water supply of drinking water and to augment the underground water supply for increasing well irrigation, percolation tanks are constructed in low rainfall zones and in scanty areas.

6.1.3 Component Parts

The following are the important component parts of percolation tank :

- Earthen bund to form a tank.
- Cut-off trench to prevent the seepage through the foundation.
- Broad crested weir of small length of 20 m to pass the surplus flow of water.

6.2 CONSTRUCTION

6.2.1 Materials Used

- Locally available soils for central core, murum and soft rock for casing, boulders and large stones as riprap for protection of upstream slope.
- The section of an earthen bund of percolation tank is shown below. (Fig. 6.1)

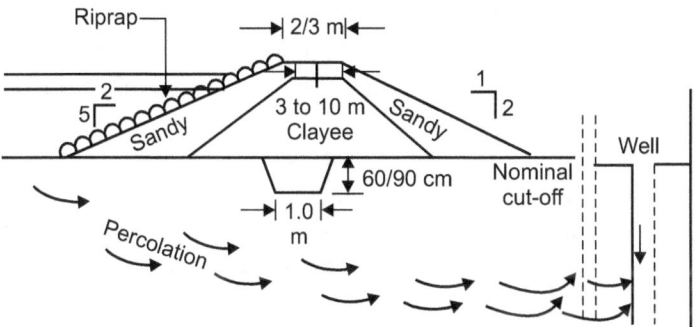

Fig. 6.1 : Section of percolation tank

- From the construction point of view, the percolation tank is similar to the irrigation tank except for providing irrigation outlet for direct irrigation. The cut-off trench is provided with the depth limited to H/4, where H is the depth of water between G.L. and F.S.L.
- The bottom width of cut-off trench may be kept as 3 m. The height of bund will not generally exceed the limit of 10 m. The drainage arrangement should be provided in the bund seat to avoid slips by saturation. Adequate waste weir should also be provided to pass the Inglis flood discharge for the safety of the tank.

6.2.2 Irrigation Benefits and Limitations

Benefits :

- The irrigation benefits of the percolation tanks are indirect as no irrigation outlet is provided for carrying out direct irrigation.
- The water which goes underground passes through unknown seams and is spread over the unknown area and partially tapped by wells at isolated places.
- The practice at present followed for finding out the area likely to be benefited is to assume 15 acres per Mcft of storage, after deducting evaporating losses.

Limitations :

- There is uncertainty about the command area.
- Low efficiency as compared to flow irrigation.

Hence, percolation tanks are recommended where other schemes are not feasible.

6.3 BANDHARA IRRIGATION

- The Bandhara irrigation scheme is a minor irrigation scheme in which direct irrigation is practised.
- A bandhara is a masonry diversion weir of small height generally 1.2 to 4.5 m constructed across a nalla or a small stream.
- The object is to raise water level in the stream so that the water enters into a small main canal taking-off from the upstream side of bandhara.
- It is the cheapest and most economical type of irrigation. It has been largely practised in Pune, Nasik, Dhule and Jalgaon Districts. Over one stream, there may be series of bandharas, one below the other.
- Thus, flow of water from isolated catchments which cannot be economically included in major irrigation schemes is effectively utilized.
- It provides supplementary irrigation for Kharif and Rabi crops during the deficiency of rains. The irrigating capacity of each bandhara may vary from hectares to about 400 hectares.

6.3.1 Site of Bandhara

- The selection of site is very important for the success of bandhara irrigation scheme. The following are the requirements for an ideal site for bandharas :
   (a) The site should be near the area to be irrigated. This reduces the length of canal and avoids canal losses.
   (b) The site should be preferably below the confluence of two or more streams to have good supply of water.
   (c) The site should preferably be just on the upstream side of steep bed slope.
   (d) The section of stream at the site should be straight, narrow and well defined. The natural banks should be high enough to avoid submergence of marginal land.
   (e) At the site good foundation should be available for the construction of bandhara.
   (f) Good culturable command should be available at the site.
   (g) The cost of construction should be within the yard stick.

A typical cross-section of bandhara is shown in Fig. 6.2.

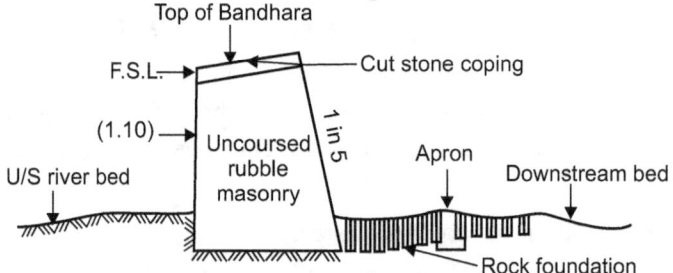

Fig. 6.2 : Cross-section of bandhara

6.3.2 Component Parts and Layout

Following are the important components of a bandhara irrigation scheme. (Fig. 6.3)

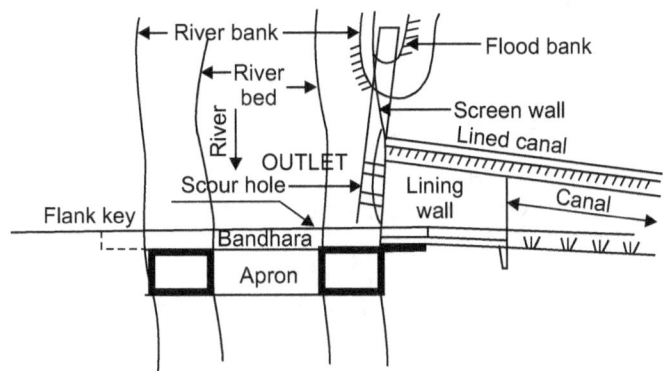

Fig. 6.3 : Layout of bandhara

(a) The bandhara,

(b) Screen wall and outlet,

(c) The flood banks,

(d) Canal on lining wall (off-taking canal).

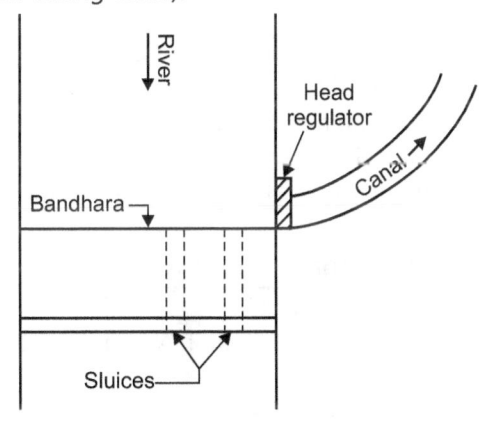

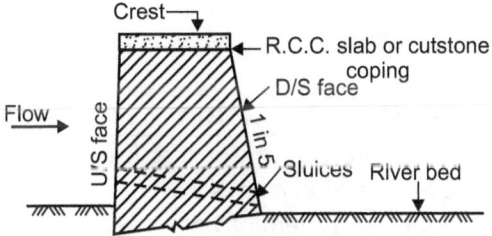

Fig. 6.4 : Bandhara irrigation system

6.3.3 Design of Bandhara

(1) The bandhara should be designed as low dams. The section of bandhara is usually trapezoidal in shape.

(2) Crest width of bandhara should be kept equal to $\sqrt{H}$, where, H is the height of bandhara; subject to minimum of 1.2 m.

(3) The discharge flowing over bandhara is given by

$$Q = 1.7\, l\, H^{3/2}$$

where, l = Length of bandhara.
h = Height of water above the crest of bandhara.
Q = Discharge in cumecs.

(4) Scouring sluices of suitable sizes should be provided at the bottom to clear the silt.

The section of bandhara should satisfy the usual conditions of stability.

1. **Screening Wall and Flood Banks :** At the main canal side of bandhara there is a masonry screening wall constructed at right angles to the bandhara on upstream side. Top of this wall is kept about 0.3 m above the H.F.L. so that flood water may not outflank the bandhara on upstream side. Flood embankment is provided from the upstream end of screen wall to confine the flood water in the stream.

2. **Offtaking Canal :** The canal starts from the outlet in the screen wall. The side wall on the right side of this canal is called lining of wall and has its top above the downstream H.F.L. so that downstream flood water may not enter the canal.

3. **Chain of Bandhara :** In this scheme, a series of small weirs of bandharas are constructed across the river or stream and a canal taking-off at each bandhara from one side only. Thus, there can be number of bandharas on the same river or stream called as chain of bandharas. The available water in the monsoon is made use of. The bandhara irrigation system is very economical. The area served by each bandhara varies from a few hectares to 400 hectares. The length of canal system is restricted to 8 km. The canals terminate in a low lying area called Thal.

6.3.4 Advantages of Bandhara Irrigation

- The system of irrigation is economical.
- Small quantities of water which would have otherwise gone waste is utilized to a maximum in this system.
- The length of canal and distribution system being small, seepage and evaporation losses are very less.
- The area to be irrigated being close to the source, it yields a high duty and intensive irrigation.

6.3.5 Disadvantages of Bandhara Irrigation

- The irrigable area for one Bandhara is more or less fixed and hence, even if greater quantity of water is available for irrigation it goes waste.
- If the river is non-perennial type, the system of water becomes seasonal and unrealiable in summer.

- Small source of water is dammed up for irrigation, hence population living on downstream of Bandhara which depends upon the river or stream for water supply goes without water during dry period.

6.3.6 Types of Bandhara

There are two main types of bandharas :
  (1) Temporary, seasonal or kachcha bandhara.
  (2) Permanent or pucca bandhara.

(1) **Temporary, seasonal or kachcha bandhara** : It is a practice to construct a kachcha bandhara at the selected sites, observe its performance and if found successful, replace it by a pucca bandhara.

(2) **Pucca bandhara** : The pucca bandharas are constructed in stone masonry, brick masonry or mass concrete. There are two types of pucca bandharas as;
  (a) Solid bandhara,   (b) Open Bandhara.

6.3.7 Solid Bandhara

- The height of the bandhara in masonry wall varies between 2.5 m to 3 m without shutters and 1.5 m to 2.5 m with shutters.
- The top width is kept equal to 3 m to 4 m which permits the bullock carts to cross the stream during dry season.
- A batter is provided on both faces. Shutters made of thick wooden planks or mild steel plates, automatic or manually operated, of height upto 1 m are sometimes provided on the top of the bandhara. It helps to raise Full Supply Level (F.S.L.) without increasing the affluxed high flood level (A.F.S.L.).
- The height of bandhara depends upon Afflux = A.F.S.L. − H.F.L. Afflux is decided arbitrarily and usually limited to 1 m.
- On the downstream side of the bandhara, an apron of concrete blocks is constructed, to protect the foundation from scouring action of overflow. If exposed rock exists in the bed, the apron is unnecessary and the cost of the foundation reduces.

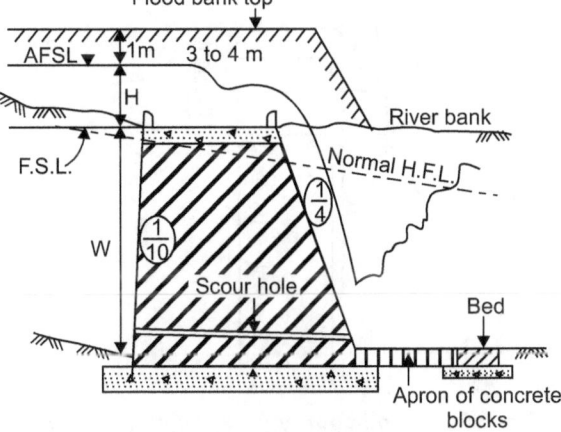

Fig. 6.5 : Cross-section

6.3.8 Kolhapur Type Bandhara (K.T. Weir)

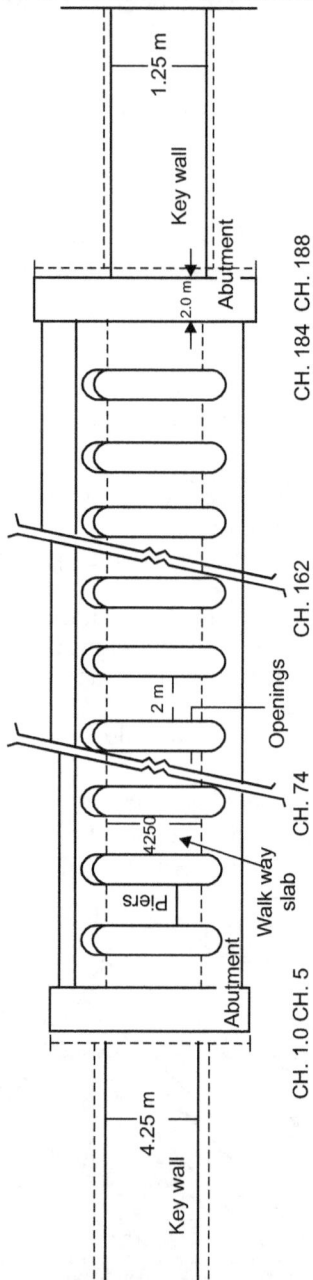

Fig. 6.6 (a) : Kolhapur type bandhara (overview)

PLAN IN DETAIL

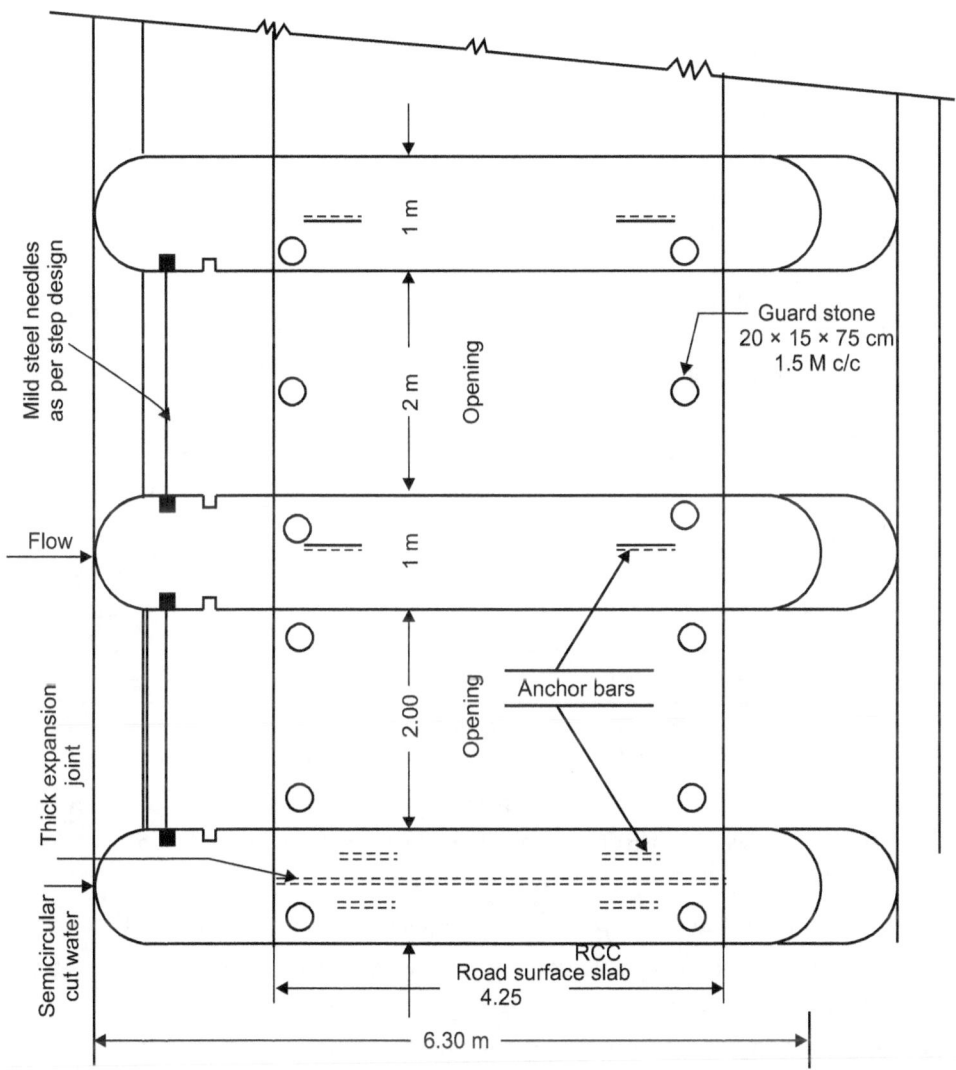

Fig. 6.6 (b)

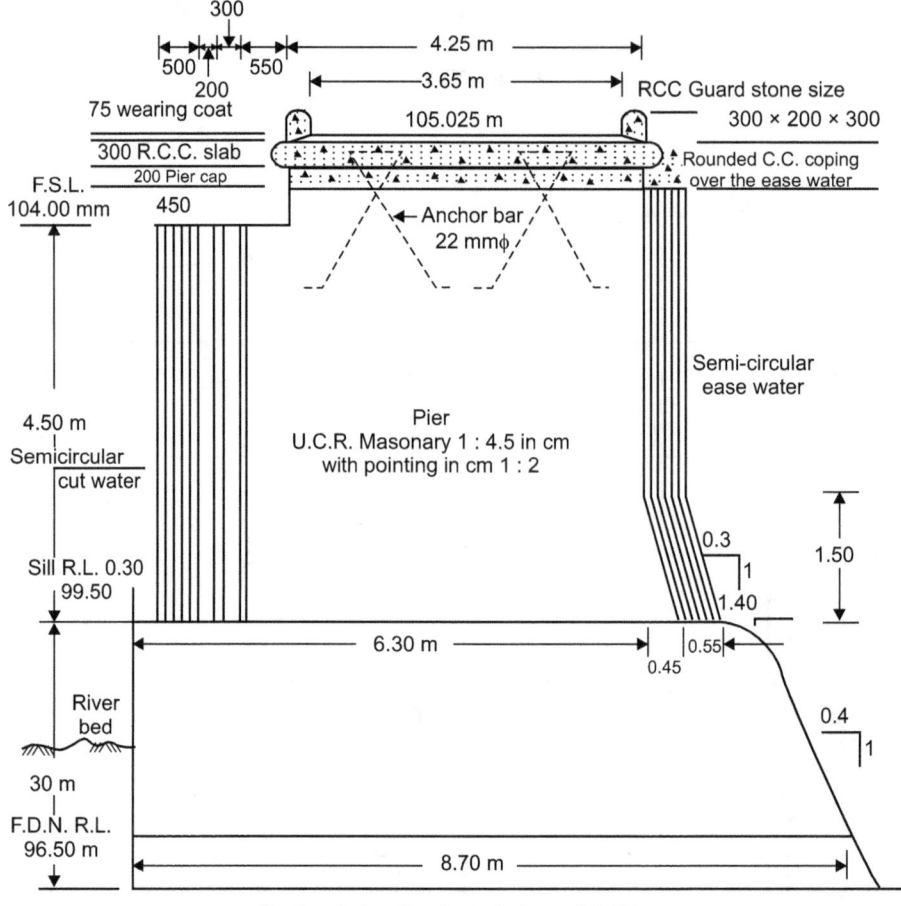

Sectional elevation from chainage 5 to 74 m
(23 Piers and 24 Openings in 69 m length)

Fig. 6.6 (c)

- It is a fully open weir consisting of a number of piers having side grooves for fixing wooden needles.
- The needles are put across the piers for the required height to form a continuous weir.
- The height of weir can be changed by removing the needles or putting additional needles.
- The needles are to be taken out during the floods season so that there is no accretion of levels and the rise of flood levels upstream of the weir.
- Sometimes double set of grooves are kept in the pier and two sets of needles are provided. The gap in between the two rows of needles is closed by ramming earth to make it water tight.

- These types of bandhara are commonly constructed in Kolhapur district and are termed as Kolhapur type weirs. Now-a-days K.T. weirs are also constructed in other districts of Maharashtra.

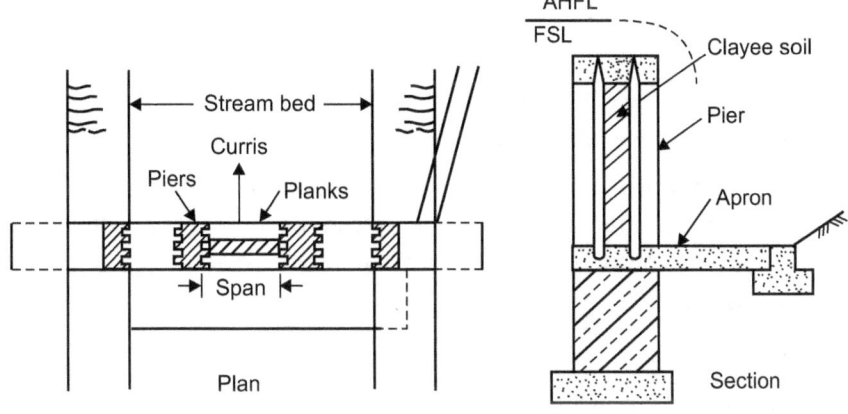

Fig. 6.6 (d)

Selection of Site for K.T. Weirs :

The following conditions should exists for selecting a site for K.T. weirs :

- Availability of good rock at the site giving easy foundation conditions.
- Availability of some post monsoon flow. Discharge observations should be arranged before selecting the site.
- The bed of nalla or stream is practically flat or with a very mild slope idea being to have a large storage of water with a small height of bandhara.
- Some well irrigation should exist on the banks on upstream side.
- Inclination of the people to practise lift irrigation direct from the storage or from wells on banks.

Construction of K.T. Bandhara or K.T. Weirs :

- A plan and section of a K.T. weir is given in Fig. 6.6. This is a structure similar to Barrage type construction. The sufficient openings are kept in nalla portion so that there is no afflux or hindrance to the monsoon discharge.
- Masonry piers with regular grooves are provided with standard opening of 2 metres. These openings are blocked by means of needles in two rows filled with puddle in between them. The needles are placed in the grooves provided in piers.

- The size of wooden needle 15 cm height, 5 cm thick and 2 m in length. These wooden needles are placed into the openings at the fag end of monsoon to store the post monsoon water.
- It is necessary to restrict the number of openings because of the considerable difficulties involved each time in placing the wooden needles at the fag end of the monsoon and removed of them just before the monsoon.

The Height and Top Width of Bandhara :

- The height and top width of bandhara are sometimes provided taking into consideration of other utilities of this structure such as bridge-cum bandhara. The width of bandhara is 2 m if it is to serve as footbridge and 4 m if it is treated as road bridge.

Replacement of Needles :

- The wooden needles are required to be replaced in about 5 years time.
- The recurring expenditure is heavy on these needles. In order to avoid this expenditure, experiments are being carried out recently to provide R.C.C. needles or mild steel needles depending on the availability and economics of material and on the local conditions.
- These K.T. weirs have become very popular especially in the sugar factory areas with a result that the co-operative sugar factories have come forward to bear the expenditure on the construction of these bandharas initially and to get the expenditure reimbursed after a period of 5 years or so depending on the convenience of the government.

6.4 LIFT IRRIGATION SCHEMES

Before any lift irrigation scheme is planned, designed and executed, it is necessary to consider following important factors.

- **Source of Water Supply :** The source of water supply, is the most important factor to be considered before the implementation of the scheme. The source should be reliable and the discharge available during lean period should be sufficient to irrigate the proposed land during that period i.e. the source should also be dependable.

  The quantity of water available from the source should be ascertained by gauging the site for a number of years. Usually 'area-velocity' method is adopted for the determination of the discharge. Any commitment on the upstream or downstream of the source for any other purposes should also be considered.

- **Suitable Site for the Intake Well :** Suitable site for the construction of intake well in the bed of the source should be available. It should also be easily accessible at any season of the year after its construction.

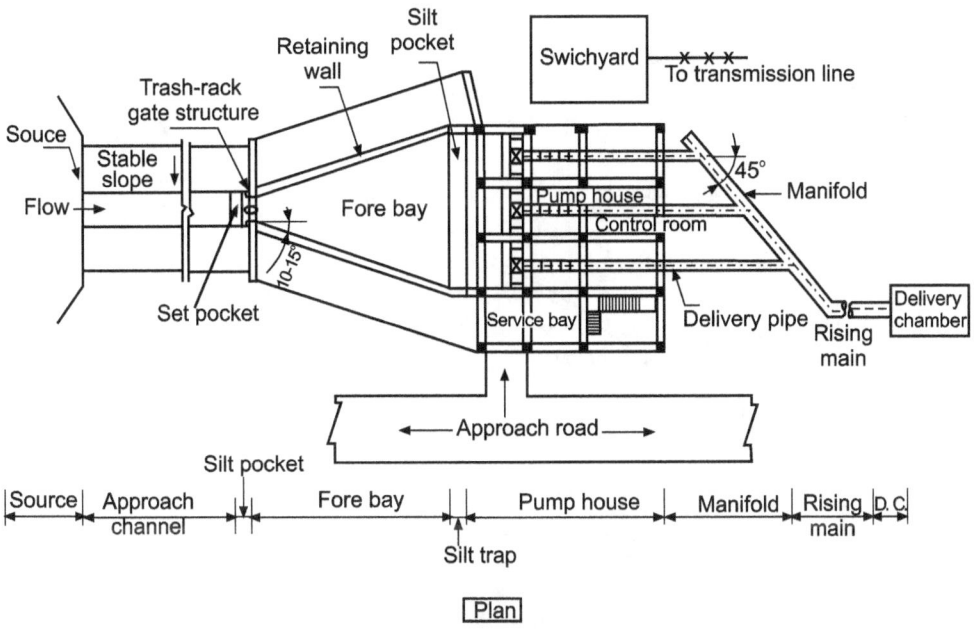

Fig. 6.7 (a) : General layout of L.I.S.

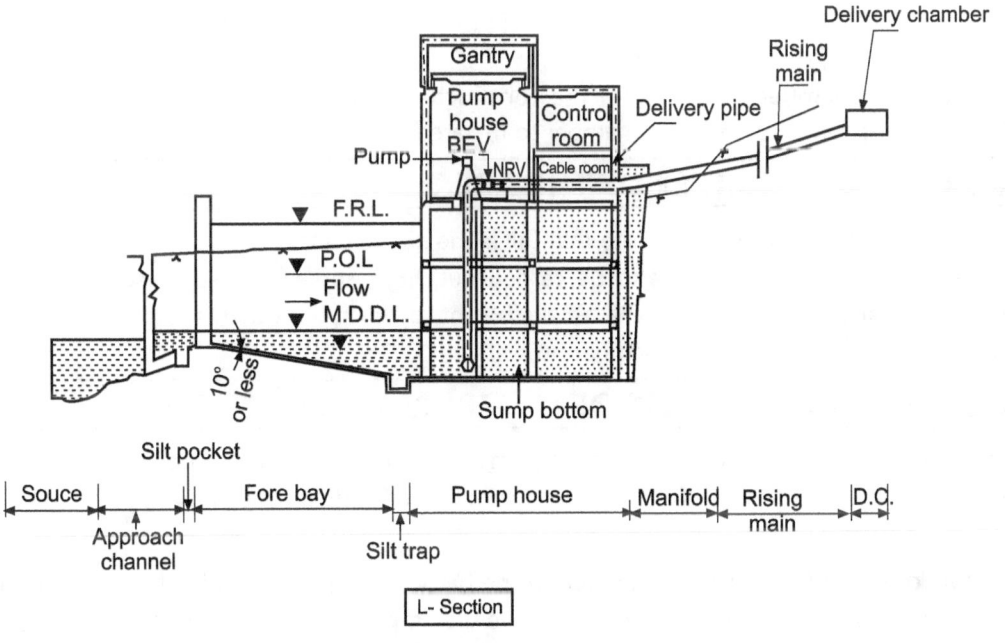

Fig. 6.7 (b) : General layout of L.I.S.

UNIT VI | 6.13

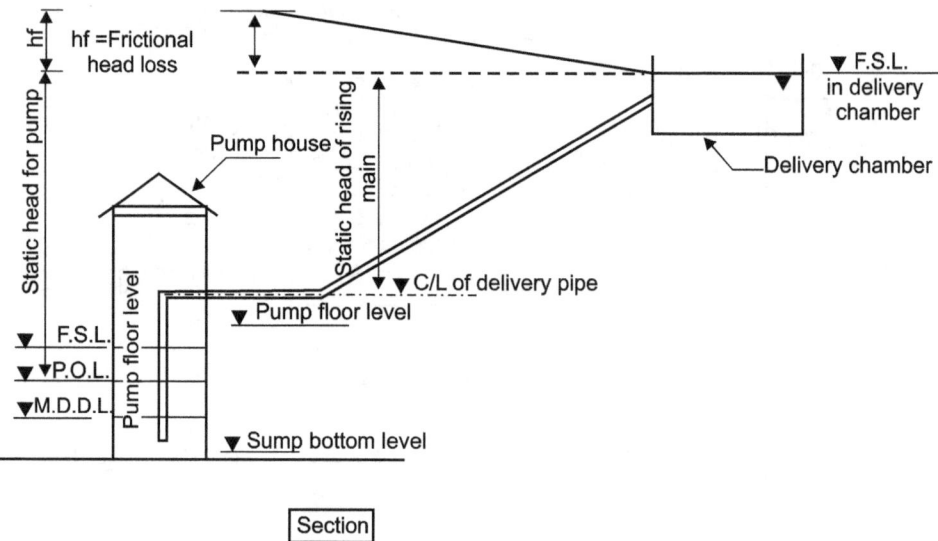

Fig. 6.7 (c) : Controlling levels of L.I.S.

- **(iii) Nature of the Rising Ground :** The ground over which the rising main is to be laid [Fig. 6.7 (a), (b) (c)] should not be too steep, but it should be gradually rising, to avoid the effect of back flow and water hammer effects in the rising main. The length of the rising main should also be small.
- **(v) Delivery Chamber :** The site for the construction of delivery chamber should be such that water can flow from this chamber to the area to be irrigated by gravity.

6.5 CONTOUR SURVEY OF THE AREA

After the selection of a particular site that fulfils the above consideration, a rigorous contour survey of the command area is to be carried out. Such surveys assist in ascertaining the exact command area under the scheme, the height to which the water is to be pumped and the construction of an efficient distribution system.

6.6 COMPONENT PARTS OF LIFT IRRIGATION SCHEME

Fig. 6.7 (a), (b), (c) shows a schematic diagrams of a section of a lift irrigation scheme, with river as a source. It consists of the following component parts for the efficient functioning of the scheme.

- **Intake Well :** It is a well constructed in the bed of the river at a suitable site to tap the water (from the source). It should have its upper portion constructed above the minimum water level, expected at any time and the bottom portion embedded well below the bed of the river.

- **Intake Pipe Line :** The purpose of the intake pipe is to convey the water collected into the intake well, to the Jack well which is constructed to lift the water to the rising main.
- **Jack Well :** The water from the intake well is carried to the jack well as shown in the figure. Suitable care is to be taken to see that the jack well is stable and does not settle. It should not be submerged by the waters in the river during the periods of high floods.
- **Centrifugal Pump, Suction Pipe :** A centrifugal pump with suction pipe provided with (non-return) foot valve is housed into the jack well. The level of the foot valve should be always below the minimum water level in the river.
- **Rising Main (pipe) :** It is a delivery pipe of the centrifugal pump that transmits water from the jack well to the delivery chamber cum pumping house for the next stage. The length of the rising main should be small and the (rising) gradient of the pipe should not be too steep, to avoid the back flow, cavitation and water hammer effects in the pipe line. The alignment of the rising main should avoid the necessity of excessive cutting or excessive lowering of the pipe.
- **Delivery Chamber (Cum Pumping House for the Next Stage) :** The water from the rising main is delivered to this chamber. The elevation of the delivery chamber should be such that the water can easily flow into the distribution system (that leads water to the area to be irrigated) by gravity flow.

  Another centrifugal pump may be installed in the delivery chamber if the water is to be lifted to the next stage of the lift irrigation scheme.
- **Distribution System :** The water may be conveyed to the command area (i.e. the area that can be irrigated by gravity flow) either by irrigation (gravity) canals or by suitable underground distribution system depending upon the site conditions etc.

6.6.1 Data Required for Design of L.I.S

1. **Administrative Approved Copy of the Scheme.**
2. **General Layout of Scheme/Pump House :**
   - Source of water.
   - Controlling levels of L.I.S. : MDDL, FRL, MWL, HFL of source and FSL at delivery point.
   - Details of approach channel.
   - Contour map of water conductor system.
   - Longitudinal section of water conductor system.
   - Length of rising main.
   - Bore holes/Trial pits data from source to D.C. (Certified by the Geologist).
   - Location of switchyard.
   - Approach road.

3. **Pump House Structure :**
   - Weight of pump, weight of motor, Gantry load details.
   - Safe bearing capacity of foundation strata.
   - Block out details and locations at pump floor, control room floor.
4. **Rising Main :**
   - Approved alignment, plan and longitudinal section of rising main.
   - Bore holes/trial pit details.
   - Aunty surge derives and their locations

6.7 CLASSIFICATION OF LIFT IRRIGATION SCHEMES

The lift irrigation schemes are classified as follows :

- Temporary or small schemes in which it is necessary to shift the position of the pumping unit from one level to the other depending upon the rise or fall in the level of water in the source.
- Permanent Large Schemes where (permanent) wells are constructed for the installation of pumping units.

The area under command in the former case is usually small as the supply of water from the source is seasonal or limited. The latter method is usually adopted for large command areas where there is assured supply of water from the source, throughout the year. The Fig. 6.7 (a), (b), (c) shows different sections of a lift irrigation scheme applicable for the latter case.

The drawbacks of the arrangement for temporary scheme are as follows :

- Applicable for small areas i.e. less command area.
- During sudden high floods in the source of water supply, there is every possibility of submergence of the entire unit i.e electric motors including power lines or diesel engine sets, if it is not shifted to safe higher levels.
- Shifting of the pumping unit at different levels depending upon the level of water in the source becomes laborious and expensive.

6.8 DESIGN CRITERIA

For the design of the large lift irrigation schemes [as shown in Fig. 6.7 (a), (b), (c)], the following criteria should be adopted:

- Source of water supply should be reliable and dependable.
- Suitable site for the construction of intake well should be available in the river bed. Necessary arrangement should be made to prevent the entry of floating matter and silt into the well.

- Even in the dry or lean season, there should be sufficient amount of water entering into the intake well.
- The level of the inlet pipe conveying water from intake well to the jack well should be above the silt level in the intake well. i.e. it should allow to flow silt free water from intake well to the jack well by gravity.
- The diameter of the inlet pipe should be sufficiently large (greater than 450 mm) to avoid choking of the pipe due to silt etc.
- The jack well should be installed at such a place that under no circumstance it is flooded by the water. i.e. this well should be located such that its top is above the high flood level of river.
- There should be convenient access to the jack well throughout the year.
- It should be possible to install the pumping unit on the top of the jack well without any difficulty.
- A square shape pumping unit is to be preferred to the circular one.
- Requirements of the power (for lifting the water) and the number of pumping units. Power required to pump the water depends upon
    (a) The lift of the pump (H) in metres.
    (b) The amount of the water to be lifted in m³/sec (i.e. Q) and
    (c) The efficiency of the pump (η_0) i.e.
    $$P = \eta_0 \cdot \gamma \cdot Q \cdot H$$
    The total gross head (H) will equal to the difference in level between the minimum water level in the source (river) and water level in delivery chamber plus the head losses in both suction and delivery pipes, losses in the bends, reducers, reflex valves, foot valve etc.
    At least minimum two pumping sets should be installed so that one will be working and other will serve as a stand by unit. Use of the characteristic curves supplied by the pump manufacturers should be made in selecting the appropriate type of pump.
- The static suction head usually varies from 3 to 4 m and the total suction head is to be limited to 8 m. The delivery end of the pipe should be suitably connected to the rising main by one or more Y junctions.
- Proper arrangement of a sluice and a reflex valve is to be provided to regulate the discharge and to avoid removal of water from the rising main.
- The appropriate size (i.e. diameter) of the rising main should be selected for the given discharge. The head loss due to friction should be limited to 0.3 m for every 100 m length. Appropriate type of pipe wall will depend upon the pressure head it has to resist Tills pressure is to be decided by sketching a hydraulic gradient line from the beginning and end of the rising main.

- The type of pipe of required thickness may be of concrete spun pipes or concrete coated steel pipes. At the bends, the concrete thrust blocks are required and at the summit points, air valves are required. Usually the rising main is buried underground with proper cover.

- All water from the rising main should be delivered into the delivery chamber, constructed of stone or brick masonry, with minimum losses. The water from the delivery chamber should flow into the distribution system by gravity.

- The distribution system essentially consists of either contour or ridge channels (depending upon the topography) leading water to the distributaries and then to the field channels by gravity flow. In cases where construction of such channels and its maintenance is difficult and costly the water may be conveyed through efficient pipe distribution system. However, it adds to the cost of the scheme.

- Economics of the lift irrigation scheme is to work out by comparing the benefit of the scheme to its entire cost (i.e. initial capital cost and maintenance cost). The ratio of benefit to the entire cost of the scheme should be slightly greater than unity for the scheme to be beneficial.

6.9 WATERSHED MANAGEMENT

Watershed is a natural unit drain, draining run-off water to a common point, by a system of streams or rivers. A watershed is a closed hydrological unit, consisting of the geographical area that feeds a river or stream. Thus, watershed development consists of the integrated treatment of this unit. These treatments include measures to reduce soil erosion, increase rain water retention and conservation, regeneration of the depleted biomass through a forestation, improving soil quality, fertility and water retention capabilities of farmlands, social participation and sustainability.

Watershed is defined as 'that geographical area which feeds water to a drainage line (like a rivulet, stream, river etc.)'. However, more than being only a geographical area, it is also the area from where the community draws sustenance. The quality and health of a watershed, therefore directly affects the quality of the life of the people. Watershed development involves the conservation, regeneration and judicious utilization of natural resources. It seems to bring about an optimum balance between the demand and use of resources. It therefore involves interactions between various components like Human Resources Development (Community Development; with particular attention gender specificities), soil and land management, water management, crop management, a forestation, posture and fodder management, live stock management and related areas.

Bringing about a balance between the often-competing demands of these various sectors requires a consensus among all those living within a particular watershed and commonality of purpose on how to meet these demands in sustainable manner.

6.9.1 Aim and Necessity

- Protect, conserve and improve the land resources for efficient and sustained production.
- Protect and enhance water resource, moderate floods and reduce silting up of tanks, increase irrigation and conserving rainwater for crops and thus mitigate draughts.
- To utilize the natural local resources for improving agriculture and allied occupation or industries. To improve socio-economic conditions of the local people.

6.9.2 Objective of Watershed Management

The main goal of Watershed Management – sustainable management of natural resources to improve the quality of living for the population – is to be accomplished by the following objectives:

- Supply and securing of clean and sufficient drinking water for the population;
- Provision and securing of access to sanitation;
- Improvement and restoration of soil quality and thus, raising productivity rates;
- Reducing the impact of natural hazards (especially in the context of climate change);
- Improvement of the income of the population with simultaneous regeneration of natural resources;
- Improvement of infrastructure for storage, transport and agricultural marketing;
- Improvement of physical health (supported by clean drinking water, access to sanitation improved nourishment);
- Advancement of (environmental) education and self-help;
- Improvement of an effective management of the financial resources available for environmental and international co-operation.

6.9.3 Program of Watershed Development

- Obstructing the rainwater and increasing ground water storage.
- Development of ground water resources at low level.
- Watershed development program can be done on a scientific basis.

6.10 TYPES OF WATERSHED

- Mini watershed
- Intermediate watershed
- Macro watershed

- **Mini Watershed :** A watershed covering an area ranging 25 hectors to 150 hectors, is termed as Mini watershed.
- **Intermediate Watershed :** A watershed covering an area ranging 150 hectors to 750 hectors, is termed as Intermediate watershed.
- **Macro Watershed :** A watershed covering an area ranging 750 hectors to 1500 hectors, is termed as Macro watershed.

6.11 DEMARCATION OF WATERSHED

The watershed can be marked from source of the stream i.e. from the ridge to the basin. Most of the time the village boundary is considered as the watershed boundary in between two villages.

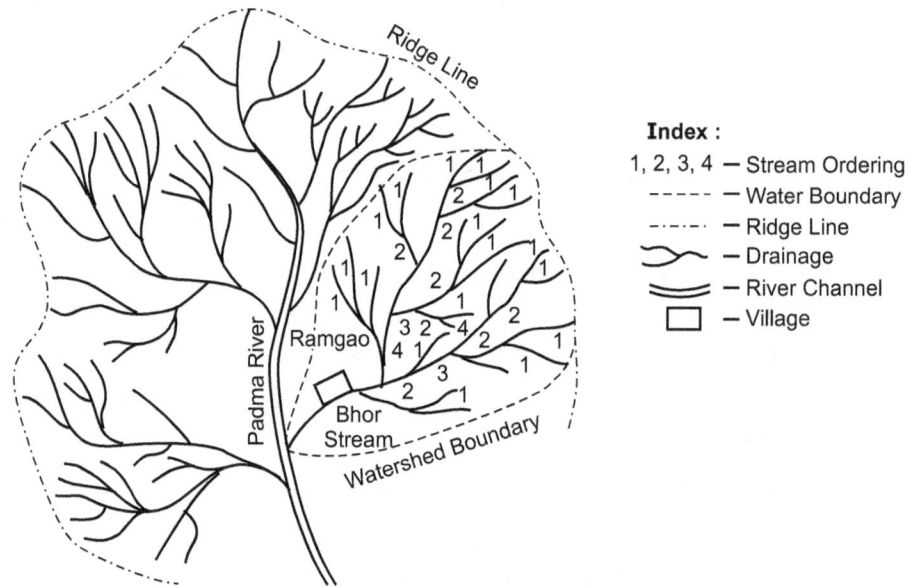

Fig. 6.8

The demarcation of a watershed is made in such a way that all the gullies and drains in the watershed from source (ridge line) to the basin (bottom) should be collected in a single drain and accordingly the boundary can be marked (Fig. 6.8) . For example in Fig. 6.8, a Bhor stream is a tributary of a main river i.e. Padma river. It is 4th order stream, comes under Ramgaon village boundary. Therefore, a village boundary becomes a watershed boundary. But most of the times a watershed can have more than one village boundary.

Topography and geological conditions of the area play an important role in creating groundwater potential. This aspect is described as :

(i) Hilly, (ii) Undulating, (iii) Plain.

6.12 WATER STRUCTURES

6.12.1 Present Status of the Measures on the Watershed Development

Project Study :

Different measures have been taken on the watershed project study. These measures have been taken for conservation of soil and to increase the ground water potential. The effectiveness of these measures depends upon the technical knowledge used during the construction, according to the purpose of the measures taken, and quality of the construction.

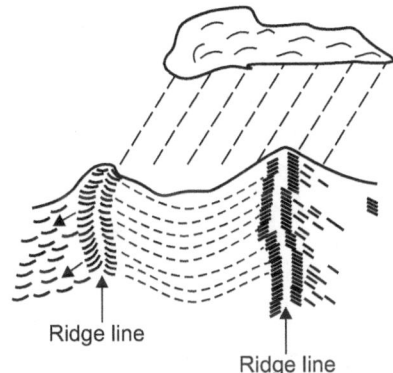

Fig. 6.9 : Soil conservation structures

As mentioned above, following measures have been taken for the conservation of soil and to increase groundwater potential.

6.12.2 Measures Taken for Soil Conservation

(a) Gully Plugs

(b) Continuous/Staggered Contour trenches and

(c) Contour Bunds

6.12.3 Measures Taken for the Increase of Ground Water Potentials (Water Conservation Structures)

(a) Nala Bunds

(b) Earthen check dams

(c) Masonry check dams

(d) Gabions and Percolation Tank

These structures have been constructed very recently on five micro watersheds.

Development projects studied and it is expected that they would function effectively for a long time in future. From these points of view, the observation of these measures is carried out. These observations are given below in brief.

Gully Plugs :
- Gully plugs, by using random rubble; have been constructed across the gullies on the hill slopes almost on all the watershed development projects studied.
- In the area of Siddeshwarwadi, beneficial Gully plugs constructed by the forest department have become very much beneficial.
- Towards upstream of the gully plugs, soil is deposited in the gullies which have become shallow.
- On the bank of the gullies, grass and bushes area grow vigorously due to the increase of soil moisture.

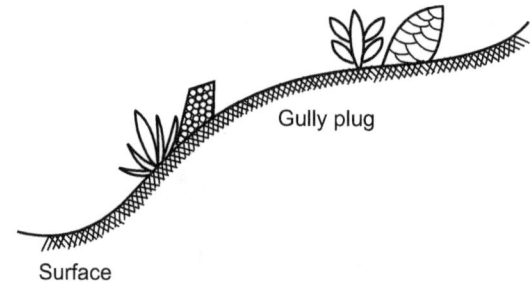

Fig. 6.10

- It is a common observation that, loose rocks used in construction of gully plugs are dislodged and are carried away along with the water and is laid down on the bed of the gully.

Continuous/Staggered Contour Trenches :
- Soil is an important material in the development of watershed, hence it is essential to control soil erosion. Therefore, Continuous Contour Trenches is one of the best solutions for the same.
- Contour trenches should be aligned along the contour so that, rain water remains accumulated for sometime in the contour trench and gradually percolates in the downstream region of the contour trench.

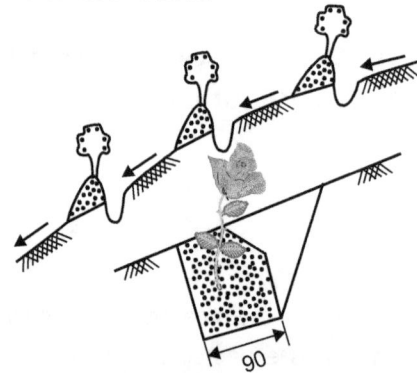

Fig. 6.11 : Refilled continuous contour trenches (C.C.T.)

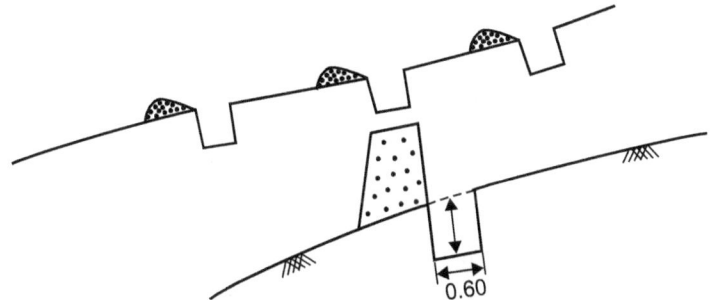

Fig. 6.12 : Open continuous contour trenches

- On the southern slopes of the hill, contour trenches that are taken by the forest department can be considered as ideal ones.
- The soil is deposited in the trench and tress of Subabhul grow luxuriantly on the mountain. While on the slope of the hills in Mandwa ghat on way to Ambajogai, it is clearly seen from distance that contour trenches divert from the contour.

Loose Boulders :

In upper reaches area the loose boulder structures are constructed to reduce the velocity of water flowing on hill.

Mounds :

The soil and the murum excavated from the trench is stacked along the downstream edge of the trench forming small ridge or mound, on which forest trees are planted.

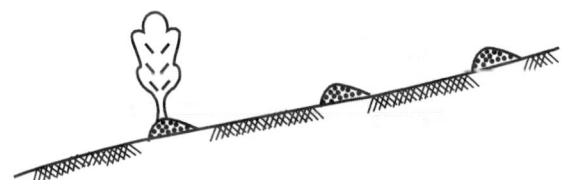

Fig. 6.13 : Earthen mounds

Staggered Contour Trenches :

- In the area, where slope of hill is rather steep and intensity of rainfall is high, in that region staggered contour trenches are taken.
- The length of every contour trench is about 4 m having interval little less than 4 m between the two.
- Another row of contour trenches is taken alternatively to the previous ones at the lower level.
- The dimensions of these staggered contour trenches are similar to the continuous contour trenches.

Crescentric Contour Trenches :

They are also provided in the foot hill regions. The arms of the crescent always point towards the higher level whereas the kink of the crescent is at the lower. Therefore, the maximum height of the bund is always at the kink and gradually it becomes less and less towards the arms.

Contour Bunds :

In the region of foot hills where slopes are flat and are covered by medium to coarse-grained soil, continuous contour bunds are provided. These bunds are very short and are constructed by scrapping the soil from the same area. As these bunds are aligned along the contour, the velocity of the water coming from the higher reaches gets reduced and whatever soil is removed from the higher level gets deposited towards upstream of the bunds.

Vanrai Bandhara : This structure is constructed by using cement bags. It is a temporary and low cost structure, constructed on the stream slope within 3% and 1 to 1.5 m stream bank height.

Gabbian Structure : The structure which is constructed by using stones randomly and is covered with mesh is known as gabbian.

The structure is constructed across the stream which has width of not more than 10 m. The height of the stream is not more than (1 m or) 1/3 of depth of stream.

Nala Bund : This is a masonry structure constructed across the stream. For this structure the required width of stream bed ranges from 30 m - 5 m.

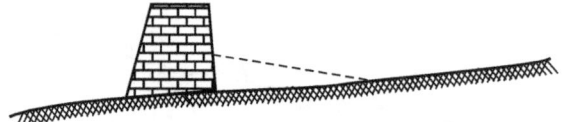

Fig. 6.14 : Nala bund

Earthen Dams :

It is made up of earth material and has length equal to the width of the stream. This is known as an earthen structure. During construction of earthen check dam, engineering principle such as zone and quality should be controlled.

It is observed, in a number of watershed areas that the earthen check dams have been constructed without following engineering principles for providing zones and without observing quality control while using the material for construction.

At the earthen check dam, outlet is located at the side of the higher level, where rock occurring is to release excess quantity of water that cannot be stored in the check dam.

- If erodable rock occurs in the region of outlet and along the tail channel extensive, erosion to tail channel takes place - forming waterfalls.

- Sometimes erosion of the tail channel occurs almost touching the body of the earthen dam. If proper maintenance is not carried out, there is every possibility, that entire earthwork would be washed away.
- It is also observed that the extensive silting has occurred in majority of the earthen check dams, creating watertight blanket over the floor of the reservoir, and therefore no percolation takes through the reservoir area.

Masonry Check Dams :
- Masonry check dams constructed in the watershed area are of different dimension.
- Across the major Nalas, high masonry check dams are constructed where as, across the minor Nalas small and short check dams are constructed.
- It is observed that while constructing the check dams across the major streams some engineering principles are followed. However, while constructing small overflow structures, no engineering principles have been followed.
- It is also observed that in case of some check dams, quality control was not taken into account during the construction. In case of Check Dam, voids occur in the body of Check Dam, through which water percolates and Check Dam becomes empty. Similarly, at another Check Dam, no proper bond between the foundation rock and the base of the Check Dam was achieved. Therefore, Check Dams become empty by developing leakage from the junction between the foundation rock and back base of the check dam.
- It is also observed that in some of the Check Dams constructed on various watershed development projects, erosion at the toe has taken place. This indicates that supervision and maintenance are lacking.

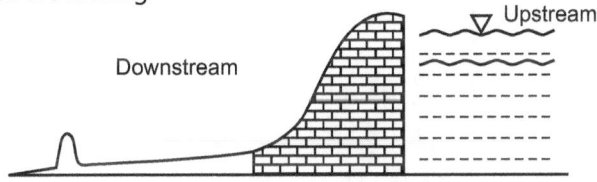

Fig. 6.15 : Masonry check dam

If these structures continue to function for a long time to serve the purpose for which they have been constructed, their repairs are necessary for which suggestions have been made afterwards.

Percolation Tanks :
- The percolation tank is a major structure constructed in watershed areas for recharging the ground to increase the ground water potential. Therefore, geological conditions play important role in their functioning.
- Percolation tanks have been constructed side by side across the tributaries of the main stream.
- The percolation conditions are very much favourable at the site of percolation tank but cut-offs have been taken only upto shallow depth. Therefore, as soon as water starts accumulating in the percolation tank it becomes empty by developing profuse leakage through foundation.

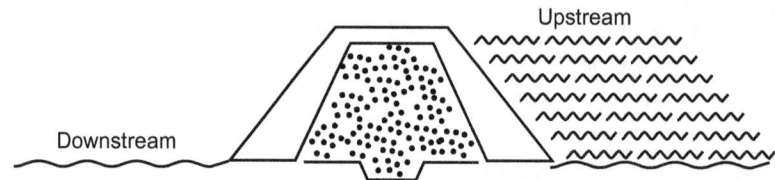

Fig. 6.16 : Percolation tank

- A deep cut-off has been taken by the villagers immediately towards upstream of the wall of the percolation tank to stop profuse leakage that was taking place from the foundation rock. However, by taking new deep cut-off the percolation from the foundation rock is almost stopped and the area immediately towards downstream of percolation tank is deprived of getting any benefit.
- From the above observations of the present status of the measures taken in various watershed areas, it is clear that measures certainly require repairs and modification to make them meaningful and useful.

Farm Pond : The pond constructed at higher elevation in farmer's field to collect the extra flowing water during rain is known as farm pond. It stops surface run-off and stores large amount of water which result in ground water recharge and increase in yield of field.

It is a geographical unit draining at a common point by a system of streams, called watershed.

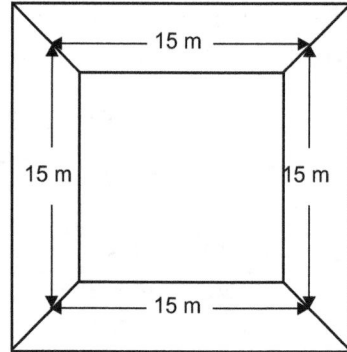

Fig. 6.17 : Farm pond

Aim and Objective :

- Protect, conserve and improve the land resources for efficient and sustained production.
- Protect and enhance water resource, moderate flood and reduce silting up of tanks, increase irrigation and conserving rainwater for crops and thus mitigate draughts.
- To utilize the natural local resources for improving agriculture and allied occupation or industries, so as to improve socio-economic conditions of the local residents.

Program of Watershed Development :

- Obstructing the rainwater and increasing ground water storage.
- Development of ground water resources.
- Watershed development program can be done on the scientific basis.

Gulley Plug   **Continuous Contour Trenches CCT**

Check Weir   **Farm Pond**

Check Dam   **K. T. Weir**

Photos

K. T. Weir (Kolhapur Type Weir) :

Kolhapur type weir is a typical water conservation structure, in which open gates are provided for easy operation to dispose the excess water during flood condition.

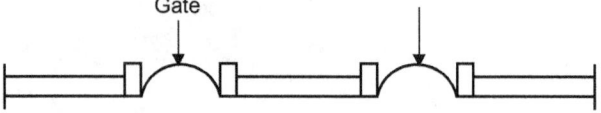

Fig. 6.18 : Kolhapur type weir

6.13 ELEMENTS OF WATERSHED

Topography :

Topography of the area play important role in increasing ground water potential. The geomorphic structure present in the area should be described. The altitudinal range in the watershed projects such as highest and lowest elevation, should be reported. The type of the drainage pattern and slope of the area is also studied under this section.

It is categorized as (i) Hilly, (ii) Undulating and (iii) Plain topography.

Rainfall Data :

As referred in the criteria for selection of watershed, the area for proposed watershed should be a draught prone area, and there should be a scarcity of rainfall. So last 20 years rainfall data of watershed area is collected to know the back history of the same. For the selection of watershed, this rainfall data should be below the average rate. Rainfall is very important parameter to recharge the watershed.

Climatic Conditions :

Data is collected from the nearest meteorological station. The following data is collected to check the climatic conditions of the study area:

1. Normal rainfall of the area in a year.
2. Highest intensity/hour of rainfall in the last 10 years (mm).
3. Highest rainfall in 24 hours in last 10 years (mm) and average rainfall is calculated.
4. Temperature maximum and minimum in three seasons i.e. summer, monsoon and winter.

During climatic studies the following points are taken into consideration:

- Whether the climate is hot or cold.
- Dry or moist.
- Microclimatic zone boundaries within the watershed are also studied.

6.14 ROOF TOP RAIN WATER HARVESTING

Rooftop Rain Water Harvesting is the technique through which rain water is captured from the roof catchments and stored in reservoirs. Harvested rain water can be stored in sub-surface ground water reservoir by adopting artificial recharge techniques to meet the household needs through storage in tanks.

The Main Objective of rooftop rain water harvesting is to make water available for future use. Capturing and storing rain water for use is particularly important in dryland, hilly, urban and coastal areas. In alluvial areas energy saving for 1 m rise in ground water level is around 0.40 kilo watt per hour.

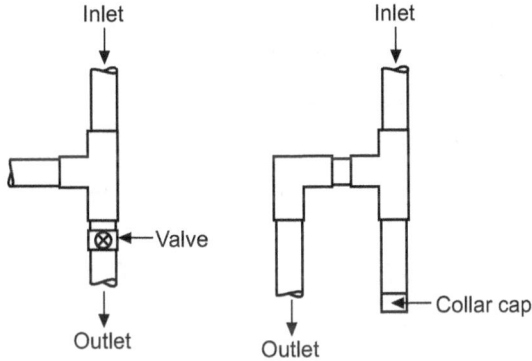

Fig. 6.19 : Rainwater harvesting

6.14.1 Need for Rooftop Rain Water Harvesting

- To meet the ever increasing demand for water.
- To reduce the runoff which chokes storm drains.
- To avoid flooding of roads.
- To augment the ground water storage and control decline of water levels.
- To reduce ground water pollution.
- To improve the quality of ground water.
- To reduce the soil erosion.
- To supplement domestic water requirement during summer, drought etc.

6.14.2 Advantages of Rain Water Harvesting

- Provides self-sufficiency to your water supply.
- Reduces the cost for pumping of ground water.
- Provides high quality water, soft and low in minerals.

- Improves the quality of ground water through dilution when recharged to ground water.
- Reduces soil erosion in urban areas.
- The rooftop rain water harvesting is less expensive.
- Rainwater harvesting systems are simple which can be adopted by individuals.
- Rooftop rain water harvesting systems are easy to construct, operate and maintain.
- In hilly terrains, rain water harvesting is preferred.
- In saline or coastal areas, rain water provides good quality water and when recharged to ground water, it reduces salinity and also helps in maintaining balance between the fresh-saline water interface.
- In Islands, due to limited extent of fresh water aquifers, rain water harvesting is the most preferred source of water for domestic use.
- In desert, where rain fall is low, rain water harvesting has been providing relief to people.

6.14.3 Simple Formula to Workout the Run-off from a Catchment Area

$$Q = A \times I \times C$$

where,
- Q = Total quantity of water to be collected (cu.m.)
- A = Roof top area (sq.m.)
- I = Average monsoon rainfall (m)
- C = Co-efficient of run-off

Collection Efficiency: Efficiently the rainfall can be collected depends on several considerations. Collection efficiencies of 80% are often used depending on the specific design.

6.14.4 Components of the Roof Top Rainwater Harvesting System

The illustrative design of the basic components of roof top rainwater harvesting system is given in the following typical schematic diagram.

The system mainly constitutes of following sub-components :

1. Catchment.
2. Transportation.
3. First flush.
4. Filter.

6.14.4.1 Catchment

The surface that receives rainfall directly is the catchment of rainwater harvesting system. It may be terrace, courtyard, or paved or unpaved open ground. The terrace may be flat RCC/stone roof or sloping roof. Therefore the catchment is the area, which actually contributes rainwater to the harvesting system.

6.14.4.2 Transportation

Rainwater from rooftop should be carried through downtake water pipes or drains to storage/harvesting system. Water pipes should be UV resistant (ISI HDPE/PVC pipes) of required capacity. Water from sloping roofs could be caught through gutters and down take pipe. At terraces, mouth of the each drain should have wire mesh to restrict floating material.

6.14.4.3 First Flush

First flush is a device used to flush off the water received in first shower. The first shower of rains needs to be flushed-off to avoid contaminating storable/rechargeable water by the probable contaminants of the atmosphere and the catchment roof. It will also help in cleaning of silt and other material deposited on roof during dry seasons. Provisions of first rain separator should be made at outlet of each drainpipe.

6.14.4.4 Filter

There is always some skepticism regarding Roof Top Rainwater Harvesting since doubts are raised that rainwater may contaminate groundwater. There is remote possibility of this fear coming true if proper filter mechanism is not adopted. Secondly all care must be taken to see that underground sewer drains are not punctured and no leakage is taking place in close vicinity. Filters are used for treatment of water to effectively remove turbidity, colour and microorganisms. After first flushing of rainfall, water should pass through filters. There are different types of filters in practice, but basic function is to purify water.

6.14.4.5 Sand Gravel Filter

These are commonly used filters, constructed by brick masonry and filleted by pebbels, gravel and sand as shown in the Fig. 6.20. Each layer should be separated by wire mesh.

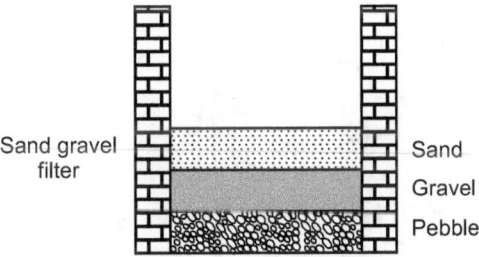

Fig. 6.20 : Sand gravel filter

6.14.4.6 Charcoal

Charcoal filter can be made in-situ or in a drum. Pebbles, gravel, sand and charcoal as shown in the Fig. 6.21 should fill the drum or chamber. Each layer should be separated by wire mesh. Thin layer of charcoal is used to absorb odour if any.

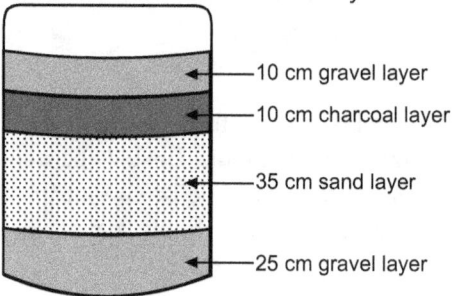

Fig. 6.21

6.14.4.7 PVC- Pipe Filter

This filter can be made by PVC pipe of 1 to 1.20 m length; Diameter of pipe depends on the area of roof. Six inches diameter pipe is enough for a 1500 Sq. feet roof and 8 inches diameter pipe should be used for roofs more then 1500 Sq. feet pipe is divided into three compartments by wire mesh. Each component should be filled with gravel and sand alternatively as shown in the Fig. 6.22. A layer of charcoal could also be inserted between two layers. Both ends of filter should have reduced of required size to connect inlet and outlet. This filter could be placed horizontally or vertically in the system.

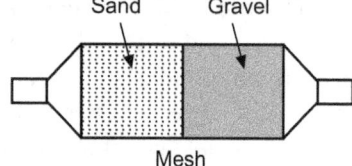

Fig. 6.22 : PVC pipe filter

6.14.4.8 Sponge Filter

It is a simple filter made from PVC drum having a layer of sponge in the middle of drum. It is the easiest and cheapest form of filter, suitable for residential units.

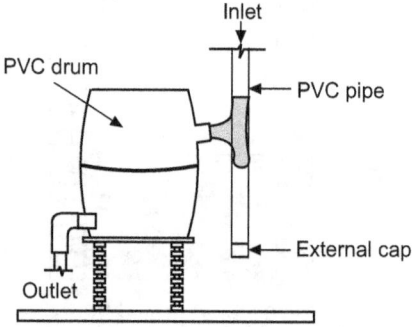

Fig. 6.23 : Sponge filter

6.15 METHODS OF ROOF TOP RAINWATER HARVESTING

Storage of Direct Use :

In this method, rain water collected from the roof of the building is diverted to a storage tank. The storage tank has to be designed according to the water requirements, rainfall and catchment availability. Each drainpipe should have mesh filter at mouth and first flush device followed by filtration system before connecting to the storage tank. It is advisable that each tank should have excess water overflow system.

Excess water could be diverted to recharge system. Water from storage tank can be used for secondary purposes such as washing and gardening etc. This is the most cost effective way of rainwater harvesting. The main advantage of collecting and using the rainwater during rainy season is not only to save water from conventional sources, but also to save energy incurred on transportation and distribution of water at the doorstep. These also conserve groundwater, if it is being extracted to meet the demand when rains are on.

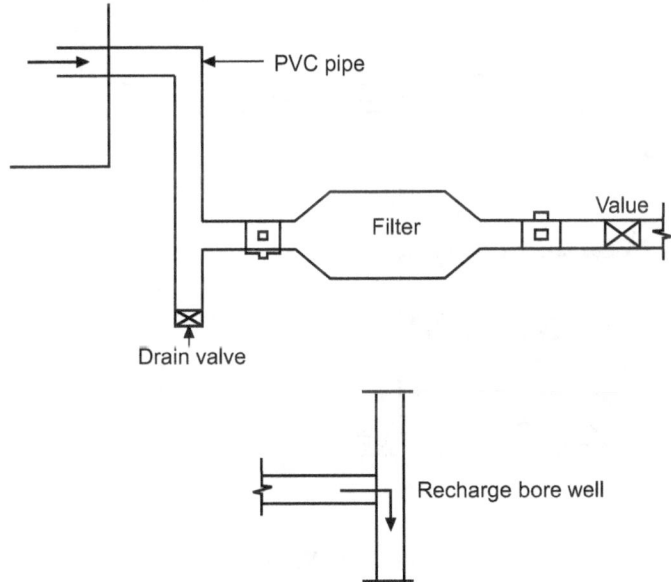

Fig. 6.24 : Flow diagram of rainwater harvesting

6.15.1 Recharging Ground Water Aquifers

Ground water aquifers can be recharged by various kinds of structures to ensure percolation of rainwater in the ground instead of draining away from the surface. Commonly used recharging methods are:

(a) Recharging of bore wells,

(b) Recharging of dug wells,

(c) Recharge pits,
(d) Recharge trenches,
(e) Soak ways or Recharge shafts,
(f) Percolation tanks,

6.15.2 Recharging of Bore Wells

Rainwater collected from rooftop of the building is diverted through drainpipes to settlement or filtration tank. After settlement, filtered water is diverted to bore wells to recharge deep aquifers. Abandoned bore wells can also be used for recharge.

Optimum capacity of settlement tank/filtration tank can be designed on the basis of area of catchement, intensity of rainfall and recharge rate as discussed in design parameters. While recharging, entry of floating matter and silt should be restricted because it may clog the recharge structure. "First one or two shower should be flushed out through rain separator to avoid contamination. This is very important, and all care should be taken to ensure that this has been done."

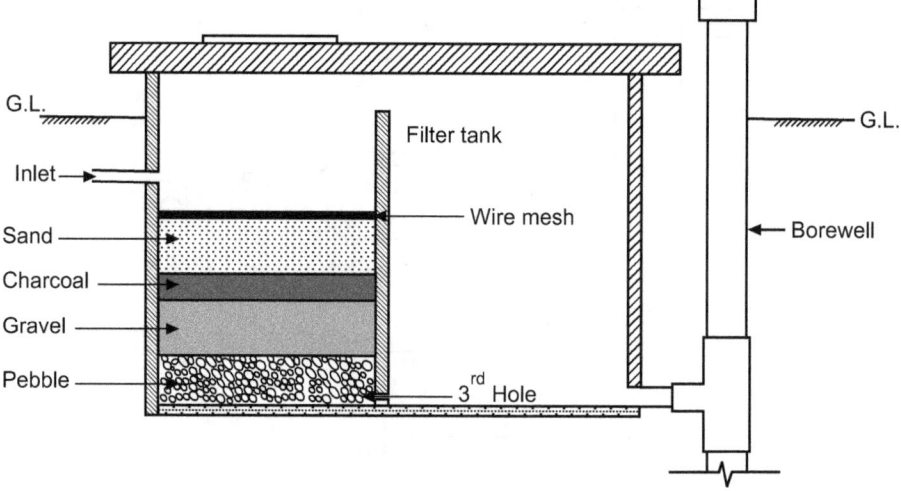

Fig. 6.25 : Filtration tank

6.15.3 Recharge Pits

Recharge pits are small pits of any shape rectangular, square or circular, contacted with brick or stone masonry wall with weep hole at regular intervals. Top of pit can be covered with perforated covers. Bottom of pit should be filled with filter media.

The capacity of the pit can be designed on the basis of catchment area, rainfall intensity and recharge rate of soil. Usually the dimensions of the pit may be of 1 to 2 m width and 2 to 3 m deep depending on the depth of pervious strata. These pits are suitable for recharging of shallow aquifers and small houses.

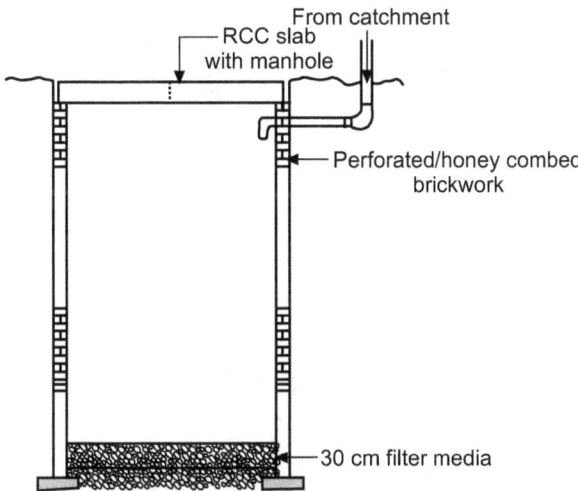

Fig. 6.26 : Typical recharge pit

6.15.4 Soak Away or Recharge Shafts

Soak away or recharge shafts are provided where upper layer of soil is alluvial or less pervious. These are bored hole of 30 cm diameter upto 10 to 15 m deep, depending on depth of pervious layer. Bore should be lined with slotted/perforated PVC/MS pipe to prevent collapse of the vertical sides. At the top of soak away required size sump is constructed to retain runoff before the filters through soak away. Sump should be filled with filter media.

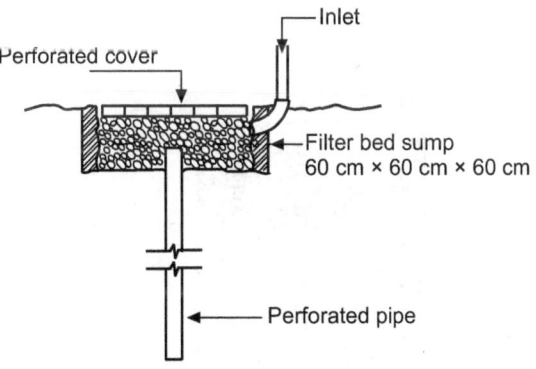

Fig. 6.27 : Recharge shafts

6.15.5 Recharging of Dug Wells

Dug well can be used as recharge structure. Rainwater from the rooftop is diverted to dug wells after passing it through filtration bed. Cleaning and desalting of dug well should be done regularly to enhance the recharge rate. The filtration method suggested for bore well recharging could be used.

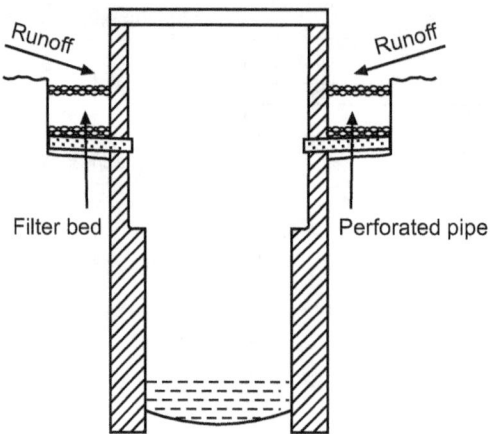

Fig. 6.28 : Recharging of dug wells

6.15.6 Recharge Trenches

Recharge trench is provided where upper impervious layer of soil is shallow. It is a trench excavated on the ground and refilled with porous media like pebbles, boulder or brickbats. It is usually made for harvesting the surface runoff. Bore wells can also be provided inside the trench as recharge shafts to enhance percolation. The length of the trench is decided as per the amount of runoff expected. This method is suitable for small houses, playgrounds, parks and roadside drains. The recharge trench can be of size 0.50 to 1.0 m wide and 1.0 to 1.5 m deep.

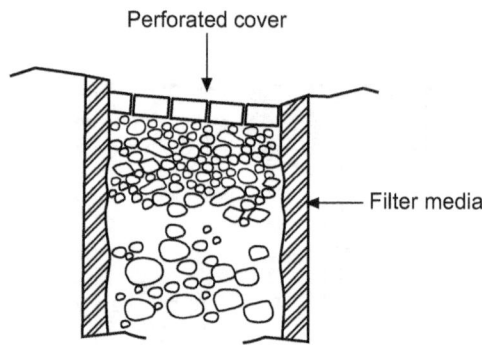

Fig. 6.29 : Recharge trenches

6.15.7 Percolation Tanks

Percolation tanks are artificially created surface water bodies, submerging a land area with adequate permeability to facilitate sufficient percolation to recharge the ground water. These can be built in big campuses where land is available and topography is suitable.

Surface run-off and roof top water can be diverted to this tank. Water accumulating in the tank percolates in the solid to augment the ground water. The stored water can be used directly for gardening and raw use. Percolation tanks should be built in gardens, open spaces and roadside green belts of urban area.

THEORETICAL QUESTIONS

1. State the considerations for the selection of the site for bandhara.
2. State the components and use of bandhara scheme.
3. Explain the types of bandhara.
4. Explain how percolation tank differs from irrigation tank.
5. Draw a layout of bandhara irrigation scheme showing the catchment area, irrigation canal and other component parts.
6. What is Kolhapur type weir ? State the conditions favouring location of such weirs.
7. Describe with sketches the construction of K.T. weir.
8. What are the requirements of site selection for a percolation tank ?
9. Explain necessity and importance of percolation tank.
10. Differentiate kachcha bandhara and pucca bandhara.
11. What are the requirements of a site for percolation tank ?
12. Draw a neat sketch of percolation tank.
13. What do you mean by lift irrigation scheme? State its necessity.
14. Explain the various factors to be considered while preparing a new lift irrigation scheme.
15. Draw a neat line sketch in section of a permanent lift irrigation scheme and state the function of each component part of the scheme.
16. Classify the lift irrigation schemes and state the merits and demerits of each.
17. State the various design considerations for the preparation of a permanent lift irrigation scheme.
18. Explain the meaning of economics of lift irrigation scheme and state the criteria for the justification of the execution of such scheme.
19. Write notes on water lifting devices used in lift irrigation schemes.
20. Explain necessity of watershed management work.

21. Explain the types of structures involved in watershed management.
22. Define watershed.
23. Explain roof top rain water havesting and ground water recharge.
24. Write short notes on the following:
    (ii) Zoned earthen embankment.
    (ii) Watershed management.

www.ingramcontent.com/pod-product-compliance
Lightning Source LLC
Chambersburg PA
CBHW082037230426
43670CB00016B/2682